ARCHETYPAL IMAGINATION

STUDIES IN IMAGINATION
A series edited in collaboration with
The Institute for the Study of Imagination

———————————

The Planets Within, Thomas Moore

Facing the World with Soul, Robert Sardello

Book of the Heart, Andrés Rodríguez

ARCHETYPAL IMAGINATION

Glimpses of the Gods in Life and Art

NOEL COBB

Lindisfarne Press

Published by Lindisfarne Press,
RR4, Box 94 A1
Hudson, NY 12534

Library of Congress Cataloging-in-Publication Data

Cobb, Noel.
    Archetypal imagination: glimpses of the gods in life and art /
Noel Cobb.
    Includes bibliographical references.
    ISBN 0-940262-47-9
    1. Archetypal (Psychology) 2. Psychoanalysis and the arts.
I. Title.
BF175.5.A72C63 1992
155.2'6—dc20   92-12751
                                                 CIP

10 9 8 7 6 5 4 3 2

Cover: "Nightwatchman at Gateway Bay." Collage by Noel Cobb
with Eva Loewe and Mick Lindberg.

Printed in the United States of America

CONTENTS

For Eva

INTRODUCTION

by Thomas Moore

When the early Greek philosophers inquired into the nature of things, the world and their own experience, they asked: "What are the *archai?*" What is the ultimate nature of things? They were not asking for a final explanation; they went beyond explanation to *logos,* to myth. They searched not only for the ultimate physical particle but also for a poetic cosmology, where flux and strife could be taken as ultimate constituents.

It is in this context that I understand "archetypal psychology"—not as a psychology of archetypes that fits modern experience into traditional symbolic forms, but as a poetical work through which we can imagine our experiences and the world around us with as much depth of insight as imagination allows. Freud's use of mythic images such as Eros and Pleasure, the Primal Scene and the Phallus is an inchoate archetypal psychology, which loses track of the *archai* only when its mythic imagery is taken literally and personalistically. Jung was radically more explicit in placing myth at the center of his theory and his method, but the systematization of his thought also obscures Jung's pursuit of the *archai.* That is to say, the archetypal nature of his work is lost in the move from myth to system. In my view, James Hillman uniquely tries to keep the archetypal quality of his work intact in his theory and in the manner in which he explores ideas about psychology.

Hillman's writings spell out his theory, which focuses in part on keeping imaginal pursuit of value and insight free of literalisms. As he says, imagination is its own ground, though the temptation in modern thought is always to tether images to some nominalistic procedure such as quantitative analysis or

to some literal experience such as actual childhood, for valida-
tion. It isn't easy in this century to trust and value imagination
for its own sake.

Hillman intentionally has not founded a school of psychology, nor has he instituted training programs. Founding schools
and instituting programs is a familiar modern approach, but it
is not the way of Hillman's Platonic and Romantic ancestors,
for whom the concealed and the mysterious are as important
as the revealed and understood, and for whom the individual
genius should not be sacrificed for common language and understanding. One wonders, and sometimes worries, whether
Hillman's subtle honing of an imaginal approach to psychology will survive as others find his re-visioning of psychology
and of culture appealing, and turn it into a practice. Hillman
like Jung sustains the originality and subtlety of his work with
a vast knowledge of history, philosophy, and religion—in
other words, with a mind schooled in tradition and classical
precision of thought. And this humanities background and
method are not now in vogue among psychologists.

It is on this point that I am encouraged and inspired by the
writings of Noel Cobb. He is obviously devoted to the work of
Hillman, which he knows extremely well. At the same time, he
follows his own genius. Like Hillman, Noel Cobb traveled in
his early years, both geographically and intellectually, in
search of a way of working and thinking adequate to his own
rich and lively imagination. Like the mythic journeys of Odysseus, his odyssey has brought him to a position where he can
write about imagination and soul with authority. This book,
among other things, establishes him as one of the trustworthy
fathers of archetypal psychology.

With the strength of his personality and the warm, Hermetic
nature of his vision, Noel Cobb fathers an "academy" known as
the London Convivium, a lovely word taken from Marsilio Ficino, a key Renaissance ancestor of soul psychology. This kind
of school, modeled on the Platonic and Renaissance academies,
centered on an individual rather than an idea or a program,
seems suited to a psychology of soul. Cobb also reveals himself

8

to be a magus in his ability to evoke a spirit and conjure a community, making London one of the geomantic poles for the establishment of a truly archetypal psychology.

To me, Noel Cobb's writing makes two important and unique contributions to the maturation of archetypal psychology. The first has to do with therapy. Many who read Hillman and other archetypalists wonder how to put this intricate and sometimes gossamer theory into practice. Do we give up the traditional form of the consulting room? Do we strive to banish the symptoms of people who come to therapy? Do we use mythology as the fundamental language of analysis? To put it in the language I have suggested here, in therapy how do we find the informing *archai* of a person or a society?

Cobb offers no system of therapy, for that would be inconsistent with a soul-centered psychology; but he does offer some important guidelines. For example, quite beautifully he says: "Soulmaking follows no program; we can only await the appearance of the transforming image, that messenger from the unknown, which, unheralded, makes a sudden entry into our lives, like the annunciation of the crimson-robed Archangel Gabriel to the Virgin." Or making the point negatively, he says: "a proper *logos* for psyche is not the dry, logical rhetoric of imageless abstraction which has asphyxiated both academic and clinical psychology." In contrast, he presents a true imaginal therapy, through which the unheralded image itself makes soul. This approach is opposed to those that either dismiss images altogether, or pressure them into appearing through various manipulative techniques, or interpret them according to some preferred theory. As Cobb says, "The diagnostic outlook is no less destructive to the landscape of soul than chain saws and bulldozers are to the Amazonian rain forests." With this receptive attitude toward images, in the style of Virgin Mary's fiat— *let it be* —Cobb offers an essential foundation for archetypal practice, a centering on beauty and on a profound appreciation for the crafted image.

Noel Cobb also expands the very meaning of therapy, showing us in some detail how the various arts enrich and nourish the soul. He says forthrightly that a film has affected him therapeutically, that a painting gives him a glimpse of the nature of soul, and that a piece of music portrays the very structures of soul that we experience as part of our own identity. Concretely he brings psychology into the world and away from exclusive attention to matters of individual personality and history.

Noel Cobb performs the extremely important task of speaking for pathology, whether it is the Dionysian experience of the "fundamental dissociability of the psyche" (Jung), the "lunar" validity of the Medusa archetype of life, or the conviction that we cannot separate beauty from pain. Images do not have to be positive and wholesome in order to be soulmaking. Cobb has a cultivated taste for pathology's beauty, and for that very reason he is a trustworthy guide toward soulful therapy.

The second contribution of this book is its love of art. Where else are you going to find in one volume on psychotherapy serious, devoted, insightful reflections on Lorca, Tarkofsky, Schumann, Munch, Shakespeare, Sewell, Dante, Corbin, Rumi, Rilke, Ficino, Novalis, and Orpheus, to say nothing of extended treatments of mythic images of Medusa, Persephone, and Dionysos? Noel Cobb finds soulmaking in art. He sees the artist as psychologist and psychotherapist, as doctor of the soul in the ancient sense. He doesn't just generalize about art; rather he presents artists of various kinds doing their detailed work of making images. "When we work with a love for [our images]," he says, "assured by their love for us, we are engaged in soulmaking." Who loves images more than artists? Yet how often do we turn to artists for guidance in the ways of the soul? How often do we regard their typically conflicted lives with the eyes of a student, rather than with the superior judgments of someone who knows better?

Noel Cobb's taking of psychology deep into the world of art, his strong distaste for psychological reductionism, is a remarkable contribution. It allows us to see that art is psychopompic—it guides the soul more deeply into itself. It is profoundly therapeutic, because it explores the psyche with precision and infinite detail and variation. It is not caught up with the myth of health, but is concerned with the presencing of beauty, in Cobb's sense that includes pain and pathology. To track the heart and mind of the artist struggling with imagery and with the challenges of life is to watch the prototype of an engagement with imagery that any of us might experience as we become drawn into the creative but demanding process of soulmaking. It is in his defending of the artist and the artist's imagery that Cobb allows his emotions to fire up his writing, so that anger, devotion, hope, and pleasure quicken his ideas.

Readers of this book have the opportunity to learn how to think archetypally, in Hillman's sense, and how to practice soulfully. In this book they will enter a house of poets, who are the best instructors in the imagery of the psyche. They will learn to deepen and expand their notions of therapy. And they will discover how rich and how soulfully rewarding is the work of the mythmaker and the artist.

It is no wonder that Noel Cobb is devoted to the god Hermes—guide of souls, inventor of music, angel of eloquence, and master of fictions. In his beautiful prayer to the god, he calls him a "hanger-out-in-doorways." In this richly stuffed book Cobb takes psychology to the threshold and invites it into the world, where the artist is bold enough to live, where its language may have more life and its images more independence.

The Struggle Out of the Cocoon

*from "Received" Analytical Language to the Speech
of Archetypal Imagination*

This book may be the first of its kind in England. Written over
the past eleven years, it clearly shows signs of a struggle. This
struggle was, and is, to free the imagination of a psychotherapist, myself, from the dead weight of our century's unconscious presuppositions about the nature of psychology and its
subject matter.

This struggle is a vital activity for a practicing psychotherapist. Training, of whatever kind, opens up some perspectives
and blinds one to others. Every school teaches certain perspectives—humanistic, personalistic, transcendental, analytic, existential, reductive. We do not always examine these viewpoints
for their mythological backgrounds. Myths are the archetypal
sources for all psychological events, including our psychologies themselves. This book, however, is not about the archetypal dominants manifesting in these different schools. It is
rather a look at the way archetypal structures of consciousness
inhabit and inform our culture.

The book is a record of the last decade of my continuing
struggle with the received language of psychology, during this
time with the language of C.G. Jung. I was familiar with this
kind of "spell" before I met the work of Jung. All through my
twenties I had been under the hypnotic spell of Freud and his
way of seeing, of speaking and of thinking. During my thirties,
I shook off that spell with the help of the existential psychiatry
of R.D. Laing, travels in wild places and the quite foreign,

13

metaphysical systems of the East, namely Ch'an and Vajrayana Buddhism. Returning to the West, I entered my forties full of the excitement of discovering the work of C.G. Jung. Jung became the bridge over which I travelled in order to re-enter the Western tradition. In particular, his work in alchemy, as tricksterish and idiosyncratic as it is, did much to inspire me—and still does.

However, I gradually began to realize that I was succumbing to yet another spell. After my own analysis and training analysis, both Jungian, I found that my essential originality simply would not be contained in being a Jungian. For one thing, I missed the eccentricity, the wildness and startling oddities of thought and speech that I was used to from my artist and poet friends. I began to feel that the Jungian world is a closed world—closed in the sense that nothing new can really happen since the origin of Jungian thought, Jung himself, is dead. All that can really happen is the codification of his thoughts, the amplification of his ideas and the endless illustration of his insights through lectures and seminars and books. After writing *Prospero's Island: The Secret Alchemy at the Heart of the Tempest* (London/Boston: Coventure/Sigo, 1984) at the end of the 1970s, I felt that I could no longer surrender my independence to a Jungian identity. The spell was breaking.

Discovering James Hillman's work in the early 1980s, I found that much of it was itself a critique of Jung and an attempt to wrest from the work of Jung something which, twisted into a new shape, might become part of a truly contemporary psychology, not born of a single father, but fathered by many. I now had a potion which would effect the alchemical *separatio* from Jung I desired.

This new psychology has been named *archetypal psychology* by Hillman, but although he has named it, he does not lay claim to it and has repeatedly said that he does not want to found a new school. The whole idea of codifying archetypal psychology, standardizing its style and creating a system which could then be taught in training institutes and universities and be the subject of doctoral theses and manuals of

14

therapeutic method is in total contradiction with its nature. It can only thrive and keep its essential character as an active, loosely defined, but invisible, academy. Unsystematized, open-ended and in the process of being created by many minds, archetypal psychology appealed to me as something I could engage with creatively.

Such words as bricolage, imaginal, underground, Renaissance, pluralistic, postmodern, polytheistic and aesthetic have been used in describing archetypal psychology. Adolf Guggenbuhl-Craig, Raphael Lopez-Pedraza, Patricia Berry, David Miller, Mary Watkins, Robert Sardello, Alfred Ziegler, Peter Bishop, Ginette Paris, Thomas Moore, Enrique Pardo, Bianca Garufi, Wolfgang Giegerich—these are but a few of the contemporary thinkers who have been associated with archetypal psychology. Henry Corbin has been given equal status with Jung as being one of archetypal psychology's fathers. Sources further back in time include Marsilio Ficino, Plotinus, Proclus, Plato and Heraclitus.

For me, the built-in mercurial inconsistencies and slipperiness of archetypal psychology are just right. It is probably a temperamental thing. If there is a spell, it is one which allows for a wide variety of improvisations, concoctions and inventions within the spirit of the, dare I say it, tradition.

The chapters in this book map the course I followed to arrive at my present point of view. Much of my writing has derived from lectures delivered through the 1980s at two important venues—The C.G. Jung Analytical Psychology Club of London and The London Convivium for Archetypal Studies, the latter a charitable trust created for the purpose of airing new ideas in archetypal psychology. Here, Chapter 1—centering on the film *Andrei Rublev* by the Russian Andrei Tarkofsky—bears a connection with the Jung Club; and chapters 2 through 5—looking at the life and art of Edvard Munch, Federico Garcia Lorca, Robert Schumann, Dante, Jalal 'uddin Rumi and others—were developed from papers presented at the first four annual conferences of the Convivium, 1987 through 1990. In chapters 6 and 7, which comprise part II, my focus shifts

somewhat to center more wholly on the life of the mythic figures Persephone and Orpheus. For me, Chapter 7 is perhaps
the most important piece in the book, being my own attempt to
describe the nature of archetypal psychology and to situate it
in relation to my own mythology, "mythod," experience and
pathology.

Many people have contributed to the making of this book.
The strongest shaping influence, of course, has been the contact with James Hillman, in the beginning through my study of
his writings, but later through seminars, lectures and conversations. I owe an enormous amount to his extravagant, precise
and generous imagination. Another spiritual influence of the
same generation has been the poet Robert Bly, whose friendship and inspiration have profoundly mattered in my life since
our first meeting more than thirty years ago.

Others, whose influence may not seem so apparent, yet
which exists because so gratefully received and absorbed by
me, are Axel Jensen, Jan Greve, R.D. Laing, the Venerable
Khamtrul Rinpoche, Buntie Wills, Kathleen Raine, Jules Cashford, Anthony Rooley, Dave Tomlin and Mauril Wirratunga.
The greatest contribution to this work has come, however,
from my partner, Eva Loewe, whose aesthetic imagination
combined with her passionate care of soul is unparalleled in
my experience. As all who know her have experienced, Eva
opens door after door into the Soul of the World when one is
in her delightful presence. Working at my side, often throughout the night without sleep, Eva has helped create the London
Convivium for Archetypal Studies, five annual international
conferences and four issues of the journal *Sphinx*. To share
with her the imaginal worlds of poetry, art and music in Rumi
or Rilke or Lorca, in Schubert, Schumann, Chopin, Brahms and
Mahler, or Klimt and Khnopff and Munch and Rembrandt,
has been the greatest experience of my life. Instead of our practices in psychotherapy suffering from this passionate devotion
to the imagination and to the living roots of culture, they
have thrived and deepened. Our "patients" have understood
that what matters is not the petty and contrived concerns of

transference nor the narcissistic preoccupations of trumped-up "victimizations," but the individuation of the angel (Corbin). These essays are not about our psychotherapeutic practice. They are about what informs it, and what gives us the heart to go on.

N.C., HAMPSTEAD, LONDON
SPRING EQUINOX, 1992

ARCHETYPAL IMAGINATION

Prayer to Hermes

Old knower of roads, chief connoisseur of pathways,
Traveller! Over all the herms and cairns of memory
Your smiling, ectoplasmic form
Hovers like a silent sphinx of starlight.

Dream peddler! Comrade of outlawed night! Daimon!
Whimsical hinge of the floating world!
I think I have always coveted your quicksilverness,
Gypsy trickster with eyes of modest diamond.

You angel of mischief and hanger-out-in-doorways!
You spectral familiar of the shades of hell! Chthonios!
Diaphanous master, rattling your handsome knuckle-bones
Inlaid with moons of mother-of-pearl!

Playmate of the Muses, blessed by oracles of bees,
You ornament dread death with necklaces of poetry.
And just when roads are blocked, the situation lost,
You sidle up with visions rich as eyes in peacocks' tails.

Rogue! Shameless one! Father of all ithyphallic pride,
Arch-fiend of staid propriety!
You honour the darkness of the perfumed garden.
You hide the drunken lovers in a cloud of credibility.

Swift as death, you always appear in the nick of time!
O breath of the breeze, O brilliant flash from the depths!
Nothing is safe from your light-fingered touch.
Cattle-rustler! Wily Highwayman! Thief of every certitude!

Dusty celestial! You of the Seraphic voice
And helpless fits of laughter! Verdigris and gold,
You beckon ever on. Who can resist you?
O, Cornerless corner of the King's Highway!

Hermes, hear me! Work through my work. Let me be
Among those who carry out transfiguration on the earth.
Give my speech an eloquence. Let my life end well.
And grant me knowledge of the way to return.

1

ECHOES OF AN
IMAGINAL BELL

Reverberations of
Andrei Tarkofsky's
Andrei Rublev

As Herman Hesse says in *The Glass Bead Game*, "Truth has
to be lived, not taught. Prepare for battle!"...Indeed, Hesse's
words...could well serve as an epigraph to *Andrei Rublev*...
For us the story of Rublev is really the story of a "taught," or
imposed concept, which burns up in the atmosphere of living
reality to arise again from the ashes as a fresh and newly discovered truth.

—ANDREI TARKOFSKY, *Sculpting in Time* [1]

*Ropes and animal skins hanging from the sides of a church wall.
Sounds of a faintly tolling bell mingling with the hiss of gas and the
murmur of men struggling with what we only later realize are the
moorings of a gigantic, primitive balloon. A man in winter furs
comes rowing a kayak, reaches the shore, jumps out, runs to the
church, panting, up the staircase. "Am I in time?" He climbs to the
belfry and out over the edge to drop into a strange harness, while far
below a crowd of people streaming from different directions begin
beating the men with the ropes, gesticulating, apparently determined
to stop the balloon from taking off. They shout, "Burn them alive!"*

This chapter developed from a talk to film students at a London Polytechnic in
1986; the material was first published in 1987 in *Harvest*, the journal of the C.G.
Jung Analytical Psychology Club of London.

But they are too late, it is airborne! The man in furs dangles in harness as the balloon floats away from the church. Awestruck at the space between himself and the earth, he cries, with all the reverence of someone who has seen an angel, "I'm flying. I'm flying!" And we look from his perspective at the marshes below and their dark, glinting channels reflecting grey skies. We are sailing fast now in the silence, over the open fields and houses, churches and little streets, out over a wilderness of lakes and marshes. On the water ominous shapes in boats holding motionless oars look up: slower now, gases hissing as the altitude drops. Yes, it's going to come down, the descent is faster now; it's going to hit the ground at some speed. Then, the thud, and we see as in a dream a horse fallen on its back, rolling over in slow motion. It's down. The gases sighing out their last breath into the lake at the water's edge. So ends the first, "Prologue," section of the film *Andrei Rublev*[2] by Andrei Tarkofsky.[3]

To someone who questioned the value of the life of the imagination Baudelaire is supposed to have replied, "Three days without bread, yes. One day without poetry, never!" But as we are constantly being reminded—by Ethiopia, Cambodia, Lebanon, Afghanistan, North Ireland, South Africa and Iran—there is, all around us, in Mr. Kurtz's words, "the horror, the horror!"

It is a mark of his great courage and a belief in what John Keats called "the Heart's affections and the truth of the Imagination" that Tarkofsky made this film. *Andrei Rublev* is purportedly the story of one of Russia's great artists of the fifteenth century. I say "purportedly" because very little is actually known about the life of Rublev, the icon painter. This has obviously been a thorny problem for the Soviet authorities for they withdrew the film from the 1971 Belgrade Festival because "it did not correspond to historical truth." That says everything about the fear of the imagination in 1971 in Russia. *Hamlet* and *Richard III* are not great plays because they "correspond to historical truth." But *Andrei Rublev* is not a newsreel from the Middle Ages. It is an imaginal biography of a Russian artist.

Tarkofsky had this to say about his film in a 1967 issue of the Soviet journal *Film Art*: "I do not understand historical films which have no relevance for the present. For me the most important thing is to use historical material to express ideas and to create contemporary characters." It is clear that Tarkofsky did not see contemporary history in the same way as the Soviet authorities saw it.

So what is the film about? In the same journal, Tarkofsky says that "in *Rublev* we want to describe the process of the artist's relationship with his world...Rublev put man first. He looked for God in Man, and saw Man as the house in which God lived."

In *Andrei Rublev* we enter a Russia which is imaginally true. Tarkofsky is being true to his imagination, not to the official Soviet fiction of what is history. And what Russia is this? It is a Russia suffering under the invasion of the Mongol hordes; a Russia subjected to barbaric atrocities; an occupied, oppressed Russia. In it we see the Imagination struck dumb, speechless, unable to say a thing; no voice with which to tell, to laugh, or to sing—unable to make anything at all out of the unspeakable horror.

I want to make a comparison between what is going on in this film and what ought to be going on in psychotherapy. Because in one form or another, this is also how the psyche presents itself every day in the consulting room: it has lost its tongue, it can not give voice to the imagination; it cannot imagine a way to live with itself; it simply cannot go on any longer. And to add to the horror: the faint, nearly strangled cry of the soul often does not even get an echo from the general practitioner, the British National Health Therapist, the deadpan analyst or the anti-imagination psychiatrist. As the American analyst James Hillman has said: "Dreams are extraordinary, unbelievable; fantastic things happening all the time...they walk into therapy with these images, these absurdities, this surrealism, and it's translated into the deadest, dullest most serious, most unimaginative...a bore, an utter bore."[4]

For the soul to survive, we must *make something* out of what has happened to us. Poetry according to the ancient Greek root, *poiesis*, means "making." In a letter to his brother, Keats wrote: "Call the world, if you please, 'the vale of soulmaking.' Then you will find out the use of the world." A therapy of *soul-making* would answer Hillman's call, would echo Baudelaire's commitment—"One day without poetry, never!"

Three monks walk in a solid downpour across the countryside, dressed in long skirts and black cowls. They come across an inn in which a buffoon, banging a hand drum and deliriously singing obscene and satirical songs, has been entertaining a motley crowd of peasants. The monks ask if they can take refuge from the storm. They find seats against a rough stone wall while the buffoon goes out in the rain for a wash. Three mounted officials ride up, tether their horses and arrest the buffoon. They drag him away and fling him head first against a tree where he falls unconscious. They heave him onto one of the horses and leave —though not before one of them returns to the inn to locate the buffoon's lute, which he finds and smashes against a tree. They ride off across the skyline. Lower down in the frame of the picture we see the three monks walking away from the inn. End of scene one: "1400—The Buffoon."

It would not matter terribly much to me if I never see another film. You'll never get me to trade my memories of walking through the dappled shade and sunlight of the covered bazaar in Uzbeki Tashkurgan or exploring the sinister wilderness of the Ahaggar mountains of the Sahara for a scintillating cinematic travelogue. And I would always prefer seeing Shakespeare on the stage to seeing Shakespeare on the screen. I would always prefer the pleasure of turning over the words of a good novel on my tongue and delighting in the interplay of word and image to seeing the film version in widescreen technicolor and full, "glorious" Dolby sound. And yet, perhaps those crudely crafted, quaint film travelogues I saw in my childhood did point the way to mysterious, foreign countries. And it has happened that a film has actually moved me very deeply, acting upon me psychologically, even psychotherapeutically, in ways which I would not be able to distinguish from similar effects of traditional great art. One such film is *Andrei Rublev*.

As a psychotherapist I am aware that therapy is going on all the time, both inside and outside the walls of the consulting room and that seeing a film can be strangely therapeutic, releasing the imagination into life and making those connections upward to the realm of the spirit and downward into the realm of the body—connections which have been lost, atrophied, ruptured or paralyzed. And if it can do this, it is because something has struck home, an image in the heart lifts up its head and comes alive, something vibrates in the soul, sounding its voice and resounding with the experience of being touched, awakened, moved. Tarkofsky's film is actually about all this: the healing of the imagination in a man who has lost faith in everything and especially in the artist-in-himself. Nowadays, if you were that man, you would risk being literally labelled "severely depressed," or maybe even "borderline psychotic," or "schizoid with paranoid tendencies," or if you happen to be very unlucky and uncompromising, "catatonic schizophrenic." How much truer the ancient, primitive expression for a member of the tribe in this state of speechless darkness: "He is suffering from a loss of soul."

As I have suggested, I see the true heart of psychotherapy as a "making" akin to the work of poetry, as a *psychopoiesis*, or what Keats called a "soulmaking." Like Hillman, I see psychotherapy as a work which should model itself on the crafts and should take its analogies from the arts rather than from medicine, physics or technology. No "cure," no "treatment," no "repair" or "adjustment of faulty functioning," but something crafty and seaworthy, imaginative and well-fashioned, as well as aesthetic and deft. A work on the imagination by the imagination, for imagination. And this is certainly what is going on in this film, *Andrei Rublev* by Andrei Tarkofsky.

One of the previous trio of monks has arrived at a large, empty cathedral. His name is Kiril, and he is a brother monk of Rublev's monastery. He has come to look for Theophanes, the Byzantine-born, master icon painter. He finds him asleep on a bench in the dim cathedral. Theophanes thinks the visitor is Rublev; he has heard tell of him, but Kiril explains that Rublev is back at the monastery. Theophanes, the Greek, old and frosty-bearded, tells Kiril, "I'm going to die soon. I dreamt of an angel. He said, 'Come with me.'" The old master wants

25

*to go to Moscow to paint in the Church of the Annunciation. He
needs help and asks Kiril to come. Kiril tells him that he cannot come
unless he has permission from his monastery. If Theophanes could
only send a messenger to beg for him in front of everyone, Kiril might
be allowed to come. However, when the messenger arrives, he asks
Rublev to come to Moscow instead, and Kiril, sick with envy and
rage, sits blackly in his room while Rublev makes ready to go. Andrei,
who is young and almost beardless, takes leave of his old friends. A
bell knells as he goes. Kiril also departs raging, cursing the monastery for its materialism and battering his dog to death on his way out.*
We realize that Kiril and Rublev were two of the monks in the
first scene.

The third scene of the film is entitled "1406—The Passion
According to Andrei." *The artists are in the forest, gone there to
collect what they need for making glue for their stone-ground pig-
ments. We see how severe and strict young Rublev is in his understanding of morality. In an argument with Theophanes, Andrei is
horrified to hear the old master suggest that perhaps a woman should
give in to her attacker if she is being raped. As they argue, a silent,
visionary sequence of the Crucifixion appears in a deep, snowbound
landscape. A melancholy Russian song hangs dreamily in the air.
Brueghelesque peasants follow Christ grimly through the snow up a
long hill. The profile of the hill looks like the edge of a deep gash with
rivulets of blood running over the snow. A young woman with long,
streaming hair hugs the legs of Christ as he climbs towards his death.
A heavy cross is dropped in the snow. A sign in Russian is nailed to
the head of it. Christ is laid out. The woman sobs and clings to him.
The soldiers try to pull her away. She is the only person to show any
emotion.*

*Back in the forest, the artists gather their pots and brushes. On the
way back to their camp, they stumble upon a band of pagan worship-
pers, running naked through the trees, carrying torches into the
river. Thinking the people are casting spells, Andrei goes after them
to watch. In the woods he meets a naked girl who throws herself down
on her back in front of him. He is mesmerized and stands immobile
until he suddenly sees that his trousers have caught fire from the embers he's standing in. Later, in a nearby barn he sees another girl,*

naked except for her fur, jumping over a smouldering bonfire, muttering spells. Two men appear and grab him. Thinking he must be a church spy, they tie him to a post in the barn and leave him. The girl in furs appears again and tries to arouse him by rubbing herself against him. He says, "To be naked is a sin!" "Is love a sin?" she asks. Then she adds, "Tonight, everyone should love!" and kisses him. Andrei asks to be untied. When the girl obliges, he stalks off into the night. At the river a narrow, wooden dugout, carrying a ritual sheaf of grain and decked with candles, is pushed out into the current and passed from hand to hand between two lines of torch-bearing, naked men and women. Andrei turns up at dawn in the artist's camp covered with scratches from his night out.

Two years later: "1408—The Last Judgement." *We are in the cathedral of Vladimir. The walls, freshly prepared, are wonderfully white and empty. All is in readiness for Rublev's artists to paint the flowing murals for which he was so famous. But Andrei himself is absent; he will not begin work. Consternation. The head priest cannot understand. The Grand Duke has ordered that it be done. Two months have passed without anything happening. And the others will not begin without him. Where is Andrei? A fellow artist finds him standing in the middle of a vast field. Burning midday sun. All around them the buzzing of thousands of bees —forming a background of orchestral excitement to their solo voices. Andrei explains that he cannot paint the required scene of Hell and the Last Judgement. He cannot frighten the people with such things. A disembodied voice speaks the famous passage from Paul's letters to the Corinthians beginning: "Though I speak with the tongues of men and angels, and have not Love, I am become as sounding brass or a tinkling cymbal."*

The Grand Duke pays a visit to the church. He insists that the work be good, to outdo the cathedral in his brother's town of Zvenigorod. All the while he speaks, his small son is yelling at the top of his voice and beating his father in the face. The Duke pays no attention. Soon after, we see a band of artists in the forest on their way to Zvenigorod. They are fed up with waiting for Andrei and they have defected from Vladimir. The Duke, however, has got wind of this and has sent his men to find them. The Duke's men encounter the artists on their way through the forest and chase them down among the trees

until they have caught and blinded, with daggers, one eye of each art-
ist. Only Sergei, a young apprentice, escapes.

In the cathedral, Andrei, in an act of outraged despair, perhaps at
the blinding of the artists, flings a pot of paint over the empty, white
wall and asks a boy to read to him from the scriptures. The boy reads
aloud from those same letters to the Corinthians, this time the pas-
sage on the subordination of women to men (for men are first before
God) and the ordinance that women must keep their heads covered
when in prayer as a sign of respect, while men need not cover theirs.
Meanwhile, a peasant girl with a disfigured lip wanders into the
church, carrying a sheaf of grain. She sees the spattered mess on the
wall and, breaking into sobs, goes straight to it and caresses it in a
wild, terrified grief, as if it were the body of Christ and she,
Magdalene. From her gestures and inarticulate groans, we realize
that she must be mute; she has no words. Andrei notices the monks
looking at her with reproof and asks, "Is she a sinner because her head
is not covered?" It is clear that he does not agree with the words of St.
Paul. He rushes out of the church and into the rain. The girl follows.
End of scene four.

Andrei is in deep conflict. No longer is he the young artist
with the peach fuzz beard and the severe, moralizing judgments. The saturnine world of the Old Testament Yahweh has
been unable to completely suppress the stirrings of *anima
mundi*, the soul of the world. Andrei sees *her* now for the first
time, embodied in the shape of the wild-eyed, dumb peasant
girl. And he has fallen in love. In recognizing soul in the dumb
girl, Andrei has come awake to soul within himself. But the
dumb girl does not only stand for the state of Andrei's soul; she
is also an image of the great soul of Russia.

A mad, wild girl has ever been—since the days of burning
Troy and the distraught stare of night-eyed Cassandra—the
poetic image of a world in pain: the agonized writhing of *anima
mundi*, whether it be Magdalene's Palestine, Dido's Carthage
or Ophelia's Denmark. The incoherently moaning, mute girl is
a living image born from the stony despair of a world in confusion. In gnostic terms it is the cry of the world soul, Sophia,
lost in the dark coils of materialism.

Soulmaking follows no program; we can only await the appearance of the transforming image, that messenger from the Unknown, which, unheralded, makes its sudden entry into our lives, like the annunciation of the crimson-robed Archangel Gabriel to the Virgin in the icons of those anonymous artists, like Andrei Rublev, who were painting in the Middle Ages.

The incomparable Sufi poet Jalal 'uddin Rumi, thinking of the Virgin as a symbol of the heart of the mystic, describes the apparition of the archangel in these words:

> Before the apparition of a superhuman beauty,
> Before this Form which flowers from the ground like a
> rose before her,
> Like an image raising its head from the secrecy of the
> heart...

The Virgin, beside herself with fear, seeks refuge in the realm of the invisible. But the angel says to her:

> Before my visible Form you flee into the invisible...
> But truly my hearth and dwelling place are in the
> Invisible...
> O, Mary! Look well, for I am a Form difficult to
> apprehend.
> I am new moon, and I am an Image in the heart.
> When an Image enters your heart and establishes itself,
> You flee in vain, the Image will remain within you,
> Unless it is a vain Image without substance,
> Sinking and vanishing like a false dawn.
> But I am like a true dawn, I am the light of your Lord...[5]

What can we hear in Rumi's words? First, that trying to run away from the angel is like trying to run away from oneself and one's true dawn. Second, that when the heart acknowledges the presence of an image and takes it in, breathes in the angel's breath, as it were, the heart is inspired and a new life is born. As Rumi says, "there is born within...a spiritual Child having the breath of Christ which resuscitates the dead." The divine breath of the Imagination.

We must remember that image is not just some object or other out there; it is not the same as a picture, not the same as an optical, visual thing, not at all the same as what modern psychology refers to as "sense data." Nor is it an optical event, an afterimage, or even the same as memory. *It is neither inside us, nor outside us, but somewhere in between.* What I am reaching for is that sense of the image we can find among the ancient Greeks and again in the Florentine circles of the Renaissance— the image considered as the way in which the heart perceives.[6]

This appreciation of image is precisely what we are losing, what we see mirrored in this film, in our anaesthetized, soulless world, and no amount of supertechnological wizardry and cinematic manipulation can bring it back. Edward Casey has written that "the image is not what we see but the way in which we see." And writing about "Image Sense,"[7] Hillman reminds us that although an image is like a picture, it is not identical with it. The difference, he says, is clear if we think of dreams. In the dream I am immersed in an entire world; I am in the scene, whatever it is; but next morning I can distance myself from it by picturing it as an event. Thus images may become pictures, just as pictures can become images.

Something becomes an image through an act of "taking in," breathing, becoming inspired by the world. This process, as Hillman[8] points out, is the essence of the aesthetic response— in the original Greek sense of *aithesis,* which at root is a gasp and "Ahh!" of wonder and recognition, a sniffing, a breathing in of the world. Without this taking in of the world, there is no awakening in the heart, no poetry, no making, no craft or crafting. Events remain events, soulless occurrences; they do not become experiences. Pictures remain two-dimensional happenings of form and composition, unless through soul they become images.

Images are angels—or rather *diamones,* those ambiguous beings of the middle realm, neither Gods nor mortals, but capable of mediating between them, and intermediaries also between the realm of divine intelligence and the physical senses. Images are living presences, like animals, not pictures, not even moving pictures, but worlds alive and embodied and particular. I am trying to describe what the French philosopher of Persian mysticism, Henry Corbin, called the *mundus imaginalis*, the realm of the imaginal, "the world intermediate between the corporal and the spiritual state and whose organ is the Imagination."[9]

Tarkofsky's Russia has inherited the centuries' old fear of images that we see already present in Rublev's Russia. And the same is with us today in the English-speaking world, though it may often be disguised in a corrosive contempt for the psychic reality of the image or a Haephaestian-Promethean fantasy of manipulation through techniques—such as the "guided daydreams" of the transpersonal psychologies which often leave the individual choked on his own psyche, baffled by its reality when he has been taught only how to depotentiate images by absorbing them into the ego. Our culture is inherently iconophobic, iconoclastic. Christianity, since the time of the Nicaean Council in A.D. 787, has fought desperately against the power and reality of the image. We allow images only when they have been safely devitalized, approved (by whichever authority we obey) and passed. In A.D. 787 the Byzantine army was busy rampaging through the countryside, destroying household icons and any private images they could find. The phobia goes far back, however, to our Jewish, Middle Eastern roots in the Ten Commandments and the injunction against the crafting of idols and idol worship. The word "idol" is simply a foreshortened version of *eidolon*, the Greek word for image.

Jung noticed that the fantasy life of the soul, its spontaneous symbol formation, is inseparably linked with polytheism. Thus, we can see that the Judeo-Christian war against images and especially against the psyche's spontaneous, image-producing capacity, has also been a war against polytheism, an iconoclastic *jihad*, backed by the power complex of patriarchal monotheism. The early church only tolerated images which were venerated as allegories of the doctrine, not as images in their own right. Later, the Reformation and the rise of Puritan

Protestantism carried the iconoclastic tendency even further, as evidenced in the intense hatred of Cromwell's roundheads, who smashed all images they found in English churches as works of the Devil.[10]

It seems that in all cultures iconoclasm is religiously linked with totalitarian monotheism, whether religious or political. Witness the wholesale destruction of icons in Maoist China, when door to door collections of Taoist and Buddhist bronzes were melted down into artillery and airplane metal to fight the Koreans; the systematic annihilation of icons in Tibet under the Red Guards' reign of terror; the recent defacing of the magnificent Buddhist statues of Angwor Wat in Cambodia. Islam, of course, has practiced defacing icons for centuries. Witness the thousands of defaced Buddha statues all through the foothills of the Himalayas and the Hindu Kush wherever the invading Muslim armies have passed. Iconophobia can be of a far more insidious kind, however—through the dogmatic coercion of "re-educating" the people by leading them to reject and disregard the images of their own traditions, as well as their own spontaneous images.

When I told Francis Huxley that I was planning to give a talk on Rublev he told me how on a visit to the Rublev exhibition at the Tretyakov Gallery in Moscow he had noticed a figure in one of the murals which he took to be St. George. The figure, however, had wings. And since, as far as he could recall, wings were not traditionally associated with saints, only angels, he turned to the girl who had been assigned as his guide and asked her whether she could tell him why St. George had wings. "I'm sorry," she replied, "I cannot tell you. I was brought up an atheist and I don't know anything about these things." A history-less soul has a soulless history.

In spite of the fact that the choice of images which artists of Rublev's time could paint was severely limited, artists could still express themselves, just as church musicians of the Middle Ages had to compose without using certain outlawed intervals, like the *diabolus musicus*, the diminished fifth. And one class of images which the Church could not completely suppress was the angel, that celestial being who, though godlike, was not quite God and, though featured like a man, was not human either. The angel is not an invention of Christianity. It has appeared in the Vedic times of India, the Persia of Zoroaster, the Pharaonic dynasties of Egypt and in the writings of the Hebrews. However, in Tarkofsky's Russia, angels have been left far behind—as valueless relics of an outmoded past, beings we have evolved away from. But this is simply cutting off one's nose to spite one's face. For without contact with soul images, we lose consciousness of psyche and have no image sense, no nose for the imagination. As Hillman writes, "History is psychology because tradition is always going on in the soul."[11]

I shall never forget the words of my friend, the late August Lange, who, after surviving four years of the Second World War in the concentration camp of Sachsenhausen, returned to his home in Oslo and was appointed Cultural Attaché for Norway in Moscow. He told me one quiet Sunday afternoon as we were discussing his favorite subject, history, "You know, progress is the worst thing humanity ever invented."

I have found in my own practice, time and time again, that an individual's imagination came to life after a period of paralyzing misery at that moment when he began to experience a psychic connection between himself and history. Then his wings began to grow and he could begin to imagine life anew.

A wide river. On the far side, tents, horses, men and bustle. Sudden shouts. "The Tartars are coming!" And now, moving into the foreground, hundreds of horsemen, quivers, bows, horned helmets. They are looking for a place to ford the water. From the opposite bank the leader of a local army directs the Mongols downriver. The leaders of the two armies meet in midstream on horseback. The Russian leader, we realize, is the Grand Duke's brother. He assures the Mongol warlord that the town of Vladimir, his brother's town, is empty and can easily be taken. The Mongol smiles. They urge their mounts into a wild race over the plain—one white horse and one black horse, but both riders hell-bent on destruction.

In a short time it is all over: the gates of the city wide-open, roofs aflame, corpses everywhere. Whistles and war cries mingle with the

33

thunder of hooves as the Mongols enact the massacre of the innocents. In one of the most unforgettable scenes in modern cinema, we see the great cathedral door being bashed in by a battering ram made from the trunk of a single gigantic tree. Inside the cathedral, those who have escaped the massacre outside are huddled together, kneeling in prayer. Andrei, who has just found the mute girl and brought her inside, kneels with the people as the doors finally give way and crash open, allowing the Mongol warriors to enter. The people part in pandemonium as swords flash in an air of smoke and screams. The Mongols urge their horses further into the cathedral, cutting men and women down on all sides. Andrei, seeing a Mongol carrying the mute girl up a stairway, grabs a battle ax and follows him. Seconds later the body of the dead and bloody Mongol slithers down the steps. Immobile and smiling, the young Mongol warlord watches the carnage from his horse near the entrance of the cathedral. His eye alights on the murals, and he turns to the Duke's brother, who has aided him in this horrific betrayal. "Who's the woman?" he asks, pointing at the mural. "The Virgin Mary," comes the answer. "And who is that in the box?" "That's her son." "A Virgin with a son? Ha-ha!" The Mongol laughs, derisively.

One of the monks, tied to a wooden platform, is being interrogated as to the whereabouts of the monastery's gold. He says there is none. He is bound with strips of cloth like a mummy until only his mouth remains uncovered. A ladle full of molten metal is lifted from a nearby cauldron and poured down his throat. Silence. His body, tied to a horse, is dragged across the cathedral floor and out into the sunlight. Having desecrated the church and believing everyone to be dead, the Mongols ride off, leaving a smouldering shambles behind. A bell rings softly as if in a dream somewhere. A riderless horse wanders into the silent cathedral, its hooves echoing ghostlike among the corpses. Andrei sits among the dead on the cathedral floor. He sees an old book and opens its charred pages to read. Nearby, the only other survivor, the mute girl, sits playing with the plaits of a dead woman, rocking with terror. The ghost of Theophanes appears, and Andrei recounts his dream for him. A bell tolls absentmindedly, as if underwater. He tells his old teacher that he has been blind till now and that he has worked day and night for the people, "but are they human?" He

34

cannot grasp his contemporaries' monumental disregard for life. He says: "I will never paint again." The ghost answers, "Why? So they burned your icons. Know how many of mine they burned? You're committing a great sin." Finally, Andrei says, "I didn't tell you the worst…I killed a man—a Russian—when I saw him dragging her off." Theophanes reaches out and touches Andrei's arm—why is this such a powerful image?—*and says, "Evil is part of human nature. Attacking evil is attacking human nature." He adds, "Learn to do well. Relieve the oppressed." Andrei says, "I will take a vow of silence! I have no more to say to people." Then, "Didn't you go to Heaven?" Theophanes looks tired. "It's not as you imagine." Andrei is sunk in despair. He addresses his last words to Theophanes, his old master: "Russia. Russia. She endures all. She will endure all. Will this last? Will it?" Theophanes looks very tired now. "I don't know. Forever, most likely." He gazes raptly at one of the murals on the cathedral wall. "Still, all this is beautiful."* Cut. End of scene five: "1408—The Raid."

"Still, all this is beautiful." The teacher's words echo in our ears as the next scene unfolds: "1412—The Silence." But we know that Tarkofsky's story has reached the gates of the underworld—this silence can not be one of Transcendence and Tranquility. It can only be the silence of an utter agony of the soul, the silence of the scream that cannot be screamed. It is the silence of the grief-crazed, dumb girl and the mute hell of the monk being dragged across the cathedral floor after the molten metal touched his throat.

We are again in Rublev's monastery. It appears that the devastation of the country by the Mongol hordes is not the end of what Russia must endure. Now in the hollow ache after the savage rape of the soul, famine is born. Three years have passed without harvest. In the Andronikov monastery a group of hungry monks sit, eating rotten apples around a bare table. Kiril has returned. He tells the monks that in Vladimir the people are so starved that they are eating rats. Kiril has been wandering the country, ill from a chill he got when wolves chased him into a lake. He hears that Andrei has also come back and that he has "brought his Holy Fool with him to have his sin with." Outside in the snow the mute girl searches for any forgotten scrap of

35

thrown-out food. A dog sniffs the ground. She eats snow. She is sitting on a log, munching a rotten apple when the Mongols return through the gates which someone has left open. They are spirited and in good humor, obviously well-fed. They play cruel games with the dogs, letting them go beserk over a piece of dried horsemeat. The Mongol chieftain throws the girl a bit of meat, laughing uproariously when she bites hungrily into it. The marauders' vitality and wildness attract her—or is it simply the promise of food? The chieftain jokingly claps his horned helmet on her head and wraps her in a stolen robe. She spins through the snow in delight as the Mongols laugh. Andrei appears and anxiously tries to dissuade her from engaging with them, but she spits at him and shoves him away. Then as the horsemen prepare to ride off, she lets herself be pulled up on the chieftain's horse. In a whirlwind of whistles and yells, the Mongols gallop away, the dumb girl with them. End of scene six.

The anima vanished. Psyche—hypnotized by brutality disguised as heroics and by violence disguised as glamour—has let herself be duped into betraying Eros, her true lover. Tarkofsky has followed Rublev to the nadir of the artist's journey, through the great gates of communal faith into the Valley of the Shadow of Death, into the halls of Hades, where horror is omnipresent and where no light shines in the unrelenting, smokey gloom; where eros is without soul and soul has lost love. And he has left Rublev there, in the voiceless, speechless darkness.

Rainer Maria Rilke wrote of this agony of intense loneliness in *The Notebook of Malte Laurids Brigg*: "Even during the time when poverty terrified him everyday with new hardships, when his head was the favorite toy of misery, and utterly worn ragged by it, when ulcers broke out all over his body like emergency eyes against the blackness of tribulation, when he shuddered at the filth to which he had been abandoned because he was just as foul himself: even then...his great terror was that someone would respond to him."[12]

I would like to suggest that the bell-making scene in the film of *Andrei Rublev* is one of the most poetically alchemical scenes in the history of the cinema. Now, it would not be that if it were lifted out and shown on its own. Its great beauty and power to move us are inseparably tied to the place it has in the film. It needs the huge, silent Russian darkness of Rublev's mind in which to toll. In this silence the bell can be heard. Like a master composer, Tarkofsky knows precisely how to time the entry of an image so that all that has gone before will create the best acoustical space for the new sound to vibrate in. The bell, like an image of soul itself, will reverberate far beyond the immediate hearing of it. A bell is not a natural phenomenon. It must be cast. And to make it, a variety of objects, ores and metals, must be cast together. Thus, the bell is a true symbol; our word "symbol" is derived from the Greek words *sym* meaning "together" and *balein* meaning "to throw or cast"—thus *sym-bol* means "thrown or cast together."

In Russia, that land of unfathomable horizons, bells were believed to address the deity directly, hence the truly enormous ones cast to give greater strength to prayer. The world's largest bell, called Tsar Kolokol, was made in Russia. It weighed two hundred tons. Big Ben, by contrast, weighs a mere thirteen tons.

Bells have been with us a long time. The oldest surviving one was found at Babylon and is thought to be five thousand years old. Bells were probably made as soon as men had begun to cast metal, and when it was discovered that the magical mixture of tin and copper we call bronze gave an especially sonorous tone to a bell, bronze became *the* "belle" metal. Big bells were not cast until the eighth century A.D., but as bellcasters became more adept, increasingly subtle differentiations of bell sound were created, even in large bells.

European bell making was originally a monastic craft, but by the time of the Renaissance, bell making was almost entirely secularized. The introduction of gunpowder in the fourteenth century and the subsequent demand for cannons surely aided this process. In Russia, bell founding dates from the thirteenth century, so that by Rublev's time, bells weighing many tons could be cast. Like pottery, bell casting was a craft fraught with potential disasters. A cracked bell, like a cracked pot, has always been the symbol of something fundamentally flawed. When we have faith in someone's integrity, we say that he or she is "sound as a bell." When we have understood something well, we say that it is "clear as a bell." So, if clarity and soundness and the feature of being able to address the deity directly are attributes of the bell, its connection upward to the spiritual realm is obvious. Its spiritual side is also manifest in its legendary power, in many cultures, to induce rain or to dissolve storms, to thwart demons and to lift spells.

The bell connects downwards into the physical realm through its resonance, its power to set things ringing. Round as a belly, the bell seems pregnant with new life, ringing in the birth of the New Year as it rings for the resurrected Christ. A bell rattle may be a baby's first toy, tool (of communication) and musical instrument. But its hollow, cavernous shape with the free-swinging clapper is most of all an image of the voice: open mouth and visible tongue. Not from the mouth of a cultured, articulate orator, but rather from the wide-open gape of a bellowing, booming being, bringing forth the utterance of some pure, primeval, original sound: *Bim-Bom!* "In the Beginning was the Word."

The storm god Ba'al of Canaanite mythology creates the thunderbolt, *baraqu*, so that his subjects may hear his commands. In Sumerian, the pictogram *gu* stood for voice and thunder and was originally the expression for "word" and the voice of Enlil, Lord of Storm.

The bell *tells*, or tolls, the story of mortality. Not only does it tell the time, striking the passing hours, but it rings out the Old Year and funereally intones for another passing citizen. Traditionally, it was what called the community to gather together, for prayer, for weddings, for sacred celebrations.

The bell as mediator, *angelos*, the voice of imagination, calling us to the Word, calling us to wake up to the world. The bell as *memoria*, vast storehouse of memory images, the Akashic archives of Mnemosyne, Great Memory, mother of the muses. Does that ring any bells? Not to forget the bell as alarm, warning gong of unattended dangers, fires, hidden reefs, prowlers, fools, thieves and lepers. But also the bell that says "all's well!": the cow bell, the church bell, the dinner bell, the sleigh bell. The loved and dreaded knell, summoning us to heaven or to hell. "And therefore never send to know for whom the bell tolls; it tolls for thee."

Bell binder, bell rose, bluebells, Canterbury bells—flower bells that toil and toll soundlessly in the wind. Bells that swell like bellies that bell, boils and bubbles that could spell troubles. The explosive expansion of *bell*ow and *bel*ch. There's something in *bell* that wants to come out. We say in England "The hops are in bell" to mean that they are in flower. Something wants to blossom into being. A bell asks to be rung. The soul of a bell is like a genie in a bottle, jumping up and down, begging to be let out. A silent bell is like a sleeping image itself, its sound gone to rest in its visible form.

I hope I am managing to evoke an archetypal sense of the bell. In English there is something resoundingly numinous even in the name. Its range of resonance stretches from the animal undertones in the guttural bark (the "bell") of a rutting stag all the way to the divine overtones of the oldest of Gods, *Bel*, God of lightning, *belitz*, blitz. And somewhere between the rutting stag and the God of lightning stands the bellicose consort of Mars, *Bellona*, Roman Goddess of war.

Perhaps, then, the ancient Sumerian-Babylonian god *Bel* is really the God of the bell. Babylon was, of course, named after *Bel*, whose temple, *Ba-bel* (meaning "Father Bel"), stood on the pyramid in the center of the city, *Ba-bel-lon*.

And then the Goddess of the bell would be *Bel*'s consort, *Belit*. For the bell symbolically, at any rate, is completely bisexual: lingam and yoni, phallus and vulva. Its ringing is a kind of *mysterium coniunctionis*, or sacred marriage, of opposites, and this wedding, the archetypal one, is what it celebrates with its annunciating sound. I do not know if the world's oldest surviving bell, which was found in Babylon, was once sacred to *Bel*, and this is not my point. If anything, the bell in Tarkofsky's film is analogous to the imagination, and as imagination it is more akin to feminine soul than masculine spirit. But certainly, the bell speaks in tongues, many tongues, and its proliferating progeny of tones rises from the bowels of the deepest earth below to the crowning glories of the highest heavens above. So it is totally appropriate that Tarkofsky should introduce the bell-making scene at the end of his film, and it is totally miraculous, a stroke of magnificent genius.

In fact, though this is the whole moment of revelation and truth for Andrei Rublev, as Tarkofsky sees it, Rublev is not at all central now—any more than he has been earlier. Like the anonymous artist he was, Rublev is seen as only peripheral to the main action, as a bystander, a spectator who at least once is noticed because he is in the way. In all he appears only nine times in this long last scene, and five of these appearances are only momentary. But these brief glimpses of Rublev are so telling—they say all there is to say. In removing Rublev from the center of the stage of his own story, Tarkofsky has made a move very like what archetypal psychology has done in decentralizing the ego, seeing through the self-centered, monopolizing tendency of the ego of modern ego psychology and dethroning this megalomaniac concept from its autocratic rule over all other figures and inner persons of the psyche, creating in fact the basis for a truly polytheistic psychology. The bell-making scene unfolds exactly as if it were a dream of Andrei's, and (temporarily) the main characters in it are a boy and a bell.

The year is 1423. There has been another devastation of the country. The Black Death has decimated the population. Two of the Duke's men are out searching for someone who can cast a new bell for the cathedral. They come across a boy of perhaps fifteen years among some deserted huts. They ask, "Does Nikola, the bellmaker, live here?"

The boy answers, "He's not here."

"Where is he?"

"Dead—plague took ...mother, my sister..."

"Where's the bellmaker, Gavrila?"

"He's dead, too. Only Fedor's left—and he's dying."

The officials confer. They've looked everywhere. There's no one to cast the bell. They have given up and are riding off when the boy shouts, "Take me with you! I'll cast the bell!"

40

"Are you crazy?"

"Take me to the Duke! It'll be a marvellous bell! And...I know the secret! My father told me the secret on his deathbed!"

The men, perplexed and desperate, turn around and look back. They've changed their minds. The boy will get his chance, but God help them if he's lying. The Duke will skin them alive.

Outside the city walls the boy gathers the workers and ceremoniously pounds a stake into the ground, asking: "Shall we dig together?" The men murmur and withdraw. One says: "We're bellcasters, not diggers. It's not our job."

The boy answers, "Know what my father said? 'Bellcasters must dig the casting pit.' Then he died." The men are unmoved. Some leave; a few stay to help dig. One day the pit is finished. In the darkness at the bottom of the deep, empty pit the boy lies, spread-eagled, in happy exhaustion. Faint bells ring somewhere in the distance. Suddenly, a snow white bird explodes in flight across the screen, as if the dove of the Holy Spirit had suddenly manifested. An image of annunciation?

But the problems are only beginning. The men don't want to waste time looking for the clay. They would rather use whatever clay they find, but the boy insists that they keep on searching. We see him standing by a bank of clay, testing it between his fingers and listening to the sounds it makes when he squeezes it. "That's not the clay," he says. "Let's keep looking!" In the end they all leave him. What is this strange obsession—that no clay is good enough? They don't understand. Holding up the project for months, for what? Can't we just get on with it? "No!" the boy says. The right clay must be found.

And the rains have begun again. Morishka, for that is his name, drags himself along through the torrential downpour still looking for the clay. Investigating the steep slope above the river, he misjudges a foothold, slips and is suddenly flying pell-mell on his back down the long incline, stopping only when his flight-path throws him into a bush. But now, groping around in the slippery stream bed, he notices—what?—that he has landed in a new clay field. And this is exactly the right sort of clay! Lying in the stream with the rain beating down on him and covered in mud, he shouts ecstatically to the obscured sky: "I've found the clay!" And just here, at this precise moment, we catch our first glimpse of Andrei. He, too, is out in the rain, trudging along

41

beside a horse-drawn cart which is transporting cabbages to the monastery. The monk lifts his rain-soaked, hooded head and looks in the direction of the sound. There, behind curtains of rain on the opposite bank of the river, a boy lies shouting in the mud. That's all. A cry in the storm.

But with the clay, the work can proceed, and next we see the casting mould being built up into the shape of an enormous bell. The boy supervises the work, bargaining for rope with one of the Duke's officials. The man says the expense may well ruin the Duke. The boy answers, "Buy it anyway!" Hurrying back to the casting pit, he collides with Andrei, who has been attracted to all the bustle, and growls, "You're in the way, father!"

Quelling a minor mutiny by sending one of the workers off to be whipped, the boy crumples in fatigue at the bottom of the pit. But he is aware of someone looking at him. It is Andrei silhouetted against the skyline. The two stare intently at each other. We see Andrei from the boy's point of view as someone in a "superior" position, looking down on us. The boy is irritated by this silent monk and shouts, "Why are you staring?" Andrei, immersed in the enormous ocean of his silence, makes no answer. Exasperated, the boy jibes, "Lost your tongue?" Distant sound of whiplashes and cries form the background to this second brief meeting.

A female voice caresses the notes of a Russian lullaby, and we glimpse Andrei silently hovering among the smoke and fires of the makeshift foundry. The boy sleeps, only to find when he is called awake that the great meltdown of metal has begun. The boy tells the Duke's man who is weighing the silver plates that he needs another eighteen pounds of silver. The official doesn't want to comply. "What's eighteen pounds, more or less?" But the boy is adamant, confident that he holds the highest cards. "Only I know the secret!"

This conversation is interrupted by a commotion close by. The buffoon, from the earlier inn scene, has returned from prison where he has been for the last 10 years. As punishment he has had half his tongue cut out. Catching sight of Andrei in the crowd he chases him, shouting that he knows him, implying that Andrei was the informer who caused him to come to grief. He never reaches Andrei, however, because Kiril suddenly interposes himself, falling on his knees and

42

begging the buffoon that he be beaten instead. The buffoon is so disconcerted that he drops the whole idea. Turning away, he says, "When the Duke's jester died, I refused the job. I'd rather be a carpenter."

The next frames are truly the heart of the film. We have arrived at the alchemical moment when a great multiplicity of individual things dies so that one transfiguring image may be born. It is the moment when, after all the candelabra, urns and samovars, serving plates, tureens and silver goblets have disappeared into the maws of the ovens, they are transformed into one molten mass of white-hot metal. Consciousness gives up its hoarded treasures to the furnaces of the underworld.

Now, surrounded by flame-belching ovens, directing the gargantuan exhalations of a four-man bellows, as if he were the angel of the fiery furnace himself, the boy gives the signal for the sweating stokers to release the lake of liquid bronze. The breath of the giant bellows becomes four incandescent streams, flowing down their separate channels to meet at the hole in the top of the bell-cast. The boy is transfixed. His face dissolves in a cloud of light. His attention is entirely turned inward in prayer.

Andrei's figure is now seen rising up from below to where the boy is—he has changed his position and is closer to the underworld perspective that sees images, not events. They listen and we listen—to the tiny sound of liquid metal trickling its way into the depths of the cast. For a flash we are reminded of the negative image of the molten metal being poured into the monk's mouth in the cathedral of Vladimir.

I am reminded at this point of the awakening of the human embryo's heart at the end of the first month of pregnancy. On or about the twenty-eighth day of the embryo's life, its heart begins beating. Just like that. Nobody knows why. It just starts beating. Tarkofsky has captured something of that mystery in this scene. We know, from the ecstatic luminosity in the boy's face, that something has been born. Before this, the bell was only a conception. Now the image has entered the world. It is embodied. Of course, the casting of the image could go wrong. Air bubbles could form as the metal solidifies, creating pockets of weakness; the whole thing could crack upon cooling, and so on. So the boy prays. And this prayer is directed to someone. Prayer is an act of imagination.

Considering prayer as an archetypal act, Hillman writes:

> By praying we move out. As Coleridge insisted, the intensity of Western subjectivism requires a personal divinity to whom we address our hearts. We are saved by these divinities, psychologically, for we are saved from the personalism of feeling by bringing those feelings to persons who are not we, who are beyond our notion of experience...They who give experience and are its ground...We talk to them, they to us; and this "dialogical situation" which constitutes prayer (in distinction to worship, idolatry, ecstasy) as a psychological act is, in Corbin's words, "the supreme act of the Creative Imagination."[13]

There are many things going on in the story at this point: Andrei Tarkofsky has imagined Andrei Rublev being saved from his crushing "personalism of feeling" through the image of a boy praying. Has Rublev forgotten those "powers beyond our notion of experience?" And does he now remember them? "By prayer we move out." And if one cannot pray? What is it that lifts a soul damned in the hell of its own unbearable suffering out into the fragrant air of life renewed? We stand before an unfathomable mystery. What did Beethoven hear in the unutterable loneliness of his deafness that allowed him, no, inspired him, to go on to create some of the most sublime music ever written? Here, psychology no more than theology can tell us what happens. It is perhaps only the rustling of an angel's wing in the darkness of our despair that calls us out of the personalism of our feeling. The image as angel. The image perceived, really perceived, and taken in, taken to heart, the true organ or home of perception, according to the Greeks. When this happens, we are no longer imprisoned in the "single vision and Newton's sleep" of the ego. Rilke's great poem on the panther is another way of saying this. He is, of course, writing about the real panther, the imaginal one within us all.

His sight from ever gazing through the bars
has grown so blunt that it sees nothing more.
It seems to him that thousands of bars are
before him, and behind them nothing merely.

The easy motion of his supple stride,
which turns about the very smallest circle,
is like a dance of strength about a center,
in which a mighty will stands stupefied.

Only sometimes when the pupil's film
soundlessly opens...then one image fills
and glides through the quiet tension of the limbs
into the heart and ceases and is still.[14]

We know at the end of this poem that not only is the image still but that the restless animal also is still. It is the same stillness we feel at the moment the bell is cast. We do not even need to see the actual bell, the image has already established itself in the heart. Of course, there will be all the excitement about the unpacking of the bell, the raising it up out of the pit and its being hung on high for all the people to see and to hear. But even its yet unheard sound is in some strange way the echo of an imaginal bell. *The bell already exists. It sits inside its shell like a nut grown invisibly within its husk.*

And the bell must cool. Big bells take days to cool. Only when the great heat has left, can the husk be broken. The boy, of course, is there with his spear-shaped shaft, grimly silent as he feverishly cleaves apart the giant shell of this numinous bell-fruit. And there it stands, the great bell, gleaming darkly as the carapace cracks apart. Unspeakably relieved that it seems whole, he leans his head on its broad bosom, beside the emblazoned emblem of Archangel Michael, and falls asleep.

For once, we do not catch a glimpse of Andrei. But at this stage, where is he? Why isn't he there for the moment of the bell's birth? He isn't there because he is at the monastery, being harangued by Kiril, who has been allowed to return on the condition that he copy the scriptures fifteen times. Kiril is confessing his jealousy of Andrei and

*begging his forgiveness. Kiril, like Schaffer's Salieri in relation to
Mozart, realizes that Andrei has a divine gift. He is disturbed because
Andrei has stopped painting. To his mind Andrei is a sinner for not
painting. "Look at me with no talent," he says. Andrei moves to leave.
"Why are you silent?" Kiril cries. "Curse me, but speak!" Andrei
turns and looks at him. Somewhere in the far distance a bell rings.
Kiril seems somehow to have finally understood something, for he
nods in assent to Andrei's unspoken reply.*

*Hundreds of people are making their way toward the great super-
structure from which the bell will hang when it has been raised out
of the bell-pit. Myriads of ropes are attached to the bell through pul-
leys in the scaffolding. On all sides gangs of men hold the ropes at
the ready. Morishka is asked to give the signal, and like the conductor of a spectacular opera, he raises both arms and drops them as a
sign to begin. Sounds of wood creaking under the strain. And just
now the Duke's train with its nobles and ecclesiastics emerges out of
the city gates and makes its way toward the scene. The crowds of
peasants fall to the ground on their faces. Silence. The great bell
hangs, majestically positioned, for all to see. The white-robed, Russian Orthodox priests begin their ritual of anointing the bell. The
boy walks nervously alone amongst the crowd. As the Duke rides
closer to have a better look, the boy is pushed forward by the workers.
He kneels in the mud in front of the Duke's horse. The man glances
in annoyance at him and urges his mount forward, snarling, "Move,
blockhead!"*

*The time has come for the bell to be rung. The entire assembly falls
silent as a strongman leaps into the pit to swing the ponderous clapper. Its huge weight glides back and forth in slowly widening arcs.
The only sound, apart from the faint groaning of metal, is the conversation of two Italian courtiers, who are speaking in their own language, saying they don't think the bell will ring. They break off
abruptly when one of them notices a beautiful girl in the crowd and
says, "Guardo cuesta bella ragazza!" And just as these words are
spoken, we see the back of Andrei's head in its black cowl, and the first
incredible boom-m-m of the bell rings out as he turns to face us, eyes
gazing past us at—what? The bella ragazza, of course. And what
better way of showing the return of soul to the world of the silenced*

46

artist? There she walks, dressed all in white, leading a horse through the crowd, head turned to the right, looking directly at us and Andrei Rublev. It is only a brief moment, however, and this image is quickly submerged in the general clamor of people cheering and bells ringing, as if the ringing of this one bell somehow ignited the fuse that set off the ringing of all the bells in the world—as in centuries past the great bell in the Kremlin would set all the bells in Moscow ringing at midnight on Easter day. The crowd begins dispersing. The Duke's party rides off in pomp and splendor in their ermines and brocades. The peasants fall to the ground in obeisance.

Alone again, the boy wanders forlornly out onto the open ground beyond the casting pit. He has dropped down, sobbing, beside one of the tie posts and lies there in the mud, hugging it. But someone has noticed him. Out of the crowd Andrei alone has been aware of the boy and has seen his distress. Going to him, he kneels and takes him in his arms. The boy is saying something in his tears. Andrei bends closer to hear. "My father," the boy sobs, "never told me. He took the secret to his grave." And without realizing that he has broken his vow of silence, Andrei consoles him, ignoring the stupendous confession, saying, "What a treat for the people! You've created such joy— and you cry!" Now something has definitely broken in Andrei and a flood of words come forth—"You and I...we'll go together. You'll cast bells and I'll paint icons. We'll go to Troitsa Monastery." And, as he comforts the lad, the woman in white appears again, this time leading the horse across the distant skyline, while at Andrei's feet the logs of an abandoned campfire begin to glow, and the glowing becomes the red background of a wall mural. We are transported to the presence of the great icons of Andrei Rublev in Moscow: images of unearthly beauty, painted with a tenderness and humanity never before seen in Russian painting.

From this point on the rest of the film is in color, and the change from black-and-white underscores Tarkofsky's portrayal of the re-awakened imagination. The glowing icons, like the rekindled embers of the campfire, warm us with their imaginal fire. And we do not need to make heavy political analogies to the situation of an artist like Tarkofsky in Russia today. The echoes of the imaginal bell that was the life and work of the great fifteenth century icon-painter, Andrei Rublev, found a hearing in the soul of one of our time's greatest film-makers, Andrei Tarkofsky.

Thunder booms and crashes as if it is coming out of the eyes of Rublev's Pantocrator, bearded and enhaloed with an open book, "The Word," in his lap. The Lord of the Storm has spoken. It is one of those obliterating downpours again, and we are at the last image of the film: a group of horses grazing in the pouring rain somewhere in a river valley in Russia. And with this image of horses peacefully, freely grazing in undisturbed nature, the film ends. *Andrei Rublev* by Andrei Tarkofsky.

The horse of the imagination—not rolling over dead on the ground, nor breaking its legs, stumbling down a flight of stairs, nor being used as the mount of an iconoclastic mass murderer, nor as the seat of a jealous ego-bound tyrant, nor as a ghost horse in a cathedral full of corpses, nor as a stumbling cart horse, nor even as a mystic horse led by a woman in white, but the free, grazing-in-the-open horse. As a true lover of images, Tarkofsky has given us a profound teaching on the nature of the imagination. Like James Hillman, Tarkofsky enables us to see the imagination as "an animal mundi and an anima mundi, both diaphanous and passionate, unerring in its patterns and in all ways necessary, the necessary angel that makes brute necessity angelic."[15]

With the example of the boy of the bell who gives tongue to his own inaudible voice through passionate devotion to the image in his heart, Andrei Rublev learns how to speak again and how to imitate the bell in its fidelity to its own nature. "You and I...we'll go together. You'll cast bells and I'll paint icons. We'll go to Troitsa Monastery." As Rilke says, "Where the infinite wholly enters (whether as minus or plus), the oh so human number drops away, as the road that has now been completely travelled—and what remains is the having arrived, *the being.*"[16]

In 1930, exactly five hundred years after the death of Rublev, another great imagemaker, W.B. Yeats, wrote a tribute to the mind of the imagemakers of that time in his poem "Byzantium,"

48

which ends with these lines on the essentially reverberating nature of the image.

> Astraddle on the dolphin's mire and blood,
> Spirit after spirit! The smithies break flood,
> The golden smithies of the Emperor!
> Marbles of the dancing floor
> Break bitter furies of complexity,
> Those images that yet
> fresh images beget,
> That dolphin-torn, that gong-tormented sea.[17]

2

THE MORBID AND
THE BEAUTIFUL

Edvard Munch
Painter of the Modern Soul Life

I will never forget the first time I walked into the rooms of the Munch collection in Oslo. I was twenty-one, poor, haunted, friendless, in a foreign country, a country I had chosen to make my home—in soul-sick, self-imposed exile from America. Lonely as only a young poet can be in a country where he cannot speak the language, I would walk around for days enveloped in a misty cloud of dread, in the grip of a vertiginous anxiety that transformed the harbor streets of Oslo into the smoky mineral light of the Inferno. My forced fundamentalist childhood religion was dying an agonized death. The Void was opening.

And then—those paintings! Those paintings of Edvard Munch! What precise visionary testaments of the soul's private hells and salty torture chambers! Brushed and slapped on mammoth canvases: paint streaked, striped, pasted, daubed, even squeezed directly out of the tubes! Paintings scratched, combed, gouged; feverishly worked paintings of dissolving

This chapter developed from a paper given at the 1st Annual Conference of The London Convivium for Archetypal Studies in London, June, 1987.

faces, ghoulish, madly staring, sunken-eyed creatures; putre-
fying corpses; emaciated, consumptive, sick, dying, wounded,
bloodied bodies painted with, oh, what ferocity and sureness
of expression, and what unexpected tenderness! I recognized
them all. Oh, how did he know? How did he know the tortured, crying, crippled figures of my dreams?

And then the colors! Never had I seen such exact formula-
tions of the inner chemistry of suffering, its psychological reality somehow perceived as shapes of living color—the ghastly
grey phosphorescence of despair, the putrid green metal of
nausea, the howling reds and the sulphurous yellows of panic,
the gall-green poisons of jealousy, the hematite browns and
purples of brooding melancholy, blackened reds of congealed
hate and the bright scarlet flowering of passion. It was beautiful! Yes, there was something so utterly and fearlessly true,
such a beauty, that I found myself, in sheer wonder of being, in
this mysterious room of soul pictures, weeping unstoppable
tears of gratitude to this strange, inimitable artist.

During the following seven years of my sojourn in Norway,
I went back again and again to stand in those rooms filled with
soul paintings, breathing in their dark and pungent odors, listening to their sombre chamber music, their adagios, their incredibly yearning melodies. And each time I came away
calmer, stronger in my sense of soul. It is wonderful, isn't it?
That painting can do this? That one solitude can speak to another? Across years and years! Time doesn't count. There he
was—I could see him in his cheap pied-à-terre in Paris or Berlin, standing almost reverentially in his three-piece suit as if he
were going to church, staring into the transparent mirror of the
soul and daubing the canvas with music. Copying Nature?
Here is Munch, writing in his journal:

*We can never hope to duplicate Nature anyway—therefore it
is better to express one's own feelings. How could one possibly
paint real grief—tears that well up from the depths of a person's soul, like those of the woman I saw crying in the hospital
for venereal disease, her arm clutching a pale, naked sickly*

51

child. She had just discovered that her newborn child was doomed to die. Her contorted face, the swollen lips, her bloated crimson chin. Her eyes mere slits from which rivulets of tears were flowing. Her reddish purple nose.

That anguish-racked face had to be painted the way I saw it then against the green walls of the hospital. And the inquiring, suffering eyes of the child I had to paint just as I saw them staring out of the tiny, pallid yellow body as white as the white sheet on which it lay. I had to ignore a lot of other things such as the effects of truth to light, which is relative. Large areas of the picture were like a poster—wide expanses of nothingness. But I hoped to make the best parts, the ones meant to convey the picture's true message of pain, something even more sublime.

And then the public all laughed at the picture, saying that it was blatantly immoral, and I was once more destined to be mocked and martyred. I knew that the accusation of immorality would cause me pain, even though I had intended it to be a highly moral work. And I knew that I would be branded like a common criminal.[1]

One hundred and one years have passed since Munch painted his first great soul picture, *The Sick Child*. Perhaps now we can begin to allow ourselves to feel the depths of anguish in this work and the *pothos*, or nostalgia—for soul, behind it. Only a very few of his contemporaries could. But how glad I was to find his paintings! Immediately, he became a teacher for me, a soul guide, as did the Czech poet, Rainer Maria Rilke, whom I had recently discovered. How else could I have made it through six years of clinical psychology at the University of Oslo? Rilke and Munch were older soul brothers, telling me about the wolves I would meet in the forest, pointing out secret paths known only to initiates in the brotherhood of dark pain. Through them I began to trust my own sense of soul, to believe in the value and the nobility of the imagination, to dare to own experiences previously locked out in shame and humiliation. And then a strange thing happened. When I began to own my own soul life, I also began to see that it wasn't only mine. There was another dimension which didn't really belong to me. What freedom! To discover that I was also Everyman, Everywoman! The same currents of soul flowing through me as through the person walking beside me. We meet in this river—not the petty personal one in which so many schools of psychology get caught—but the bigger one, the greater river.

Archetypal psychology shares the concern for soul that Edvard Munch expressed. Archetypal psychology can move us to see things from the perspective of soul—to see the world ensouled and alive from end to end and to give first place to soul in our lives and psychologies. *But the work of artists like Munch also contributes to the self-discovery and individuation of archetypal psychology itself.* Great art does this because there is a transhistorical dimension of the soul. The concerns of the soul are not bound by time, nor should they be allowed to be the exclusive domain of psychologists. Even the subjects of history become subjects of soul—when they have been touched by imagination.

In fact, it is soul which deepens events into experience,[2] making soul out of history. Soul is what turns the brutal iron bruise of "what has happened to me" into the imaginal red blood of sustaining heart food.

Archetypal psychology holds that the primary metaphor of psychology must be soul.[3] As psychologists we must learn to turn to artists like Munch to deepen our understanding of soul. One soul painting by Munch simply eradicates the relevance of volumes of analysis—by Freud or anyone else. For the dry, logical rhetoric of imageless abstraction that has asphyxiated both academic and clinical psychology is not a proper *logos* for *psyche.*If we can take the meaning of the logos of psyche as *that speech or telling which is inherent to psyche herself,* then we would have to say that *the psyche's form of logos is the image.* Or to say it in another way: If, as Jung held, "every psychic process is an image and an imagining," then the stuff of which our souls are made must be images, and Edvard Munch's soul painting calls us to a reverie upon the life of the soul and its images.

The paintings of Munch not only give the soul's voice a range it had historically lacked. They bring a physiognomy of soul into play. The face of the soul moves, is alive, shows its grief, its fear, its painful vulnerability, its shy longing. Whereas before the soul had little voice or face, now it has both: the soul embodied—no longer a bodiless soul nor a soulless body.

I like James Hillman's idea that archetypal psychology's first links are with "culture and imagination rather than medical and empirical psychologies, which tend to confine psychology to the positivistic manifestation of the nineteenth century condition of soul."[4] Though it will soon be the twenty-first century, we are still not free of that nineteenth-century positivism. Witness the way artists (of any art form) are seen by twentieth-century psychologists. "So-and-so was a great artist, but look at his life!" Take Munch—not only did he suffer the dismissive prejudices of his own time; he is still being subjected to that spirit of denial in other guises. In a recent issue of *The Journal of Psychohistory*, for example, Carol Ravenal, an associate professor of art, writes that the marks, erasures, alterations and deletions in Munch's art originate in impulses to attack his mother's breast and in efforts to retrieve this breast "which was originally denied."[5] This infantile psychologism— with its simplistic, reductive, analytical dissection of Munch's artistry—is a savage attack on the imagination itself, on imagination as the organ of perception of the soul. As Jung so succinctly put it: "This figure of the personal mother looms so large in all personalistic psychologies that, as we know, they never got beyond it."[6] In other words, as James Hillman writes,

> The mother archetype itself is responsible for personalistic psychology and for loading the burdens of the archetypal upon personal figures, personal relations and personal solutions and for taking oneself so personally, one's problems and fate always as "mine."[7]

The problem with such personalistic, reductive approaches to art is that works of the imagination can only be understood and appreciated through the imagination. Ravenal consistently

ignores the imagination in Munch's work just as she ignores
Munch's own painfully articulated intention: to be a painter of
the modern soul life.

Gaston Bachelard, that marvelously original phenomenolo-
gist of the elemental imagination, gives us an entirely different
perspective, a perspective informed by a love and respect for
imagination:

> The imagination is not, as its etymology suggests, the
> faculty for forming images of reality; it is the faculty for
> forming images which go beyond reality, which sing re-
> ality. It is a superhuman faculty.[8]

"It is a superhuman faculty." Bachelard could almost be speaking of Munch when he writes that "a man is a man to the extent
that he is a superman. A man should be defined by the sum of
those tendencies which impel him to surpass the human condition...The imagination invents more than objects and dramas—it invents new life, a new spirit; it opens eyes which hold
new types of visions."[9]

It is a peculiarity of personalistic psychology, loaded as it is
with the reductive theories of psychoanalysis and object relations, that it quite overlooks imagination as the faculty of forming images "which go beyond reality, which sing reality." For
Ravenal, the significance of Munch's work doesn't lie in its aesthetic revelations of our soul life, but rather in its usefulness as
illustrative case material for a psychological paper on Mother.
Munch was mother bound. Proof is that he painted these feminine figures. These actual forms, however, are completely ignored as archetypal persons, they are just representations of
Munch's mother. But before these figures are faces of a literal
mother, they are archetypal persons, persons to whom we ultimately owe our personality. They have an autonomy and an
intentionality which does not derive from our personal parents. In speaking of these archetypal figures Jung says that we
"are obliged to reverse our rationalistic causal sequences, and
instead of deriving these figures from our psychic conditions,

we must derive our psychic conditions from these figures" (*CW* 13.299). To lose touch with these figures in their archetypal sense is to lose touch with soul. Perhaps this is the danger in becoming a professor of art. Further, to become truly adult we must stop referring to childhood as if it were the origins of what we are now. As James Hillman and Wolfgang Giegerich have both said, from the perspective of developmental theory the adult is merely "a fully developed child"! Giegerich writes:

> To be truly adult means growing up and away from childhood. Yet what does psychology do? It conceives of man as a product of his childhood, of his father and mother...If I see my origin in childhood and derive my healthy or disturbed personality from this, I remain a child psychologically, even if educationally I may be as adult as they come.[10]

Hillman remarks that "the dominance of the child archetype in our psychological thinking, besides softening the intellect, has deprived the adult of his imagination."[11]

How is an artist to answer language used against him as an artist? But can a professor of art be against art? It may be so. The world is a strange place. How then do justice to the artist? By not being reductively personal, but archetypally personal, certainly. By kneeling beside him for a time and worshipping at the same altar? Perhaps it is better to take up the mantle of imagination when it has been so beautifully offered in painting after painting after unbelievable painting. The medieval Persian dervish, Jalal 'uddin Rumi, addressed this subject:

> Today, like every other day, we wake up empty
> and frightened. Don't open the door to the study
> and begin reading. Take down the dulcimer.
> Let the beauty we love be what we do.
> There are hundreds of ways to kneel
>   and kiss the ground.[12]

Bachelard gives us a clue as to how we could evolve a method of working with painting in his book *The Poetics of Reverie*—he demonstrates a way of "dreaming oneself into things."

> The image can only be studied through the image, by dreaming images as they gather in reverie. It is nonsense to claim to study imagination objectively since one really receives the image only if he admires it.[13]

Bachelard is talking of poetry, but we can transpose what he is saying to painting. He says that we must not try to command the image as a hypnotist commands a somnambulist. It should be the other way around: "When the reverie is good, when it has the continuum of good things, it is the somnambulist in us who imperceptibly commands the action of his mesmerizer."[14]

Reverie then is a method for working on images in poetry, paintings and dreams—listening for commands from the somnambulist within.

Seeing Through Realism

We need something more than just photographs of nature. Nor should we content ourselves with painting pretty pictures to hang on sitting room walls. Let us try and see, even though we ourselves may not succeed, if we cannot lay the foundations of an art dedicated to mankind. A style of art that will fire man's imagination. An art that springs from our very hearts.[15]

When Edvard Munch wrote these words in 1890 at the age of twenty-seven, he was already an artist of the highest calibre. I make this claim on the basis of a single picture, painted four years earlier and called simply *The Sick Child*. To my mind this painting has a beauty as breathtaking as anything ever painted, a beauty as earthly as it is unearthly, a beauty never before seen in painting.

Munch packed an immense vision into his archetypal seed images. He spoke—and painted—aphoristically, imagistically and analogically. He spoke from the soul, of the soul, to the soul. And his birth as an alchemist of soul has its moment in the painting of a teenage girl in a sickbed. Forty-three years later, in 1929, the sixty-year old painter said, "In *The Sick Child* I broke new ground—it was a breakthrough in my art. Most of what I later have done had its birth in that picture."[16] At the age of seventy-four he still regarded it as his most important work and adamantly refused to sell it, saying "I will never sell it, however much money I am offered—even if someone were to put 100,000 gleaming crowns on the table in front of me, they would not get it. That picture leaves my possession only over my dead body."[17] Munch's soul was in that painting.

What we are dealing with, then, is the birth of a new vision, not only personally for Munch, but collectively, for us all. But from the point of view of archetypal psychology, let us take note that this painting had its origins in the experience of death, specifically, in the experience of the death of the beloved. Love and death—Eros and Thanatos—two angelic artisans of the theophany of beauty. Notice that it was here, in the reverie upon Death's deft theft of his sister, Sophie, that young Edvard was initiated, at the age of fourteen, into his radical vision of soul. It took nine years for the reverie to mature and the painting to be born. Metaphorical soul reality born out of literal death. It is almost as if Munch was invested with something like what the Sufis call the *khirqa,* or "mantle," of Khidr— a "transcendent, transhistorical dimension." For the Sufis this investment with the mantle is something more than an incorporation into a brotherhood in Mecca or Paris, London or New York. It is a personal, direct and immediate bond with divinity—what we would call archetypal or imaginal reality. It is an awakening to soul, to what Hillman calls "the imaginative possibility in our natures...that mode which recognizes all realities as primarily symbolic or metaphorical."[18] We could also speak of an awareness of soul-as-metaphor in the sense that Hillman uses it to discuss the underlying aspiration of the work of archetypal psychology. Or again following Keats, we could speak of "soulmaking."

"We need something more than just photographs of nature." For Munch to say these words in 1890 in Christiania was
to fly in the face of a grim Senex tradition, upheld so piously by
all those sour-mouthed, God-fearing, Bible-quoting Funda-
mentalists and blank-eyed followers of positivism, empiricism
and realism. For none of these groups had much use for metaphorical reality. The theology of that time did not teach men
and women to contemplate the nature of soul as metaphor. Not
any more than does the psychology of our time.

However, in 1886, when Munch entered *The Sick Child* in the
annual autumn exhibition in Christiania it was apparent to a
few individuals—like his two mentors, Christian Krogh and
Hans Jaeger—that something altogether new had happened in
painting. Jaeger, who was due to serve a sixty-day prison sentence, beginning the day after the exhibition opened, for writing an indecent and blasphemous book attacking the
hypocrisy of the bourgeoisie's sexual morals, came away from
the exhibition not completely understanding what appeared to
be such an unfinished work yet feeling its undeniable power to
move the soul: "What delicate colors! One wants to whisper,
'Shhh, quiet!' to people talking around one—Munch should
have called his picture 'Shhh!'"[19]

No painting from the Naturalist school could possibly have
this effect on a viewer. If one looks at the Norwegian artists
painting before Munch, one finds extreme fidelity to the so-
called real world, exquisite observation of Nature and a meticulous concern to approximate the camera's objective, empirical
eye—in Jung's terms, a great sensation function. J.C. Dahl,
Tidemand, Cappalen—all followed the tenets of realism. In
fact, there had been no native school of Norwegian painting
since the Middle Ages because Norway had always imported
its painters. It was only in 1880, the year that the seventeen-
year-old Munch made his first oil painting, that three newly returned, expatriate artists—Christian Krogh, Erik Werenskjold
and Fritz Thaulow—pledged to found a native school of Norwegian painting based on Naturalism. Six years later, Munch,
who at twenty-one had learned all they could teach him, broke

decisively with all ideas of a nationalist, Naturalist art. A few years later in Paris he jotted down his strong feelings on what painting should be about, in what is now known as his St. Cloud Manifesto. He wrote that

> *People should understand the sacred, awesome truth involved, and they should remove their hats as in a church...There should be no more paintings of interiors of people reading and women knitting. In future they should be of people who breathe, who feel emotions, who suffer and love.*[20]

Other statements made by Munch in his largely undated journals resonate strongly with the 1890 manifesto.

> *Nature is not something that can be seen by the eye alone—it lies also within the soul, in pictures seen by the inner eye...The camera will never compete with the brush and the palette, until such times as photographs can be taken in Heaven or Hell.*[21]

Munch's work of 1886, the work of a twenty-two-year-old rebel, was not only new for the Norwegians. His three great paintings of that year—*The Sick Child, The Day After* and *Puberty*—had no equal in European art whatsoever. Ingrid Langaard, in her deeply sensitive study of Munch's paintings in the critical years, firmly holds that Munch is the first artist in Europe to paint Expressionist paintings. Regarding the other contenders for the title of "the Father of Expressionism"— Gauguin, Van Gogh and Ensor—she writes that "it is however a fact that none of them had painted in this style until 2–3 years after Munch painted his first expressionist painting."[22]

This means that the point of entry, as it were, of a certain archetypal perspective, a new Western vision, was a young artist far in the north of Europe, in the provincial capital of Norway. The moving force behind Munch's vision was his experience of the death of his sister which was, at the same time, in the words of Henry Corbin, the experience of "beauty...the theophany par excellence."[23] This supposition need not seem strange, for the experience of true beauty is an experience of the divine, an experience of God, to use the language of the mystics. Corbin writes:

> Here, it should be noted, we are dealing not only with a purely aesthetic pleasure accompanied by a joyful tonality but with the contemplation of human beauty as a *numinous*, sacral phenomenon which inspires fear and anguish by arousing a movement toward something which at once precedes and transcends the object in which it is manifested, something of what the mystic gains awareness only if he achieves the conjunction, the conspiration, of the spiritual and the sensory, constitutive of mystic love.[24]

The general response to *The Sick Child* among the public and the critics was one of anger, disgust and scorn. The painting was not perceived as beautiful at all. It was considered to be an abortion, a sketch, an unfinished mess, "the ravings of a madman." Munch wrote about this time many years afterwards:

> *No other painting in Norway has ever caused such a violent outburst of moral indignation. On the opening day, when I went into the room where it hung, there were crowds of people packed round it—and there were sounds of derisive laughter. When I went out into the street, the young Naturalist painters were standing there, together with their leader, Wentzel, the most feted artist of the day..."Pretentious rubbish!" he screamed in my face.[25]*

What apparently disturbed people the most was the technique or what seemed to be the lack of technique. No one seemed to be able to take in the image: a young girl dying. Somehow the whole notion of beauty had become split off from the experience of death. Beauty had become entirely subsumed under the perspective of Apollo—clean, lofty, noble, remote from death, darkness, sickness, imperfection. Consequently the possibility

61

of beauty in death, beauty in sickness, for example, was denied. It could not be perceived. Death could only be something ugly. But Munch had seen beauty in his sister's face as she lay dying.

Yes, death is horrible. But the eye of love perceives beauty even there. To speak, as Corbin does, of beauty as a "sacral phenomenon which inspires fear and anguish by arousing a movement toward something which at once precedes and transcends the object in which it is manifested" means that the experience of beauty reminds us of something. And what calls to us in the experience, what we are reminded of, is not ultimately something from our personal past at all, but something from our Platonic childhood, the awareness of the world of archetypal forms and images, the *mundus imaginalis*. The experience of beauty is an experience of nostalgia, of *pothos*. It is a longing for the literally unattainable—an archetypal nostalgia, a nostalgia for the archetypal.[26] And the experience of beauty is so invariably associated with tears because it also reminds us that to be human is to be a prisoner of time. There is a great, bottomless well of grief in our existence as human beings, and the garden of the soul is watered by the overflowings of these wellsprings in the soul's experience of theophanic beauty. The need for beauty may be one of the soul's most vital needs. Without beauty the soul would shrivel away. But we cannot entirely separate beauty from pain. Mysteriously, the rich soil of pain often makes the flowers of beauty glow more strongly in their colors. No beauty without beast. We cannot escape into some air-conditioned palace where nothing dark ever happens and where death and illness are forever banished, no matter what the exponents of plastic surgery and wonder drugs in our brave new world tell us.

The Sick Child

My guess is that Munch's experience of beauty-as-supreme-theophany emblazoned itself on his soul so that he never forgot it. Decades later he would paint or engrave the image with no original at hand yet without deviating the slightest from it.

But to a twenty-two-year-old with no actual model for what he wanted to achieve, the task must, at first, have seemed insurmountable. After carrying the image with him for five or six years after Sophie's death, he began trying to conjure it into a material form. He worked desperately on it for nearly his entire twenty-second year, painting and repainting it twenty times. There was no thought of creating a style—this was of absolutely no concern—he simply wanted to get it right. But in his feverish insistence, he was miraculously, unconsciously evolving a new vision of painting. He wrote about this period:

> When I first saw the sick child—her pallid face and the vivid red hair against the white pillow—I saw something that vanished when I tried to paint it. I ended up with a picture on the canvas which, although I was pleased with it, bore little relationship to what I had seen. I painted the scene many times in the space of one year, scratching it out, just letting the paint flow, trying endlessly to recapture what I had seen the first time—the pale, transparent skin against the linen sheets, the trembling lips, the shaking hands.[27]

This passionate devotion to the image, this dedication to crafting it and working it until it takes on its own life, is completely equivalent to what archetypal psychology means by soulmaking. This attitude to the image, as Hillman has pointed out, is one of *dulia*, an attitude of service, not of *latria*, or worship of the image as in idolatry. This service to the image, our image work, our *dulia*, is directed to the imagination by the imagination for the imagination.

Each time we work with the images of our dreams, for example, painting them with love or speaking to them in love in a poem, we are performing an act of service. When we work with a love for them, assured by their love for us, we are engaged in soulmaking.

For Munch this work on *The Sick Child* was a unique, ritual act of soulmaking. One can hear it in his journal jottings as well as see it in the intensity of feeling in the painting itself. It

63

is almost as if for the image to be pictured in the right way, there had to be a simultaneous dissolution of the ruling archetypal structure of consciousness, the heroic, Apollonian mode. We will see later that several other Gods make their appearance, as it were, in Munch's life during this time, but one of them is certainly Eros. And with Eros a warmth enters which melts the Apollonian rules like wax.

Using the brush handle Munch scored double lines at the edges of contours in the painting, thus blurring the definition of form. By patting the incompletely dried paint with rags, he transformed it into hills and valleys. He speckled the canvas randomly with erratic flecks of white, green and red paint. In many areas he trowelled the paint in thickly and scored it with gouges. None of these techniques, however, can be understood from the outside. The only way to understand them is to become the artist oneself. We must grasp his intention, and that is only possible if we grasp his vision. By calling attention to the literal matter of the paint itself in this way, Munch is making it quite clear that he is not trying to duplicate nature. He is not trying to approximate a photographic likeness. He makes us subtly aware that he is *seeing through* the literal paint and that he is seeing by means of a different medium than the physical eye. In doing this—as William Blake did in his way— Munch is giving us an excellent equivalent to archetypal psychology's claim that the image is not *what we see*, but *the way in which we see*, what we see *through*.

In his later descriptions of the genesis of *The Sick Child*, Munch tells us of his discovery that we see by way of images when he says, "I paint what I saw, not what I see."[28] Regarding his way of working, he writes that

> *I would occasionally, either in a sick, agitated frame of mind or in a happy mood, find a landscape I wanted to paint. I fetched the easel—set it up and painted from nature. The picture turned out well—but it was not what I wanted to paint. I was not able to paint it the way I saw it in my sick mood or in my happy mood.*[29]

In other words, everything Munch did to the canvas of his painting was in order to achieve his goal: to paint what he saw with his inner eye, the eye which saw soul. It is a mark of the enormous foolishness of modern psychology that a psychoanalyst, an art critic or a professor of art could conceive of using a painting by Munch to suggest that what is actually an act of ta'wil—which among the Sufis means the transfiguration of a literal event into an image of soul—is merely the result of hypothetical childhood impulses.

Of course childhood is full of things which resonate throughout our lives. Of course the mother is critically significant for the child. Of course there is personal interchange, there is a particular relationship. But to refuse to see that the thing is *simultaneously* a reflection of a metaphorical, archetypal reality is to stay forever within the perspective of literal identification.

Analysts and critics have long been puzzled by the parallel streaks of thinned paint which were originally supposed to have run down the painting and by other lines which have been gouged horizontally across the canvas. We heard earlier what one writer had to say about this. Let us hear now what the artist said:

I also discovered that my own eyelashes had contributed to the impression of the picture. I therefore painted them as hints of shadow across the picture. In a way the head became the picture. Wavy lines appeared in the picture—peripheries—with the head as center. I made frequent use of these wavy lines later.[30]

Munch is here suggesting that his eyes have contributed to the experience of what he saw. He is not painting an object at all, neither an inner nor an outer one, but an image. More precisely, he is painting a picture of an image. It is a picture of the way in which he saw his sister. He is not painting a picture of how his sister would look in general, as through the abstracting eye of the camera. He is showing us how she appeared to him. We are being allowed a glimpse of the artist's experience of imaginal

65

reality. And that experience does not preclude representation of the real tears "that well up from the depths of the soul" to blur the sight, of the eyelashes that glisten like wet branches in the rain.

Is this why it is so hard to really see this painting, to take it in? Is it because we must look at death? Our death? And perhaps through our eyelashes and our tears? For the sister is the artist's death. She it is who beckons to him across the threshold. She it is who holds the secret memories of the feminine way to the Imaginal. She is his death in other ways as well— because through her he contemplates extinction, dissolution, the necessary desubstantiation and relativization of the ego which accompanies soulmaking. In so far as he remains true to his sister, he will remain true to what is deepest in himself. Keeping close to her, true to her constantly dissolving form, he will be able to help liberate other images of the repressed feminine from the collective prejudices of his time.

The Sister

Psychology has not paid enough attention to the immense value of the archetypal sister as agent of soulmaking. The Gretel to our Hansel lost in the woods of literal reality. The Sieglinde to our Siegfried. Isis to our Osiris. A soft and mystical moon to our fierce, rational sun. *Soror Mystica* of the alchemical opus. *Anima Mercurialis*. Agile-subtle priestess of Imaginal Mysteries. Archetypal playmate. Sharer of secrets, comrade of mythical adventures. What art can be created without her? Sappho hails her as the moon, this archetypal twin.

> Awed by her splendour
> Stars near the lovely
> moon cover their own
> bright faces
> when she
> is roundest and lights
> earth with her silver[31]

Speaking of those feminine figures imaged in ancient engravings and texts of alchemy, Bachelard says something of great relevance for the alchemy of painting:

> Alchemy is a nuanced materialism which one can understand only by participating in it with feminine sensitivity, but keeping a record, all the same, of all the little masculine rages with which the alchemist torments matter. The alchemist looks for the secret of the world the way the psychologist looks for the secret of the heart. And the soror is there to soften everything. At the bottom of every reverie, we find that being which deepens everything, a permanent being. For me, when the word sister comes up in the lines of a poet, I hear echoes of a distant alchemy. Is this a poetic text, or is it a text of the alchemy of the heart?[32]

> Come pray with me, my sister,
> To recover vegetable permanence.

Bachelard, reflecting on these two lines from a poem by Edmond Vandercammen, comments: "Vegetable permanence," what an anima truth, what a symbol for a soul's repose in a world worthy of dreams!"[33]

Looking now at Munch's painting *The Sick Child* we could similarly ask, is this a work of art or is it a hieroglyph for the alchemy of the heart?

Is there anywhere a work of art which has succeeded in catching the tremulousness of life like this? We do not even know whether she is still in the land of the living. Perhaps it is her last breath. Her consciousness wavers on the knife-edge of life-and-death. Her breathing is a whisper fainter than the whisper of breeze invisibly blowing through the curtains of the open window. Is she still with us? Shhh! How faint the china white face with its dim pools of hidden blood, seemingly ashamed to darken the translucent skin with their pale, pink shadows. The bonfire of flaming orange hair the only thing left of the terrible fevers that have racked the thin girl's body with the holocaust of consumption. She's so close to departure. The body propped up among the pillows, face turned to lie on the unconsoling snowfields of linen. Shhh! Isn't she trying to say something?

In a pen and ink drawing from 1890 Munch depicts two little children setting out to explore the world. They are holding hands and walking away from us into a wide expanse of mountainous wilderness. He called it *Bertha and Karleman,* names he used in his journals when speaking of himself and Sophie. Karleman has knee-length trousers and holds a walking stick. Bertha wears a dress and is surrounded by rows of short, wavy lines, giving her the appearance of being in a disintegrating field of intense vibration, without the solidity of Karleman.

Sophie's death at the age of fifteen must have left her year-younger brother completely desolate. They had always been close, in particular since the death of their young mother from consumption when Edvard was five and Sophie six. Munch's adult account of those early days is simple and very moving. Life in the home, in spite of the presence of their mother's sister, Aunt Karen, was very sad. The family turned in on itself. Dr. Munch, their father, turned more and more to his prayers and the Bible. The happiest times for Edvard and Sophie were when they sat drawing around the family dining table. Sophie was good at it, too. Everyone acknowledged her skill and originality.

Much of Munch's own childhood was spent in sickness and fevers. He came close to succumbing to consumption himself. In fact, he was just recovering from an attack of it when Sophie showed the first signs of her fatal illness. In his journals Munch records the memory of this time in the subterranean gloom of the sickroom in which his despairing father kept watch beside his bed:

"Papa, it is so dark, this stuff that I'm spitting." It seemed as if the entire inside of his chest was dissolving and as if all of his blood would come spurting out of his mouth—Jesus Christ,

68

Jesus Christ. He folded his hands. "Papa, I'm dying; I can't die; Jesus Christ, I must not die." "Don't speak so loudly, my boy, I shall pray with you." And he raised his folded hands high above the bed and prayed: "Lord help him. If it be Thy Will, do not let him die. I beseech Thee, Lord God, we come to Thee in our hour of need...I beg thee, Lord; I pray Thee in the name of the Blood of Jesus Christ, make him well."[34]

As Edvard slowly recovered from his near death experience, he had to watch his beloved Sophie fall prey to the dread disease and die.

If I have circled around *The Sick Child* so long, it is because I am convinced that staying in reverie before this painting attunes one in a particular way. This circumambulation of the image is also the way of archetypal psychology. Munch himself did this, in painting it six different times at roughly ten year intervals throughout his life.[35]

According to Arne Eggum, the present curator of the Munch collection in Oslo, Munch left us some 1,100 paintings, sketchbooks, drawings and watercolors with a total sum of 6,000 pictorial productions and 18,000 graphic prints.[36]

For me, the great work begins with *The Sick Child*. As it has been said, "Where there is no imagination of death, there is a death of the imagination." Thus the enormous importance of this kind of painting.

Munch met Death early. And it terrified him. It took him years to get it into an image. That's because he and Sophie were spared their mother's death, taken away to relatives. Cheated in a way. But with Sophie's death, it was different. She was there, and he was with her. She became his *psychopomp*, his soul guide to the underworld. In attempting to imagine death, he paradoxically unearthed the imagination. And what was lying buried in its depths, beneath centuries of patriarchal deadwood, was image after image of outcast feminine soul. Of course, Munch painted pictures of the feminine, not because he was mother-bound but because what he met in the underworld were feminine images largely denied any reality by the bright solar world of nineteenth century positivism—feminine images which longed for love and to be allowed to exist in their own right.

One of the first of these images to emerge is depicted in the painting called *Puberty* from the same year. This time it is a study of a girl on the threshold of womanhood. It is the first painting in which Munch suggests a state of soul through the use of shadow. The way this outsize shadow leaps across the wall behind the naked girl seated on the edge of her bed gives it a decidedly commanding and autonomous character, like an uncanny prefiguration of Jung's later idea of the archetypal Shadow. She is not an illustration of an idea or a theory, however. And she is painted with such tenderness and sympathy that it is hard to imagine that we are looking at a painting by a young man of twenty-two. Ingrid Langaard, who as always is wonderfully sensitive to Munch's pictures, writes that

> with a visionary capacity to comprehend the most secret depths in the human soul, he has—in this young girl's form—managed to give visual expression for the feelings which have possessed her and penetrated to her core. With legs pressed together and eyes stiff with terror of the Unknown which will steal her body from her by force, she tries—with a purely instinctive movement to stop the process which will so instantaneously transform her from child to woman.[37]

Medusa

The other feminine image from Munch's twenty-third year is the painting called *The Day After*. It shows a dark-haired beauty in a state of dishevelled undress, lying akimbo on her bed, sleeping off a night of revelry. Nobody in Norway had seen anything like it. What no one said, but what everyone thought, was that it depicted a prostitute whom the artist frequented. No decent woman would allow this sort of intimacy with a man outside marriage. The truth of the matter was that Munch was deeply in love with a married woman by the name of Milly Thaulow, the first in a series of women to embody a new and fascinating kind of female energy for Munch. Until 1889, when Milly left him and he left Norway for three years in Paris, he was totally enthralled by her in an increasingly torturous relationship. In Paris he wrote in his journal:

> It's been a long time since I thought of her, but still the feeling is there, What a deep mark she has left on my heart. No other image can totally replace hers. Is it that she took the perfume of life from me? Is it because she lied, deceived, that one day she suddenly took the scales from my eyes and I saw Medusa's head, saw life as a great horror? Everything which I had seen in a mist of rose now seemed empty and gray...here I felt love's burning unhappiness...I felt the executioners...and I was almost insane for several years...nature screamed in my blood...I was going to burst.[38]

Did he actually write, "I saw Medusa's head"? And did he not write that Nature screamed in his blood? To speak of Nature screaming in the blood is another way of saying "Medusa," but the experience is not yet distanced, it has no name. Phenomenologically, Munch is describing that uncannily intimate apprehension inherent in male, solar consciousness when it meets Medusa—a nameless dread. We must recognize another apparition of divinity, a theophany of fright: *Mysterium Tremendum*, the fear of the living God, or rather, the living Goddess. The name Medusa, Kerényi informs us,[39] can be translated as "The Mistress"! However, this mistress is usually considered to be the image of the absolutely intolerable. Niel Micklem, for example, writes that the "natural expression" of Medusa is "more than the human condition can stand" and that the petrifying effect of her gaze is an image of the "fixation" of what he calls the "delusional systems" in psychosis.[40] But Medusa doesn't just *represent* something—an idea, a psychological state. She is an imaginal reality, a soul image. And

71

she may also be the reason for the delusional systems that psychology devises to protect itself from a lunar, or lunatic, vision. Usually psychology panics straight into diagnosis when its tolerance level for anxiety is reached. However, if we can stand it, let us now try to hold back. By declining diagnosis, we may gain in soul. If we don't reach for our nominalist guns, we may steal a quick look in the polished shield held up to Medusa's face and see our own terror reflected there.

Munch's painting *The Scream* is not merely an illustration of borderline psychosis or of Janov's "Primal Scream." If color could be said to scream, then those streams of crimson clouds in the sky could be said to be screaming. It is a soul *in extremis*, in terror of being alive, as much as of dying. A lost soul, disinherited, no longer at home in the world. *The Scream* could well stand as an archetypal emblem over the gateway of this century's descent into hell. The lost soul of the world. The scream of *anima mundi*:

> *I stopped and leaned against the railing, half-dead with fatigue. Over the grey-blue fjord the clouds hung, as red blood and tongues of flame. My friends drew away. Alone and trembling with fear, I experienced Nature's great scream.*[41]

So Munch described the experience behind the painting in his journals. Modern man's loss of soul is reflected in the loss of soul within the very vocabulary which is supposed to deal with it, the terminology of clinical psychology and psychiatry. The language chosen to describe psychopathology has lost all sense of soul. And this soulless language has invaded even the art departments of universities. In the article quoted earlier, Ravenal comments, regarding Munch's loss of Milly and his journal entry mentioning Medusa, that "his aggression was projected as he transformed her into a castrating Medusa."[42]

I wince when I hear such language. The rhetoric itself is aggressive, like rubbing salt in the open wounds of the soul. There are five ways in which this kind of psychology denigrates soul, or psyche:

1) It pretends to explain the psyche. But we can't explain the psyche, we are the psyche.[43] Further, the soul longs for imagination, not explanation.

2) It makes the psyche a projection of the ego (inflating the ego) and denies the objective reality of the psyche. But Medusa is not a creation of Munch's or anyone else's ego!

3) It derives an archetypal figure (Medusa) from a psychic condition (aggression), rather than, as in Jung's call for the reverse, deriving the psychic condition from the archetypal figure.

4) It doesn't ask *who* Medusa is; her imaginal reality is denied.

5) It turns Medusa into a conceptual allegory, an "agent of castration"—a thoughtless idea which thoughtlessly follows Freud's thoughtless dismissal of the Medusa motif with the words: "to decapitate equals to castrate."[44]

A psychology which has no respect for the autonomous nature of the psyche doesn't deserve its name. Archetypal psychology aims at redressing this situation by invoking the Neoplatonic method of *epistrophé*, "turning about"—that is, by reverting or returning any phenomenon to its archetypal source. According to James Hillman, archetypal psychopathology returns the conditions we suffer to their true home in divine events. If we are created in divine images it follows that so too are our afflictions. This is the foundation for an archetypal psychopathology.

Following Jung's pointer that if we want to find the Gods we must now look for them in our diseases, Hillman emphasizes the double link—that pathology is mythologized and mythology is pathologized. Imagination thus becomes a method for investigating and comprehending psychopathology.[45]

Returning to Medusa, we might say that she is the archetypal experience of raw and naked life, the archetype of life itself. With her hair of writhing, squirming, wriggling, coiling and uncoiling snakes, she looks out into the world with a multiplicity of eyes, a hissing multiplicity of viewpoints. It is Apollonian solar, masculine consciousness which cannot look at her. She turns this kind of consciousness to stone, a caricature

73

of itself, a petrified monument to masculine, monotheistic vision. This masculine consciousness, cut off from the archetype of life and polycentric vision, reacts only with extreme terror and panic, as Roquentin, in Jean-Paul Sartre's novel *Nausea*, who finds that naked existence is *de trop*—"too much"—because it won't stay contained in any neat categories and is always about to bulge out of its own skin, burst its seams, obscenely and luxuriously pullulating into ever more versions of itself, in spontaneous exuberance of self-display. Jung called this archetype of life the *anima*:

> The anima...is a "factor" in the proper sense of the word. Man cannot make it; on the contrary, it is always the a priori element in his moods, reactions, impulses, and whatever else is spontaneous in psychic life. It is something that lives of itself, that makes us live; it is a life behind consciousness that cannot be completely integrated with it, but from which, on the contrary, consciousness arises. (*CW* 9.57)

Please note that I am not drawing a hard and fast distinction between anima/psyche/soul and world. My experience of soul is my experience of that part of the World Soul which is manifest to me.

Munch said that when he saw Medusa's head, he saw life as a great horror. He painted *The Scream* as a precise record of that experience. He did not say that it was his scream, but the scream of nature, or what we could call the World Soul, in him. Like Sartre's Roquentin he found life overpowering, Nature "too much"; just being alive was already unbearable.

A Meander

It is extremely difficult for masculine consciousness, the animus of Western civilization, to face Medusa and see her beauty when we have been taught for centuries that she is ugly and terrifying. For example, there is a solar myth, the myth of Perseus, in which Medusa is conquered and beheaded. Kerényi reminds us that the sun was called "Perseus."[46] When Munch names Medusa, he calls up an old *psychomachia*—the ancient soul struggle between the Solar Hero and the Queen of the Night. Perseus, more for a show of ego strength than anything else, decides to hunt down Medusa in her lair "on the other side of Okeanos, near the Garden of the Hesperides, where the realm of Night begins," and to behead her. To reach the Gorgon's cave, Perseus must track through "pathless forests and rocks"—wild, untamed country—haunt of the outcast feminine. When he finds Medusa, he avoids her gaze by looking at her image in his shield and beheads her with his sword. We have been taught to admire this feat and acclaim Perseus' courage. However, with winged sandals, which he has borrowed, an adamantine sickle sword, also borrowed, and the helmet of invisibility, he is like a high-tech mercenary facing a barefoot aborigine.

It is, we must admit, a very unequal battle. Can we not see behind this heroic, solar triumph a real fear of the "archetype of life," as Jung calls the anima?

Unity, light and monotheism vanquish the intolerable feminine with its dark serpent nest of polymorphous, polycentric vision. Micklem writes that "the way Perseus handles Medusa is a way of dealing with psychopathology."[47] He is referring to the indirect way in which the hero, using his shield as mirror, decapitates the Gorgon. The story has become an allegory, and Medusa means psychosis, an intolerable reality for the Apollonian onlooker.

Using the image of decapitation through indirection, Micklem advocates that psychotherapy not confront psychosis directly, insisting on curing the psychopathology, but approach it indirectly. So far so good. But it seems that this so-called indirect approach to psychosis is actually a screen for some very direct, decapitating action. As Micklem continues, the "therapeutic influence can only reach its centre indirectly in the far distance and darkness."[48] Now, notice the quick sword thrust of the solar-heroic mode: "It is doubtful, if, *without the aid of a physical agent*, we as therapists can decide to induce or cure it" [emphasis mine].[49] Suddenly, it is clear that all this indirection is actually an indirect plea for the use of "the preparations of psychopharmacy," which as agents of a "physical approach" must claim "pride of place."[50]

The archetypal stubbornness of psychotic soul states has become literalized in "the body's involvement as the place of immovable fixation." And thus, the use of drugs is seen to make an "undeniable therapeutic contribution towards enhancing psychic accessibility."[51]

At the risk of being labelled irresponsible and impertinent, I would say that in my experience this is certainly not the case. Naked psychosis may certainly be alarming, but the effect of "the preparations of psychopharmacy" is, in my experience, nothing more than a deceptive illusion of normalcy, which insulates and isolates one from one's own psychic reality and subtly corrodes one's sense of validity. Soulmaking is put on ice, and the individual tragically struggles with the system of medical psychiatry and its paranoid controls.

For archetypal psychology Perseus is an image of the archetypal solar hero, and it is consistent with this solar image that it should be used allegorically to defend the use of drugs to counter psychosis. For let us be clear: the use of such high-powered drugs is more than a medical intervention, it is a solar attack. "The way Perseus handles Medusa is a way of dealing with psychopathology." The solar hero invades the lunar realm of the night and murders its Queen by cutting off her head.

The mythologem is literalized when the psychiatrist, acting from this solar perspective, injects his patient with a sophisticated preparation of Dipyxl, for example, in order to sever the "intolerable" head of psychosis, "enhancing" the patient's "psychic accessibility."

And let us not forget that for the ancient Greeks, as Richard Onians reminds us, psyche was particularly associated with the head.[52] Perseus severs the connection between psyche/head and body, just as the preparations of pscyhopharmacy seem to do. The ideal aim of the Perseus perspective would be to achieve with one literal stroke of the pharmaceutical sword a liquidation of the mythopoetic imagination of Medusa, i.e., 'psychosis.' This literal stroke turns the myth of the murder of Medusa into the murder of myth.

Who, we must ask, finds the psychosis intolerable, the patient or the psychiatrist? And if we administer drugs should we not be more direct about why we do so?

Who is more crazy—mad Medusa with her directness, or supersane Perseus with his solar intolerance disguised as indirection? The plight of any psychiatrist caught in the system is very real. How can he or she move out of the archetypal solar perspective into a more empathetic, lunar one? Everything, from the architecture of the mental hospital to the journals on the psychiatrist's desk, reflects a solar perspective.

The comments of R.D. Laing, made before the Royal Society in London in 1966, about his early struggle to move into a more lunar approach to psychosis are instructive:

A woman patient who has been a patient in a mental hospital for over twenty years, approaches me at the same time each day, curtsies and hands me a piece of cardboard on which is stuck a small effigy. I take it, appraise it, smile, say "thank-you," bow, hand it back. She takes it, smiles, curtsies, walks away. Almost every day for about eighteen months the same scene is repeated.

The effigy is surrounded by captions with arrows directing the reader to different sections:

"These limbs are made with wax from my ear and hair from my armpit."

"The genital area is made with my menstrual blood and my pubic hair."

"The face is made with my tears, my saliva, my catarrh, and hair from my head."

"The body is made with my shit, my sweat, and my blood."

I played my part in this ritual to humour her, somewhat patronizing and embarrassed. I might have taken the palms of her hands and licked her sweat. I might have drunk her blood, swallowed her tears. But I was a psychiatrist. Might I now be able to show her as she showed me, how I, as she, needed to be accepted? Can I confess my tears, that I too want them to be confirmed and blessed. This patient's schizophrenic behaviour was woven out of the snot, shit, saliva, the tears and the sweat and the blood of a suffering and desire she chose to express in her way. What is our way? By giving and receiving papers at the Royal Society, perhaps. If we are normal, are we more direct and honest?[53]

The note of humility upon which Micklem's article ends, following his advocacy of psychiatic drugs in the treatment of psychosis, rings curiously hollow: "We remain in awe of the image that alters personality so far from conscious control and accept with humility the role of the intolerable in individuation."[54]

Considering that these drugs are usually given to patients against their will, where is the humility towards "the role of the intolerable in individuation"? Is a true awe and respect for the image compatible with solar heroics driven by Gorgonophobia?

I have studied the events of Munch's life in the 1880s and 1890s in great detail, and I can best see them, including the paintings he made then, as foreground. They grow clearer, somehow, as one begins to perceive a little of the swirling forces of the archetypal background. Munch was not alone in his sensitivity to the emergence of archetypal figures. Behind the sunny optimism and positivist belief in the wonders of the new technological era, there was another, darker current flowing, an erotic death wish which reached out with pale, glistening arms to pull the solar hero off the river bank and down into the depths of the soul's archaic waters. And when he refused and lashed out with his sharp intellect, she grew vengeful and demanded *his* head. Not only in Munch's work of the 1890s, but everywhere in the great Decadence of the fin de siècle, she appeared—like multiple apparitions—in image after image: whirling in a wild, brazen dance through the paintings of Gustav Moreau, Franz von Stuck, Gustav Klimt, Aubrey Beardsley; in novels like Huysman's *À Rebours*; in plays like Oscar Wilde's and operas like Strauss's. Yes, I am speaking of Herod's lovesick stepdaughter, Salome. Who is she but Medusa reincarnated? And this time out to get even with the Apollonian spiritual hero by cutting off his head! John the Baptist as Perseus aged? Why not? Isn't he portrayed as one in love with divine light and spirit, infuriating to Salome because of his rejection of her aesthetic and sensual love of the flesh?

Archetypal soul artist that he was, Munch also painted Salome in many different versions, often holding his own severed head. Yes, he knew that she was a force to be reckoned with. What folly of the psychoanalytic art critic to see merely "projection" and "castration anxiety" in these amazing paintings! Only a person truly sensitive to the psyche can see that these are "images which go beyond reality, which sing reality"! For however fearful of women Munch might have been in his relationships, he was never a misogynist; he never put women down in the way that his contemporary Strindberg did, and in his time he had many deep and close friendships with women. In particular, he was drawn to precisely those women who embodied the new feminine energy which was just beginning to seriously challenge the patriarchy's moral, legal, economic, religious and sexual structures—women who were beginning to assert their own autonomy and independence.

Of course, there were women like this in earlier times. One has only to think of Mary Shelley and her mother or Clara Schumann and her mother. But these instances were rare until the years wore on towards the close of the nineteenth century. There had also been men in those days of the late eighteenth century and the first part of the nineteenth century, especially among the Romantics, who stood up for the outlawed modes of the feminine. Three of these men also expressed an explicit love of the beauty of Medusa. One was Goethe; another was Baudelaire; the third was Shelley. Mario Praz, that great scholar of the Romantic agony, thinks that no picture ever made a deeper impression on Shelley than the *Medusa*, attributed at one time to Leonardo, which he saw in the Uffizi in 1819.[55] Shelley's poem on the head is a manifesto of the conception of Beauty among the Romantics. After exclaiming that "its horror and its beauty are divine," he adds:

> Upon its lips and eyelids seem to lie
> Loveliness like a shadow, from which shine,
> Fiery and lurid, struggling underneath,
> The agonies of
> anguish and of death.
> *Yet it is less the horror than the grace*
> *Which turns the gazer's spirit into stone...*
> 'Tis the melodious hue of beauty thrown
> Athwart the darkness and the glare of pain,
> Which humanise and harmonize the strain.
> [emphasis mine]

The 'Madonna'

Shelley's feeling for Medusian beauty, the beauty of the morbid, could almost be taken for an appraisal of Munch's unique kind of soul painting and, in particular, the most radically revolutionary soul painting of all, perhaps of the entire fin de

79

siècle, that painting of 1894 known originally as *Loving Woman* and later as *Madonna*. Of this painting, Munch wrote:

> *The woman who gives herself, and takes on a madonna's painful beauty—woman in her manysidedness a mystery to man—woman who is at the same time a saint, a whore and an unhappy person abandoned.*[56]

It is impossible to say how much Munch's bold, eccentric, erotic, outrageous and intelligent woman friends of the 1880s and 1890s directly inspired this picture. Certainly, we see something of Milly Ihlen there. And then, Oda Lasson, "La vraie Princess de la Bohème," always a good friend and confidante of Munch's during his youth in the birth-panged bohemia of Christiania. More than any other woman, though, we feel the impact of Dagny Juell. Crinkly auburn-haired Dagny, the young Norwegian music student who arrived in the early 1890s like a thunderclap among the Berlin circle of the Zum Schwarzen Ferkel and in no time had the entire group—Strindberg, Dehmel, Servaes, Meier-Graefe, Lidforss, Munch and Przybyszewski—falling over themselves for her attentions. Dagny, who, it was rumored, inspired whoever spoke to her, who believed in free love and living imaginatively. Dagny, who was nicknamed "Ducha" ("Soul" in Polish) by Przybyszewski, whom she finally married. Dagny, who wrote her own plays of feminist vision and translated her husband's novels of free love, anarchism and satanism into Norwegian; Dagny, who infuriated Strindberg to the point of paranoid obsession, and Dagny, who—the comrade—stood by Munch when his exhibitions were showered with abuse.

The *Madonna* is certainly not a literal portrait of Dagny, who had short reddish hair, not the long black snaky hair of the painting. But there is an expression of self-possessed calm and absorbed and unashamed enjoyment in the Madonna's face which may have been inspired by Dagny.

The painting was an immediate success among Munch's friends. Przybyszewski used a litho of it on the cover of his next novel, often referring to her in it as well as to Munch himself and many of his other paintings. Sigbjørn Obstfelder, Norwegian poet and friend of Munch, was deeply moved by it:

> Life has surrounded itself with a mysterious beauty and terror, which the human senses cannot, therefore, define, but to which a great poet can pray. The desire to…understand in a new way that which our daily life has relegated to a minor position, and to show it in its original enigmatic mystery—this attains its greatest heights here in Munch's art and becomes religious. Munch sees woman as she who carries the greatest marvel of the world in her womb…He seeks to depict that moment when she just becomes conscious of this in all its gruesomeness.[57]

That the painting—or should I say "icon," for it is a total revisioning of the nature of the icon—is simultaneously depicting both the conception of new life and the "little death" of orgasm, seems beyond doubt. Munch wrote about this moment in his journals, and the following passage is often cited in reference to the painting:

> The pause as all the world stops in its path. Moonlight glides over your face filled with all earth's beauty and pain. Your lips are like two ruby-eyed serpents and are filled with blood, like your crimson red fruit. They glide from one another as if in pain. The smile of a corpse. Thus, new life reaches out its hand to death. The chain is forged that binds the thousands of generations that have died to the thousands of generations to come.[58]

However shocking the picture seemed to people at the time there were some individuals who did "understand the sacred, awesome truth involved" and metaphorically removed their hats "as in a church" as Munch had wished five years previously when writing the manifesto from St. Cloud.

In Munch's theophanic vision the Goddess and the woman conspire in a single numinous form. He seems to have experienced the Madonna as—at one and the same time—*person* and *archetype*. In Henry Corbin's words, she is a "person-archetype." This theophanic conception—the only way to do justice to such a soul painting—is "of an Apparition which is a shining of the Godhead through the mirror of humanity, after the manner of the light which becomes visible only as it takes form and shines through the figure of a stained glass window."[59] This vision of the invisible in a concrete form is apprehended not by the literal, physical sense organs but by the active imagination, which is the organ of theophanic vision. For the Sufi mystics who inspired Corbin, it was a basic truth that God could not be contemplated independently of a concrete being; they held that the Godhead is more perfectly seen in a human being than in any other form and that it is more perfectly seen in woman than in man.[60] Similarly, for archetypal psychology the archetypal is in us as an image is in a mirror. And the place of this presence is the theophanic imagination that is invested in each of us.

In Munch's picture there is no separation made between the spiritual and the sensible. Christianity had split the sensual woman from the spiritual one. Either the woman was good, decent, pious and virtually sexless, or she was wicked, immoral, indecent and sexual. The Virgin Mary and the Whore Mary Magdalene split apart. What a merry thought to marry the two Marys! But what resulted in Munch's painting was an image which was neither whore nor virgin, but something altogether new. New—ironically, for she is so old, so old. We know of Goddesses before the rise of Judeo-Christian male monotheism in which pleasure-loving sensuality was one of the central attributes of deity.

This capacity to enjoy pleasure has been seen by many Jungians as part of the Witch archetype. And if we have denied the Witch then we end up pretty grim—like Puritans at an all-day prayer meeting. Women who have lost the Witch or never accepted it in their lives feel guilty for everything, especially anything to do with the enjoyment of pleasure. And men who have never claimed the Witch in themselves stay helplessly tied to Mother. So this Madonna figure of Munch's is very important. In her unashamed sexuality she looks at the world with fearless objectivity. Her bloodred halo is like the ancient Roman *flammeum*, the bridal veil flame-colored to induce love in the soul. This *flammeum* also points to the belief in the *genius* residing in the head, the belief in the life-soul or divinity often referred to as "a fire in the head." Alchemically, this reddening is also an epiphany of the *rubedo*, the crimson flush of Aphrodite in the bleached and whitened body of the work—blood returning to the head as after a faint, thoughts reddened into life, the rich blood of love coloring the pale face of austerity: Aurora. The Witch with her crimson halo holds something of the heat of passion.

Is the naked *Madonna* beautiful? Is she obscene? Is she, with her provocative stare, corpselike smile and snaky hair, morbid? Can we, as we approach the year 1994, a century later, yet look at her without wishing to cut off her hair, her head *and* her halo? As Andrei Tarkofsky wrote, "a true artistic image gives the beholder a simultaneous experience of the most complex, contradictory, sometimes even mutually exclusive feelings."[61]

The *Madonna* was—and is—shocking, disturbing and stunning because she is so multivalent. We can almost feel the gaze of that mass of invisible serpents writhing on her head. But we can also sense in her eyes the memory of a terror transcended, the image of a young girl seated on the edge of her womanly life. And the anguish-racked face of the mother with the baby doomed to die. And don't those inscrutable, heavy-lidded eyes also hide the deep grief of *The Sick Child* whispering those last painful words to her brother? During the same time that he was working on this picture, Munch entered in his journal a fictionalized account of his sister Sophie's last moments. It begins:

It was evening. Maja lay flushed and feverish in her bed; her eyes blinked and she looked restlessly around the room. She was hallucinating. My dear, sweet Karleman, take this away from me; it hurts so. Please, won't you: she looked pleadingly at him. Yes, you will. Do you see the head over there? It is Death.[62]

Writing about Leonardo's portrait "A Young Lady With a Juniper," Tarkofsky says that it is not possible to say what impression the portrait makes on us. "It is not even possible to say definitely whether we like the woman or not, whether she is appealing or unpleasant. She is at once attractive and repellent. There is something inexpressibly beautiful about her and at the same time repulsive, fiendish...It has an element of degeneracy and beauty."[63] Because we can't achieve any kind of balance in the way we look at such an image, we are precipitated into an awareness of infinity through it; "for the great function of the image is to be a kind of detector of infinity...towards which our reason and our feelings go soaring, with joyful, thrilling haste."[64]

The *Madonna* has precisely this contradictory effect upon us, and as Tarkofsky says, it acts as "a kind of detector of infinity," which depth psychology, following Heraclitus, speaks of as "the boundlessness of soul."

I was, in fact, quite dumbfounded, in reading Paul Gauguin's son's biography of Munch, to discover that he, Pola Gauguin, found an almost mystical similarity between Leonardo da Vinci and Edvard Munch. In a four-page comparison of their approach to art and their willful individuality, Gauguin succeeds in convincing me that, if reincarnation were a reality, then Munch would certainly be a good candidate for the returned Leonardo.[65] It's a strange and powerful thought. Perhaps, even that outlandish bit of speculation will make us look differently at Munch's art.

I don't think that it is necessarily any indication of the greatness of an artist's work that the critics and public consider it to be bad, but it is striking how despised Munch's work was during the time of the fin de siècle. In 1895 the *Madonna* had its first showing in Norway in Munch's only exhibition in his country for three years. The following, from the popular conservative daily *Aftenposten*, is a sample of the response he got.

He seems either to be someone who's hallucinating about art or he is some kind of joker who thinks the public a fool and makes a lie of both art and life. Even though these caricatures are laughable, the worst is that such disgusting lies are being perpetrated—which makes one quite ill and tempted to call in the police.[66]

Munch's *Life-Frieze* came together as a series during those difficult years in Berlin, first comprising only six paintings around the theme of love, but growing through additions to twenty-two paintings when it was last shown complete, in Leipzig in 1903. There each of four walls in the exhibition hall had a subtitle: "The Seeds of Love," "Blossoming and Fading of Love," "The Anxiety of Life" and "Death." There were all the great soul paintings of the 1880s and 1890s, and the *Madonna* was always prominent. Considering that this exhibition toured Europe all through the 1890s and into the twentieth century, its influence, however hated by the bourgeoisie, must have been profound. And yet we still don't know quite what to make of it all. As a true Decadent, Munch, of course, had the honor of having his paintings officially banned from Nazi Germany in the 1930s on grounds of their being "degenerate art."

Conclusion

My aim in this chapter has been to return soulmaking to beauty and to try, through speaking of Munch's work, to see beauty in connection with the more unhappy areas of soul life. I have a concern about this in my work as a therapist as well as in my work as a writer. I have noticed that the soul presents itself in the consulting room, as Hillman has pointed out, not only because it seeks love, but also because it seeks beauty, and that the beauty it longs for is the beauty of its own divinity. In those moments of hopeless agony where the soul confesses its most terrible truths, it can also stand forth in the nakedness of its being and recognize itself as pure theophanic image in the transparent mirror of the divine. In those moments I am as dumb as anyone: there is such beauty there!

In that revolutionary text, *The Myth of Analysis*, James Hillman, in speaking of the beauty of psyche, writes that

> by being touched, moved, and opened by the experiences of the soul, one discovers that what goes on in soul is not only interesting and meaningful, necessary and acceptable, but that it is attractive, lovable and beautiful. The ultimate beauty of psyche is that which even Aphrodite does not have and which must come from Persephone who is Queen over the dead souls and whose name means "bringer of destruction." The Box of Beauty which Psyche must fetch as her last task refers to an underworld beauty that can never be seen with the senses. It is the beauty of the knowledge of death and of the effects of death upon all other beauty that does not contain this knowledge.[67]

The beauty of psyche and of therapy as an aesthetic undertaking are of little concern to our modern psychologies. But in ignoring the beauty of soul, even in its most pathologized forms, we deny the soul its essentially aesthetic nature. An appreciation of the need to turn toward beauty in therapy echoes Hillman's insight: "Imagine—eighty years of depth psychology without a thought to beauty!" and his idea that "if we would recuperate the lost soul, which is after all the main aim of all depth psychologies, we must recover our lost aesthetic reactions, our sense of beauty."[68]

Andrei Tarkofsky, artist and Russian soul brother to Munch, said before his death, "I think that one of the saddest aspects of our time is the total destruction in people's awareness of all that goes with a sense of the beautiful."[69]

I close this tribute to Edvard Munch, painter of the modern soul life, with two quotations from the artist himself:

> *How beautiful life is, after all. Life that—despite everything remains a Canaanite land filled with wine and honey for me,*

and which I shall never be able to enter. I can only observe how beautiful it must be.[70]

My whole life has been spent walking by the side of a bottomless chasm, jumping from stone to stone. Sometimes I try to leave my narrow path and join the swirling mainstream of life, but I always find myself drawn inexorably back towards the chasm's edge, and there I shall walk until the day I finally fall into the abyss. For as long as I can remember I have suffered from a deep feeling of anxiety which I have tried to express in my art. Without anxiety and illness I would have been like a ship without a rudder.[71]

3

DIONYSOS AND DUENDE

Federico García Lorca
Torero of the Imagination

Were I to subtitle this chapter "Imagination and the Theatre of
the World," it would be not only to call attention to the world as
stage, life as mythological enactment, but also to recall the dramatic nature of imagination itself—its power to create and destroy reality, its terrible and beautiful masks and disguises; its
hilarity and slapstick; its astonishing capacity to originate plots
and characters; its ironic-compassionate aesthetic of seeing (and
seeing through) everything as a performance; its real tears and
laughter; its magical manner of moving the heart and its mediu-
mistic way of momentarily allowing the Gods to become visible,
while allowing us to see ourselves as metaphors of them.

El Paseo [1]

This chapter begins and ends in Dionysos—the God of Theatre
and that archetypal structure of consciousness most fundamental to a therapy that would avoid the inherent misogyny of a psychoanalysis informed by the archetypal dominant of Apollo.

This chapter was originally a paper given at the 2nd Annual Conference of The
London Convivium for Archetypal Studies, "Imagination and the Theatre of
the World," in London, June, 1988. The Spanish terms used as sub-headings
here are taken from specific, classical divisions of the bullfight and, as they are
deeply integral to the structure of this chapter, the reader is advised to pay
close attention to their definitions, given in the notes (N.C.).

Historically, the initial statement of this point of view was made by James Hillman in his 1969 Eranos lecture.[2] At that time he suggested that analytical consciousness has been governed by an archetypal structure that favors the masculine over the feminine, the principles of light and order and distance over emotional involvement—what has, in short, been called the Apollonic over the Dionysian.

Exposing prejudices in both classical scholarship and classical psychiatry, Hillman claimed that these fields are largely in collusion against the Dionysian, resulting in a repression—and thus a distortion—of all Dionysian phenomena so that they have come to be seen as inferior, hysterical, effeminate, unbridled and dangerous. If, however, Dionysos was the Lord of Souls, psychotherapy can hardly afford to labor under misleading notions of him. In fact, "this archetypal dominant is surely the *sine qua non* for any depth psychology that would be therapeutic."[3]

This is a very large statement. And since it became generally available in expanded version in *The Myth of Analysis* in 1972, I have seen no response to it among analysts of any school. That is now sixteen years ago! Could this claim be so radical that the hearing of it is immediately repressed in analytical circles?

There has been a shadow cast over Dionysos long enough. It is time for it to be withdrawn. There is shadow enough within the God. Contrary to popular belief, "the shadow is not a separated archetype but is archetypal; according to archetypal psychology, each God contains shadow and casts it according with how he or she shapes a cosmos. Each God is a way in which we are shadowed."[4]

Shadow is inevitable—and a God of shades and shadows makes this fact more evident than does a God of pure light.

In the past few years there has been a response to the call to reevaluate Dionysos, but this has not come from analysts so much as from individuals connected with the theatre and theology. Here I would like to echo Hillman's call for a Dionysian consciousness, and through the study of a modern devotee of the God, deepen the imaginal value of the Dionysian for psychotherapy.

Offering of the Cape

In this chapter I address the genius of an exceptional man, one of our century's finest poets, who at the same time was an innovative dramatist, composer-musician, artist and performer. It has been said that Federico García Lorca was the greatest poet in Spain since Cervantes.

Although he lived only thirty-eight years, Lorca left a priceless ring of keys to the Dionysian temples of the Imagination. From the *Libro de Poemas* when he was twenty-one to the *Sonetos del Amor Oscuro* when he was thirty-eight; from the youthful *The Butterfly's Evil Spell* to the posthumously performed *The House of Bernarda Alba*; from the brilliant and ecstatic talk on *Cante Jondo* in the Alhambra with Manuel de Falla when he was twenty-four, to the *El Sol* interview with Bagaria two months before his death—Lorca created Dionysian masterpieces as pure as the drops of dew on the must of a cluster of grapes, transformed into the sinuous, knife-edged scream of the gypsy *siguiriya*.[5]

The President of the Corrida Throws Down the Keys to the Toril, the Doors are Flung Open and the Bull Enters the Arena.

A poem from Lorca's *Divan del Tamarit* reads:

> There is no night in which, on giving a kiss,
> one does not sense the smile of the faceless people,
> and there is no one who, in touching a newborn child
> forgets the motionless skulls of horses.[6]

At the heart of the Dionysian mystery there is ambiguity: the God who is the principle of indestructible life, Zöe, is simultaneously the God of death and the dead (Heraclitus). And this is not the only ambiguity. We will meet others. In fact, Dionysos could be called "The God of Ambiguity." He "presents us with borderline phenomena, so that we cannot tell whether he is mad or sane, wild or somber, sexual or psychic, male or female, conscious or unconscious...He rules the borderlands of our psychic geography. There the Dionysian dance takes place: neither this nor that, an ambivalence—which also suggests that, wherever ambivalence appears, there is a possibility for Dionysian consciousness."[7]

First Passes with the Cape: Toro Levantado[8]

We must now try to follow Lorca into these borderlands of psychic geography—if we are to deepen our appreciation of Dionysos from the perspective of one who chose him and was chosen by him.

Lorca called these borderlands Andalusia, a mythic land which mysteriously and ambiguously overlaps with that part of Spain south of the Ciudad Real from the "rock of Jaen to the whorled shell of Cadiz."[9]

> This poetic land has two poles: the interior and the coast, symbolized in turn by the olive and the sea. The interior or hinterland, with its dry, parched earth, is the birth- place of tragedy...The coast with its changing mosaic of the sea, is a less fateful land...Within the interior region, Granada and Cordoba stand out in sharp relief. Seville is the capital of the seaboard region.[10]

Edward Stanton, one of Lorca's finest critics, has shown that in Lorca's work Andalusia is more than a mere theme or lyrical background. "Often," he says, "it constitutes the very marrow of his poetry. It is the touchstone of his career, his *querencia*, the place to which he always went back for vital and artistic regen- eration. The *querencia* is that place in the ring where the fight- ing bull feels most secure, most invulnerable."[11]

"I love the earth," Lorca said. "All my emotions tie me to it. My most distant childhood memories have the taste of earth" (*OC* 2.1058). This love of earth was, he tells us, responsible for his first artistic experience. While following a new plow all over the fields as a little boy, he saw the shiny steel blade pull up a Roman mosaic!

Lorca jokingly identified and named this deep emotional attachment to the earth, his "agrarian complex" (*OC* 2.1059). Remembering Jung, archetypal psychology says that within every complex there is an archetypal core and, further, that within every archetypal core there is a God. Remembering also Diotima's teaching to Socrates (Plato, *Symposium*, 203b) that the daimon is a mediating being joining the Gods and men, we ask: what is *the mediating being* between Lorca's agrarian complex and the God Dionysos? According to Stanton,

> Neither the Arabic quality of his imagination nor the regional motifs, not even the popular air of his style can adequately define Lorca's deep Andalusian essence…It resides in his fundamental attitude to life and art, in an almost pagan cult of the earth, an acute sense of human tragedy—united to a refined, graceful feeling for expression.[12]

What is it then which connects Lorca's "almost pagan cult of the earth" and his "acute sense of human tragedy" with his "refined, graceful, feeling for expression"? Does Lorca also identify this daimon?

A Series of Veronicas [13]

Sometime between the end of his law studies in 1928 and his visit to Buenos Aires in 1933, Lorca wrote his most inspired prose in the form of a talk called *The Theory and Play of the Duende*. Here he grappled with a true daimon, naming it after a familiar household spirit of Spain, adapted by the people of Andalusia to refer to a distinct quality of inspiration. Lorca quotes Goethe, who seemed to be defining *duende* when speaking of the playing of Paganini, saying it contained something *Damonisch*—"a mysterious power which everyone senses and no philosopher can explain" (*OC* 1.1098). Lorca described how all over Andalusia people spoke constantly of the *duende* and identified it accurately and instinctively whenever it appeared. He quotes his time's most honored singer of *cante jondo*, or deep song, Manuel Torre, "who had more culture in the blood" than anyone Lorca could think of, as saying of Manuel de Falla's playing of his *Nocturno del Generalife* that "all that has black sounds has *duende*" (*OC* 1.1098). Lorca adds:

> These black sounds are the mystery, the roots fastened in the mire we all know and all ignore, the mire that gives us the substance of art...The *duende*, then, is a power, not a work; it is a struggle, not a thought. I have heard an old maestro of the guitar say, "The *duende* is not in the throat; the *duende* climbs up inside you, from the soles of the feet." Meaning this: it is not a question of ability, but of true, living style, of blood, of the most ancient culture, of spontaneous creation. (*OC* 1.1098; CM 43)[14]

After these revelatory words, Lorca actually brings the two faces of the daimon into the same paragraph. Notice how Dionysos comes in:

> This "mysterious power which everyone senses and no philosopher can explain" is, in fact, the spirit of the earth, the same *duende* that scorched the heart of Nietzsche, who looked for its outer forms on the Rialto Bridge and in the music of Bizet, without ever finding it and without knowing that the *duende* he was pursuing had leaped straight from the Greek Mysteries to the dancers of Cadiz or the beheaded, Dionysian scream of Silverio's *siguiriya*. (*OC* 1.1098; CM 43)

To make an archetypal move, we could see the mediating daimon between the "agrarian complex" and the God Dionysos as Lorca's *duende*.

But the one-sidedly negative value the word "complex" often carries needs to be balanced by a more archetypal perspective. Gaston Bachelard suggests that we shift our focus on the complex from the person to the imagination. Hillman comments:

> Under [Bachelard's] scrutiny the complexes are not so much lesions or problems as emblems. In Bachelard's hand psychoanalysis shifts from an examination of complexes as disorders which separate one from the world, to an appreciation of complexes as emblems of the ways one engages and embraces the world.[15]

There is an element of ambiguity in the nature of all complexes. That element is demonstrated by Bachelard as follows:

> Originality is by necessity a complex, and a complex is never very original. It is only by meditating on this paradox that we can recognize genius as a *natural label*, as a nature being expressed. If originality is powerful the complex is energetic, imperious, dominating. It leads the man; he produces the work. If originality is slight, the complex is masked, false and hesitant. In any case originality can not be analyzed on an intellectual level. Only the complex can give a dynamic index of its originality.[16]

What constitutes the force of a complex, what gives it its dynamism, is the sum of contradictions it amasses in itself. In the case of the "agrarian complex" the supreme contradiction is the tension and ambiguity of love and coldness. "Like a true Andalusian," Lorca said of himself, "I know the secret of coldness, for I have ancient blood." But he also said, "I love the earth. All my emotions tie me to it."

If the complex is beyond intellectual grasp and not ultimately derived from the person, how then can we understand or know it? Bachelard's answer is that we can only understand the life of the passions by activating the same complexes. Here he quotes Paul Eluard: "I can understand another soul only by transforming my own, 'as one transforms one's hand by placing it in another's.'"[17]

Let us begin by placing a hand in Lorca's and allowing it to be transformed by his. Can we dwellers in cities, more dead to the world of the senses than any Sleeping Beauty rapt in her castle, can we imagine the way it might be to live in constant conversation with the lizards and bees, the river, the stars, the wind and the trees? Lorca tells us that that connection was never broken for him. "As a child," he said, "I lived very close to nature."

> Like all children I gave every object, piece of furniture, tree and stone its own personality. I talked with them and loved them. There were some black poplar trees in the courtyard of my house. One afternoon it seemed to me that they were singing. The wind was changing notes as it went through the branches, and I imagined this was music. I used to spend hours accompanying the poplar's songs. Another day I was surprised to hear someone saying my name: "Fe...de...ri...co." I looked around but saw no one. Who was making the sound? I listened for a long while and realized that the branches of an old poplar were rubbing sadly and monotonously against one another. (*OC* 2.1057; CM 132)

To the bewilderment of reductive psychoanalysis Lorca always considered that he had enjoyed a "very long, very tender, very joyous childhood that never ceased to illumine his life and art."[18] And in this we see again the presence of Dionysos—"at the centre of whose cult from the earliest times is the child, the mystery of nursing and of psychological rebirth through underworld depths."[19]

The first eleven years of Federico's life were spent outside Granada in the little town of Fuente Vaqueros on the *vega*, the fertile plain nourished by the rivers Darro and Genil that descend from the snows of the Sierra Nevada. During his childhood, as his mother was a busy schoolteacher, Federico was looked after by a servant woman from whom he undoubtedly first heard those morbistic lullabies he later wrote about

95

so eloquently: "Spain uses her very saddest melodies and most melancholy texts to darken the first sleep of her children."

Lorca's formative experience of the Dionysian must have occurred very early, but whenever it happened, it was soon linked to the black sounds of *duende* in the folk music of Andalusia. He was born into a family in which the rich musical traditions of the vega were still a vital reality. Before he was four, Federico knew dozens of folk songs by heart and had been given his first guitar lessons by his Aunt Isabel, who also taught him to sing flamenco. (He later called her "the artistic director of my childhood.") Between the ages of sixteen and eighteen, Lorca was considered the musical prodigy of Granada. Manuel De Falla is reputed to have said that everything Lorca achieved as a poet he could have equalled or bettered as a musician.[20]

In one of his first great poems, probably written before he was twenty, the poet is in conversation with "The Children." They ask him: "Who showed you the path of the poets?" And he answers:

The fountain and the stream of the ancient song.
(*OC* 1.97)

A year after the publication of those first poems, Lorca was assisting Falla in arranging the now famous first *Cante Jondo* competition at the Alhambra, in order, as he said, to prevent "the artistic treasures of an entire race from passing into oblivion." In his address, he asked the gathering to notice

the transcendence of deep song, and how rightly our people call it "deep." It is truly deep, deeper than all the wells and seas that surround the world, much deeper than the present heart that creates it or the voice that sings it, because it is almost infinite. It comes from remote races and crosses the graveyard of years and the fronds of parched winds. It comes from the first sob and the first kiss. (*OC* 1.1012; CM 30)

A Recorte[21]

It could be very fruitful for depth psychology to consider what this "deepness" of deep song is. "For archetypal psychology, the vertical direction refers to interiority as a capacity within all things...The fantasy of hidden depths ensouls the world and fosters imagining ever deeper into things."[22] We usually think of psychotherapy in terms of getting deeper into our personal messes, needs, wounds and shadows. *Deep song* is this, but it is more: it is also a way of getting deeper than the personal—into the interiority within all things. The Andalusian, Lorca says, "entrusts Nature with his whole intimate treasure, completely confident of being heard."

> Only to the Earth
> Do I tell my troubles,
> for there is no one in the world
> I can trust.
> Every morning I go
> to ask the rosemary
> if love's disease can be cured,
> for I am dying.
> (*OC* 1.1017; CM 34)

There is a pain in deep song—the gypsies call it *pena pegra*, "black pain"—which is far deeper than any personal pain, and it was this which undoubtedly opened Lorca's psyche to the universality of suffering and the need to find a language which would get beyond the limitations of the personal. The poetic image *is* such a language. Lorca did not invent this language, he found it in use among the Andalusians around him and in the poetry of the *cante jondo*. As he writes,

deep song sings like a nightingale without eyes. It sings blind, for both its words and its ancient melodies are best set in the night, the blue night of our country. It knows neither morning nor evening, mountains nor plains. It has nothing but the night, a wide night steeped in stars. Nothing else matters. (*OC* 1.1015; CM 32)

It is a song "withdrawn into itself and terrible in the dark. Deep song shoots its arrows of gold right into the heart. In the dark it is a terrifying blue archer whose quiver is never empty" (*OC* 1.1016; CM 33). As in this gypsy *siguiriya*:

> If my heart
> had panes of glass
> you'd go to the window and see it
> crying tears of blood.
>> (*OC* 1.1019)

Like the landscape of Andalusia, deep song has a harsh and terrible beauty. The songs sprout in this ancient country of dry, white dust. Lorca writes that

> we must always admit that Spain's beauty is not serene, sweet or restful; it is burning, excessive, scorched, and sometimes completely orbitless. Beauty without the light of an intelligent scheme to lean on. Beauty blinded by its own brilliance, dashing its head against the walls.
>> (*OC* 1.1076; CM 10)

Cante jondo is the song of the soul of Andalusia, and central to this soul is pain:

> Pain, dark and huge as the sky in summer, percolating through the bone marrow and the sap of trees and having nothing to do with melancholy, nostalgia or any other affliction or disease of the soul, being an emotion more heavenly than earthly. Andalusian pain, the struggle of the loving intelligence with the incomprehensible mystery that surrounds it.
>> (*OC* 1.1114; CM 105)

El Primer Tercio: Suerte de Varas, or the Trial by Lances[23]

Lorca passionately believed that the *duende* would not even appear unless it saw the possibility of death.

> The *duende* must know beforehand that he can serenade death's house and rock those branches we all wear, branches that do not have, will never have, any consolation. (*OC* 1.1106; CM 50)

The *duende's* serenade of the house of death is an image of the soulmaking promoted by archetypal psychology. "For archetypal psychology the question of soulmaking is: 'What does this event, this thing, this moment move in my soul? What does it mean to my death?' The question of death enters because it is in regard to death that the perspective of soul is distinguished most starkly from the perspective of natural life."[24]

Already as a child Lorca had discovered the importance to the soul of *personifying*, and he understood this process as archetypal psychology does—that is, as "the spontaneous experiencing, envisioning and speaking of the configurations of existence as psychic presences."[25] In a talk in 1936 Lorca spoke about "the Andalusian force, the Centaur of death," called the *Amargo*:[26]

> When I was eight years old and was playing in my house at Fuente Vaqueros, a boy looked in the window. He seemed a giant, and he looked at me with a scorn and hatred I shall never forget. As he withdrew he spat at me, and from far away I heard a voice calling, "Amargo, come!" After that the *Amargo* grew inside me until I could decipher why he looked at me that way, an angel of death and of the despair that keeps the doors of Andalusia. This figure is an obsession in my poetic work. By now I do not know whether I saw him or if he appeared to me or if I imagined him, or if he has been waiting all these years to drown me with his bare hands. (*OC* 1.1119; CM 117)

The first time Amargo appears in Lorca's work is in the 1921 collection of poems based on deep song, called *Poema del Cante Jondo*. There Amargo is a young man accosted at night on the road by a mysterious rider who wants to sell him a knife and asks Amargo to climb up on his horse and ride away with him. The poem includes this eerie, Dionysian image:

> The night becomes as thick as hundred-year-old wine. The fat serpent of the South opens its eyes to the pre-dawn, and within the sleepers there is an infinite desire to hurl themselves off the balcony into the perverse magic of perfume and distances. (*OC* 1.238; CM 120)

From his study of hundreds of Spanish lullabies and folk songs, Lorca found that the Spanish attitude to death was very un-European, very pagan. He believed that this was because Spain was a country moved by the *duende*. For Lorca, Spain was

> a country of ancient music and dance where the *duende* squeezes the lemons of dawn—a country of death. A country open to death. Everywhere else, death is at an end. Death comes, and they draw the curtains. Not in Spain. In Spain they open them…From Quevedo's *Dream of the Skulls* to Valdes Leal's *Putrescent Archbishop*, from seventeenth-century Marbella who says, while dying of childbirth in the middle of the road:

> > The blood of my entrails
> > is soaking the horse.
> > His hooves throw off
> > fires of bitumen.

to the recent youth of Salamanca who is killed by a bull and groans,

> > Friends, I am dying.
> > Friends, it is very bad.

I've got three handkerchiefs inside me
and this makes a fourth.

there stretches a balustrade of nitrate flowers where the
people of Spain go to contemplate death.

(*OC* 1.1103–4; CM 47)

From the earliest work until the end, death appears, sometimes
personified, as in the figure of the beggar-crone in *Blood Wedding*, sometimes as an invisible presence, as in the poem
Malaguena:

> Death
> enters and leaves
> the tavern.
> Black horses
> and sinister crowds
> are moving on the deep roads
> of the guitar.
> And there is a whiff of salt
> and female blood
> in the spikenards of fever
> on the shore.
> Death
> enters and leaves,
> leaves and enters;
> death
> in the tavern
>
> (*OC* 1.211)

The medieval text, *The Art of Dying*, opens with the words, "He
who has not learned how to die cannot know how to live."
Such intuitions as these were present to Lorca from very early
on. But he also needed to translate these experiences into art,
fortunately for us. Just how devoted Lorca was to this kind of
practice we can glimpse from Salvador Dali's recollections of
the young poet. Dali remembered Lorca alluding to his death

101

up to five times in the course of a single day, At night, Dali writes, his visitor would not get to sleep unless several of the house came to "tuck him in." Once in bed the poet still found ways of prolonging his exquisite conversations, but in the end he always came around to discussing death:

> Lorca acted and sang everything he spoke about, notably his demise. He staged it by miming it: "There," he used to say, "That's how I'll be at the moment of my death!" After that, he would dance a horizontal ballet that represented the jerky movements of his body during the funeral when the coffin would descend a certain steep slope in Granada. Then he would show us how his face would look several days after his death. And his features, which were normally not handsome, would suddenly acquire a halo of unaccustomed beauty...Then at the effect he had produced in us, he would smile, elated with his triumph.[27]

Considering his probable envy of Lorca and a need to give events his own twist, Dali gives a striking image of a Dionysian actor-director. This image also suggests links between Lorca's theatre, imagination and death.

It appears that when *duende* touches soul and soul touches death, it brings a new quality with it into living—a fuller, deeper resonance to experience and thought. With its roots deep in death and the underworld, *duende* nourishes the soul with life-giving images.

There is no paucity of contemporary accounts of Lorca's exuberant life force and extravagant imagination. Pablo Neruda, for example, remembered Lorca in 1968 as "the happiest man" he had known "in a rather long lifetime." He said that Lorca radiated joy in everything—hearing, singing, living.

> He was...vibrant with life, the new channel of a powerful river. He squandered imagination, he was enlightened in his speech, he made a present of his music, he lavished his

magical drawings, he cracked walls with his laughter, he extemporized the impossible…I have never seen such magnetism and such constructiveness in a human being. This marvellous and playful man wrote with a meticulous conscientiousness, and if his poetry spilled out in madness and tenderness, I know that it came from a man who had the wisdom of his ancestors, a man who had inherited all the grace and grandeur of the Spanish language.[28]

Because of its daimonic link with Dionysos, the *duende* quickens, enlivens, electrifies. But contact with that archetypal dominant is never possible without a simultaneous baptism in the dark waters of death.

With Dionysos something must always die. Understandably, what must die, or at any rate, be considerably weakened or loosened, is Apollonic consciousness, which tends toward a rational logos, hierarchy, monotheism, misogyny and a lofty distance from death and darkness.

For too long now Dionysos "has come to mean simply the opposite of Apollo," says Hillman,

> and the God has thus become in the popular, and scholarly mind too, a creature of raving maenads, communal ecstasy, lost boundaries, revolution and theatrics. Logos has to be brought in from somewhere else, e.g., Apollo…*but there is a Dionysian logos and this is the logic of the theatre*…The nature of mind as it presents itself most immediately has a specific form: Dionysian form. Dionysos may be the force that through the green fuse drives the flower, but this force is not dumb. It has internal organization. In psychology this language speaks not genetically, not biochemically in the information of DNA codes, but directly in Dionysos's own art form: theatrical poetics. [emphasis mine][29]

Theatrical poetics as the foundation of Dionysian aesthetics! For Lorca, the Dionysian theophany as *duende* was not limited

103

to any one art form, race, period, culture or style. He spoke about it in the embodiments he knew. Eventually, everything to do with *duende* coalesced around the theatre, and his own plays belong with the best theatre of any nation. Yet his characters are thoroughly Andalusian. They walk and breathe in the gorges and on the cliffs of *duende* and in the blue night of deep song. The plays are filled with images and echoes of Andalusian music and *cante jondo coplas.*

Even closer to the theatre of Dionysos is that essentially Andalusian theatre of tauromachy, the *corrida.* "The liturgy of bulls," as Lorca calls it, is a clear descendent of an ancient Mediterranean drama, a spectacular *temenos* designed to contain the untamed energy of the wild bull God. It has assumed a particular form in Spain, but in it can be heard the same groans and cries as must have passed through the onlookers in Minoan Crete as the dancer-acrobats hurled themselves in ecstatic arcs of mathematical trances over the horns of the bulls.

Bulls have always been literally sacrificed to Gods, and in some places they still are. Sometimes the bull itself is seen as God. As Kerényi has written, "to the Greeks Dionysos was preeminently a wine-God, a bull-God and a God of women. A fourth element, the snake, was borne by the bacchantes."[30] Lorca refers to the "liturgy of bulls" as an "authentic religious drama where, just as in the Mass, a God is worshipped and offered sacrifices" (*OC* 1.1107; CM 50).

The heavy air of fate which can hang over the arena during a corrida is similar to the atmosphere of all classical tragedy, the God of which is, of course, Dionysos. And Lorca's three great tragedies—*Blood Wedding, Yerma* and *The House of Bernarda Alba*—are no exception.

For a certain kind of author of tragedy, one firmly in the train of Dionysos, the bullfight stands as a stark prototype of the form.[31] All the grim potential of high tragedy is there: from the first trumpet blasts and the *paseo* of the toreros, each with their *caudrilla* of banderilleros and picadors dressed in bejeweled and gold-brocaded parade capes, to the hushed and terrible "moment of truth" when man and bull merge in a mesmeric marriage of blood and death. The bullfight, for Lorca, was the National Theatre of Spain. "Spain," he said, "is the only country where death is a national spectacle, the only one where death sounds long trumpet blasts at the coming of spring" (*OC* 1.1108; *CM* 51).

> I think the bullfight is the most refined festival in the world, it is pure drama where the Spaniard sheds his best tears and his best bile. What's more, the bullfight is the only place you can go in the certainty of seeing death in the midst of the most dazzling beauty. What would become of Spanish spring, of our blood, of our language if those dramatic trumpet blasts were to stop sounding in the ring? (*OC* 1.1128; *CM* 131)

El Segundo Tercio: Suerte de Banderillas[32]

To view theophany from within a Dionysian perspective we will keep, by necessity, to that archetypal principle of essential ambiguity: the dyadic unity, or *coincidentia oppositorum*, of wine and bull. *Serio ludere*, a Socratic maxim of Ficino, says *play seriously*.

This interpenetration of the opposites could also be called "the bisexuality of consciousness," a term employed by Hillman in his discussion of the Dionysian possibilities of a truly therapeutic psychology. Having exposed the permanent inferiority of the feminine under the rule of Apollonic consciousness, Hillman makes this startling statement: "Dionysos represents a radical shift of consciousness where bisexuality is given, a priori, with this archetypal dominant. This structure offers an end to misogyny."[33]

Recalling that Dionysos was mainly a God of women and that his cult was mainly a women's preserve, Hillman goes on to say, quoting Kerényi, that

> though he is male, and phallic, there is no misogyny in this structure of consciousness because it is not divided

from its own femininity. Dionysos "in one of his appel-
lations, is man and woman *in one person.* Dionysos was
bisexual in the first place, not merely in his 'effeminate'
later portrayals." [emphasis in source][34]

Above all, what characterizes Lorca's theatre is the warmth
and precision with which he portrays his women characters
and the depth from which the feminine speaks. Beyond that,
there is such a celebration of soul in Lorca's world, such a subtle and finely discriminating feminine awareness of the character of flowers, the emotions of trees and landscapes, the
moodiness and passion of the sky, the dreams of the wind and
the moon. And rarely has a poet had such empathy for women
and their suffering.

Modern descriptions of Dionysos often give prominence to
certain features—like the exaggerated irrationality of the religious experience—but, as Hillman points out, there are other
features deserving our attention: "stillness, the soul and death,
wine, marriage, theatre, music and dance, vegetative nature
and animal instinct, with its conservative laws of self-regula-
tion, and the flow of life into communal events."[35] We need to
keep these other features in mind or we will only be left with
an impoverished stereotype and not the creative ambiguity of
the archetypal.

Dionysos uncurls in the vine; tightens his grip in the ivy. He
is as difficult to grasp as a writhing snake. Yet he is all stillness
himself. Music comes toward him from his devotees. To be
drunk with this God is to be *entheos,* filled with the God, "en-
thused," yet completely concentrated, like a dervish walking
over a bed of hot coals. The stupid drunkenness of the heavy-
booted, ox-chested soldier is more an image of blind-drunk
Heracles, archetypal hero and athlete.

To drink without respect of Dionysian aesthetics is to further
the repression of Dionysos until only acts of ugliness and stu-
pidity are possible. Dionysos's revenge on those who reject his
bisexual consciousness is found in the conventionally 'normal'
man's bestial states of drunkenness and chronic alcoholism, as

well as in the sudden breakdowns and suicidal depressions of one-sidedly literalistic individuals. We need to know how to drink to the God, how to be drunk with him, how to dance with his spirit, how to distill his ritualistic madness into contemporary metaphor. We need a theatre and a *thiasos* (community) for the Dionysian. We forget that there is a Dionysos who presides over the feasts of the philosopher, over the *Symposia*, and this means the *Convivia* as well. The discriminating palate of the devoted wine taster, skilled in the judgment of bouquet, body and fruit is also given by a Dionysian aesthetics. "The madness of ritualistic enthusiasm is clearly to be separated from disease and insanity."[36] The repression of Dionysos leads to a kind of "black maenadism," a hysteria, in which the target is the rational Apollonian consciousness (Pentheus's head).

It is possible to see the whole of Lorca's work as a gradual refining and maturation of a celebration of the Dionysian, concurrent with the exposure of its repression in Spanish culture.

Toro Parado[37]

When the feminine is forced to live in barrenness and cannot give birth to new life, cannot conceive or be inspired, it despairs. Yerma murders her husband because he cannot understand this. He has thwarted her longing for life. Her longings break forth in a storm of Dionysian images:

> Ai, what a field of sorrow!
> Ai, what a door to beauty closed!
> I beg to suffer for a son, and the wind
> offers me dahlias of a sleeping moon!
> These two fountains of warm milk
> are two pounding hoofbeats of a horse
> within the firmness of my flesh,
> shaking the branch of my anguish.
> Ai, blind breasts beneath my dress!
> Ai, what pain of imprisoned blood
> is nailing wasps into my neck!

But you must come, love, my child,
because the water gives salt; the earth, fruit
and our womb holds tender babies,
just as the cloud holds sweet rain.

(*Yerma* II.2)

In 1988 I attended, at London's Barbican Theatre, a performance of *Lorca's Women,* a play devised by Gwynne Edwards and directed by Eve Pierce. I shall not soon forget this beautiful tribute by eight women to the poet in this century who, they clearly feel, has best understood them. The cast of six accomplished actresses created a flickering series of animated tableaux from Lorca's plays interwoven with his poetry. All the women of Lorca's Dionysian-Andalusian country were there: Yerma, Doña Rosita, Belisa, Adela, Bernarda, Lola, The Shoemaker's Prodigious Wife, The Manola Sisters, The Green Girl, The Beggar Women, The Servant, the Eloped Bride, The Mad Grandmother and—Soledad Montoya. What an astonishing pantheon. What a celebration of the sisterly love for this poet, who said he was neither all poet, all man nor all leaf, "but only the pulse of a wound that probes to the opposite side" (*OC* 1.490).

In a Dionysian consciousness the *coniunctio* of the sexes is already given. A bisexual perspective calls for equality, for democracy at the psyche's round table. And to Lorca this consciousness called for a *corrida* with the "bull" values of his own society. He did not try to hide from this realization. Speaking about his play, *Doña Rosita, the Spinster—or The Language of Flowers: a Poem of Granada in the 1900s, Divided into Several Gardens with Scenes of Singing and Dancing,* he said:

On the posters I call this play a poem for families, and that's exactly what it is. How many mature Spanish women will see themselves reflected in Doña Rosita as in a mirror! I wanted to follow the purest possible line from beginning to end of this comedy. Did I call it a comedy? It's better to say it is the drama of Spanish tastelessness, of Spanish hypocrisy, and of our women's need to repress by force into the depths of their blighted dispositions any desire for personal pleasure. (*OC* 2.727)[38]

In the landscape of Lorca's mythic Andalusia there is one element which is permanent and unmistakable. That is pain, black pain: *pena negra*. She is the suffering Soul of the World, *anima mundi*. In Lorca's *Romancero Gitano* she is called Soledad Montoya (*soledad*, "solitude"). In the musical language of *cante jondo*, she is called *siguiriya gitana*, and, says Lorca, she is the "perfect prototype" of *cante jondo* itself. The gypsy *siguiriya*, that "exact poem of tears," was always Lorca's model for great art of any kind. "*Cante jondo*," Lorca said, "is the transformation of death and black pain into art." Celebrating the anonymous coplas of *cante jondo* in his Alhambra talk, Lorca said: "In these poems Pain is made flesh, takes human form, and shows her profile: she is a dark woman wanting to catch birds in nets of wind. Black Pain is a woman of overpowering beauty who embodies that incurable pain we cannot get rid of except by taking a knife and opening a deep buttonhole in the left side."

The poet once introduced a reading of the poem by saying that "the pain of Soledad Montoya is the root of the Andalusian people. It is not anguish, because in pain one can smile, nor does it blind, for it never produces weeping. It is a longing without object, a keen love for nothing, with the certainty that death (the eternal care of Andalusia) is breathing behind the door" (*OC* 1.1118; CM 112).

Here is a translation of Lorca's poem about Soledad and her pain which Eva Loewe and I have made:

Ballad of the Black Pain

The pickaxes of roosters
were digging, looking for dawn,
when down the dark mountain
came Soledad Montoya.
Her flesh of yellow copper,
smelling of horse and shadow.

Her breasts, smoky anvils,
sighing round songs.
Soledad, who do you seek,
alone at this hour?
I seek who I seek.
What's that to you?
I want what I want,
my person and my joy.
Soledad of my sorrow,
the horse that breaks free
at last finds the sea
and is swallowed by waves.
Do not remind me of the sea,
for the black pain is stirring
in the land of the olive,
under the rustling leaves.
Soledad, how hurt you are!
How terribly hurt!
You cry tears of lemon
sour with hope and talking.
It hurts so much! I run
through my house like a mad thing
from kitchen to bedroom
my two braids on the floor.
What pain! I turn
jet black, flesh and dress.
Ai, my shifts of linen!
Ai, my thighs of poppy!
Soledad, wash your body
with waters of larks
and leave your heart
in peace, Soledad Montoya.

*

Downstream the river sings:
flounces of sky and leaves.
The new light is crowning itself
with pumpkin blossoms.

110

Oh, Pain of the Gypsies!
Pure pain, always alone,
Oh pain of the secret spring
and distant dawn!

El Tercer Tercio: Suerte da Matar [39]

During a reading of the *Gypsy Ballads* in his last year, Lorca made it unmistakably clear that for him the gypsy was an imaginal figure of the greatest importance. He said that though it is called *Gypsy*, "the book as a whole is the poem of Andalusia, and I called it *Gypsy* because the Gypsy is the loftiest, most profound and aristocratic element of my country, the most deeply representative of its mode, the very keeper of the glowing embers, blood and alphabet of Andalusian truth" (*OC* 1.1114; CM 105).

Lorca perceived a deep connection between the Gypsies, the oppressed Spanish women and the Blacks of New York's Harlem he saw during his stay in the New World:

> You Harlem! You Harlem! You Harlem!
> No anguish can equal your thwarted vermilions
> your blood-shaken, darkened eclipses,
> your garnet ferocity, deaf-mute in the shadows,
> your hobbled, great king in the caretaker's suit.
>
> (*OC* 1.460)

These figures, because of their inferior position in the world, carried soul far more truly than the smug bourgeoisie who rejected the abysmal depths of the feminine. Can we not see in this the workings of a Dionysian eros? A weakening of the dominant Apollonic-heroic mode of consciousness necessarily entails a love of what is inferior, a movement downwards and a fall away from the grandiose heights of macho, white supremacy. Hillman speaks of a "conscious bisexuality, that incarnation of durable weakness and unheroic strength that we find in the image of Dionysos."[40]

111

Lorca's opus reflects a "consciousness that requires no psychotherapy in the old sense,...a consciousness which has its bedrock in bisexuality, where those realities of the psyche called 'feminine' and 'body' are integral with consciousness."[41]

In Lorca's dramatic and poetic vision we can see a parallel to archetypal psychology's idea of a radically different kind of psychotherapy founded in Dionysian consciousness. The therapeutic goal of the *coniunctio* of this psychotherapy would now be experienced as a weakening of consciousness. A weakening "in the former sense of that notion rather than an increase of consciousness through 'integrating' the anima. The *coniunctio* now would be weird and frightening, a horror and a death, inclusive of psychopathology."[42]

Lorca's own approach to this "weird and frightening" *coniunctio* was through the struggle with his daimon, the *duende*, of which he said:

> Any man—any artist, as Nietzsche would say—climbs the stairway, in the tower of his perfection by fighting his *duende*...The true struggle is with the *duende*...But there are neither maps nor discipline to help us find the *duende*. We only know that he burns the blood like a poultice of broken glass, that he exhausts, that he rejects all the sweet geometry we have learned, that he smashes the styles...With idea, sound or gesture, the *duende* enjoys fighting the creator on the very rim of the well. Angle and muse escape with violin and compass; the *duende* wounds. In the healing of that wound which never closes lies the invented strange qualities of a man's work. (*OC* 1.10994)

For Lorca, the *duende* was at his most impressive in the bullfighter, for he must fight both death, which can destroy him, and geometry—measurement—the very basis of the festival. The bull has his orbit and the bullfighter has his, and between these orbits is a point of danger, the vertex of the terrible play.

You can have muse with the muleta and angel with the bande-rillas and pass for a good bullfighter, but in the capework, when the bull is still clean of wounds, and at the moment of the kill, you need the duende's help to achieve artistic truth.

The bullfighter who scares the audience with his bravery is not bullfighting, but has ridiculously lowered himself to doing what anyone can do—gambling with his life. But the torero who is bitten by duende gives a lesson in Pythagorean music and makes us forget he is always tossing his heart over the bull's horns. (OC 1.1107; CM 51)

In the words of Ernest Hemingway, "Bullfighting is the only art in which the artist is in danger of death and in which the degree of brilliance in the performance is left to the fighter's honor."[43]

In a commentary on Lorca's *duende* text Raphael Lopez-Padraza remembers a fellow Venezuelan, Carlos Vallalba, reflecting on the death of the philosopher Martin Heidegger. Vallalba maintained that the two horns of a bull can tell us more about death than all the works of the philosopher talking about Being-Towards-Death. For Villalba and Pedraza the maestros of teaching, the maestros of the apprenticeship into the initiation of death, are the bullfighters, the imagemakers of death. The bullfight is a "school of death."[44]

For Lorca, too, the bullfight was a "school of death." It may be objected that Lorca was not actually a bullfighter. But this does not debar him from the imaginal corrida! Ignacio Sanchez Mejias, renowned bullfighter and friend of the poet's, whose death after being gored by a bull inspired one of Lorca's greatest poems, clearly acknowledged the poet's penetrating insight into bullfighting's mythic nature.[45]

The bull and the bullfighter comprise an archetypal tandem which as image probably carries the most emotionally charged ideas of masculine values in Spanish culture. In a quite specific way it is closely akin to those trials of courage among the young braves of American Indian tribes, the lion-hunts of the

Kenyan Masai and the initiations into death among the males of many tribal cultures.

To the poet of mythic Andalusia, however, the bullight was a mine of metaphors and the arena into which the *duende,* smelling death, could most easily be lured. The style of encountering the bull on foot was a particularly Andalusian invention, originating in Ronda with the Romero family in the late eighteenth century. But Lorca, a true Orphic poet of our time, imagined the bullfight as a mythic event and returned it to its archetypal origin as liturgy. In doing this he was acting in a completely natural, Dionysian way. And for him the Andalusian poet could not be any less a torero than the literal one in the ring.

Toro Aplomado[46]

Lorca entered the last phase of the corrida of his life in March 1932, when the newly-elected Republican minister of public instruction, Fernando de los Rios, backed the poet's proposal to create a free itinerant troupe to tour the Spanish countryside in order to "save the Spanish theatre" and to bring it within reach of ordinary men and women. A government subsidy of 100,000 pesetas was awarded Lorca's company, La Barraca, the month los Rios came into office.

How could this poet, who from earliest childhood had lived in utter devotion to theatre, resist the opportunity?[47] He had no choice. Six months earlier a hopelessly uninspired production of a traditional folk play in Madrid had angered him so much that it kindled the idea of forming a theatre of strolling players who would perform all the great classics of Lope de Rueda, Lope de Vega, Cervantes and Calderon to the pueblos of Spain. And this is exactly what happened. In the four years of its existence La Barraca, "The Little House on Wheels," made, under Lorca's artistic direction, twenty-two excursions into the country, bringing many different productions to over seventy villages. Pablo Neruda, a year after Lorca's death, told how "the ancient ballads and chivalric tales, dramatized, were returned by him to the pure heart from which they had sprung. The most remote corners of Castile knew his performances. Through him, the Andalusians, the Asturians, the Extramadurans once again communed with the master poets who'd been asleep only briefly in their hearts...Through the tremendous poverty of the Spanish peasants—men that I, even I, have seen reduced to living in caves and eating herbs and reptiles—passed this magic whirlwind of poetry carrying, along with the dreams of ancient poets, grains of explosive dissatisfaction with their way of life."[48]

In November 1933 the left-wing Republicans lost power nationally to a right-wing coalition government which did not look kindly on the activities of La Barraca—in 1934 the troupe's subsidy was cut in half and it began to be heavily hampered by financial problems. That year also saw the insurrection and massacre of the Asturian miners and the closure of all Socialist clubs in the country. In Granada left-wing councillors were deposed. On December 21, 1934 the Republican newspaper, *El Defensor*, published an article by Lorca on "the theatre and the artistic vocation" clarifying his attitude about post-Asturian Spain:

> I will always be on the side of those who have nothing, of those to whom even the peace of nothingness is denied. We—and by "we" I mean those of us who are intellectual, educated, in well-off middle-class families—are being called upon to make sacrifices. Let us accept the challenge.[49]

Ian Gibson comments:

> The Right did not miss the underlying attitudes in Lorca's statement of solidarity with the ordinary people of Spain. When his rural tragedy *Yerma* was staged a week later in Madrid, the reactionary press refused without exception to acknowledge the author's talent and claimed that his work was immoral, anti-Catholic, irrelevant to Spain's problems and lacking in verisimilitude. During the opening moments of the premiere a group of noisy

115

young men tried to disrupt the performance by shouting political slogans...but the angry audience quickly silenced them.[50]

Lorca was not dismayed. *Yerma* was a success. And, without a doubt, it confirmed him as the most popular poet in Spain.

With the reinstatement of the Republicans a year later, in February 1936, Granada became a minefield of political hatred. When the premises of both the Catholic newspaper *Ideal* and a large chocolate factory were burnt down, the more conservative right-wing groups immediately began forming an alliance with the more ultrareactionary and fascist elements, enraged at the destruction of their property. "García Lorca's name was by now firmly connected with liberalism in the broadest sense of the word."[51]

At this point it is necessary to understand Lorca's importance as a political figure. It is often claimed that he wasn't a political figure, and indeed, he carried no party card. But he had become the voice of an immense number of people—not as a politician, but as a poet. He was in many ways giving a voice to the soul of Spain, especially Andalusian Spain. Lorca's comment to a friend on his last night in Madrid before leaving for Granada on the 13th of June, 1936, is a statement of pure Dionysian ambiguity: "I'll never be political. I'm a revolutionary, because all true poets are revolutionaries...but political, never."[52]

Although the poet had many friends among the communists—his fellow poet Rafael Alberti among them—his form of communism was more a Dionysian form of reaching out to the soul and the imagination of the persecuted and inferior elements of his culture. In his last published interview (*El Sol*, 10th June, 1936), he said:

No true man still believes in that nonsense about pure art, art for art's sake. At this dramatic moment in the course of world events, the artist must weep and laugh with his own people. He must put aside his bunch of white lilies and sink to the waist in the mud, to help

116

those who are looking for lilies. Myself, I am driven to communicate with others. That is why I have knocked at the doors of the theatre, consecrating my whole sensibility to it. (*OC* 2.1124)[53]

Anyone who has seen the film footage of La Barraca on tour cannot fail to be impressed with Lorca's dramatically changed appearance. Instead of the sombre, aloof and aristocratic features of a handsome Moorish prince, we are met with an affectionately smiling uncle. No longer wearing his suave velvet jacket, but clad in worker's overalls, Lorca strides arm-in-arm with members of his troupe, radiating warmth and exuberance.

Whether in his work with La Barraca, in his poetry or in his theatre, Lorca was declaring death to a certain kind of consciousness. Or one might say that he was calling for the end of an overly-bright, smug and hierarchic structure of consciousness. At this time such an enterprise was supremely political. The trouble with politics is that it tends to become incredibly "bullheaded." It can become literally dangerous and dangerously literal. Lorca knew this. In the early 1920s he had written, in a poem called "Fable,"

> Who is there who doubts
> the terrible efficacy of those horns?
> Hide your targets,
> Nature!

as if already announcing his destiny as an imaginal torero. And, as time went on, Lorca found more and more literal opposition to his concern for the soul of Spain. In April 1936, La Barraca gave its last performance. It was clear that the Western world was heading for disaster. In 1935, Lorca had said: "The basic upheavals that produce a world conflagration are already present in souls and objects" (*OC* 2.1113).

His tragic theatre painfully reveals the disturbances going on in the soul of the world. But nowhere do we find Lorca advocating a violent mass revolution; he wanted to bring to the

117

people not guns but imagination. Imagination, it turns out, is not just unreal escapism; it is a morally demanding reality of the highest order. Lorca's dedication to the dramatic logic of Dionysos, allied with his love of the *duende* as his creative daimon, would not allow him to remain a passive bystander. His deep commitment to "the Gypsy, the Negro, the Jew, the Moor which all Grandinos carry inside them" led him to make an extremely heretical statement in that last interview. Replying to the question of the capitulation of Moorish Granada in 1492 to the Christian forces of Ferdinand and Isabel, he said:

It was a terrible moment, though they say just the opposite in schools. An admirable civilization was lost, with a poetry, astronomy, architecture, and delicacy that were unequalled anywhere in the world, in order to make way for a poor, cowardly, narrow-minded city, inhabited at present by the worst bourgeoisie in all Spain. (*OC* 2.1126; CM 130)

It was precisely this bourgeoisie that was to kill him. Lorca left Madrid to return to his parents' home in Granada in mid July of 1936. By that time the atmosphere in Madrid was oppressive and ominous, filled with staccato outbursts of violence. Lorca left suddenly, hardly taking time to say goodbye to his many friends. On the night of the 12th of July, his last night in Madrid, he read his just-finished manuscript of *The House of Bernarda Alba* to a small circle of friends. The next afternoon, having abruptly decided to leave the capital, he caught the night train for Granada. He went despite friends' warnings that he would be safer in Madrid should civil war break out. What was he thinking as the train pulled out of Madrid and sped through the sultry night on its way to the country of black pain? Was he remembering the ominous experience he had recounted to Pablo Neruda a few weeks before?

Neruda wrote in his *Memoirs* that on returning to Madrid from one of the last tours of La Barraca, Lorca had called on him and told him the strangest incident:

He [Lorca] had arrived with the La Barraca troupe at some out-of-the-way village in Castile and camped on the edge of town. Overtired because of the pressures of the trip, Federico could not sleep. He got up at dawn and went out to wander around alone. It was cold, the knife-like cold that Castile reserves for the traveller, the outsider. The mist separated into white masses, giving everything a ghostly dimension.

A huge rusted grating. Broken statues and pillars fallen among decaying leaves. He had stopped at the gate of an old estate, the entrance to the immense park of a feudal manor. Its state of abandonment, the hour, and the cold made the solitude even more penetrating. Suddenly Federico felt oppressed as if by something about to come out of the dawn, something about to happen. He sat down on the broken capital of a pillar lying toppled there. A tiny lamb came out to browse in the weeds among the ruins, appearing like an angel of mist, out of nowhere, to turn solitude into something human, dropping like a gentle petal on the solitude of the place. The poet no longer felt alone. Suddenly a herd of swine also came into the area. There were four or five dark animals, half-wild pigs with a savage hunger and hoofs like rocks. Then Federico witnessed a bloodcurdling scene: the swine fell on the lamb and, to the great horror of the poet, tore it to pieces and devoured it.[54]

Notice the reverence Neruda has for this experience of his friend. The great poetic heart of Neruda responded as only a poet can respond to one he loves. He gives the truest rendition possible, pure visionary images which have their source in the *mundus archetypalis*. He tells it almost as a dream. With the artistry of Homer or Euripides. What better way to celebrate his friend? Neruda was a fellow Dionysian and loved Lorca as only a younger brother could. Their friendship as it manifests in their writings is one of great beauty.

After Lorca's death, Neruda tended to see this event as a vision life offered the poet of his own death. We might add that, even more than this, it is like Jung's visionary premonitions of World War I, an image of the massacre of innocents which was soon to happen throughout the whole of Spain and, beyond, throughout the whole world.[55] Lorca may have been pondering this as he travelled home, back to his mythic *querencia* in Andalusia. Perhaps he was thinking of his friend, the bullfighter Ignacio Sanchez Mejias, who was killed after returning to the ring from a seven-year absence. Lorca knew that his friend's death was completely destined. He had told Marcelle Auclair:

> I foresaw it all from the moment Ignacio told me of his decision to return to bullfighting…Strangely, I'm not revolted. Ignacio's death is like my death, an apprenticeship for my own death. I feel a peace that astonishes me. Perhaps because I have been intuitively warned? There are moments in which I push my vision of Ignacio's corpse to the point of imagining it destroyed, torn to shreds by worms and brambles. Finally, I encounter a silence that is not nothingness, but mystery.[56]

Or perhaps Lorca was recalling these haunting lines from his great lament for Ignacio:

> But now he sleeps without end.
> Now the moss and the grass
> Open with sure fingers
> the flower of his skull.
> And now his blood comes out singing;
> singing along marshes and meadows,
> sliding on frozen horns,
> faltering soulless in the mist,
> stumbling over a thousand hoofs
> like a long, dark, sad tongue,
> to form a pool of agony
> close to the starry Guadalquivir,

Oh, white wall of Spain!
Oh, black bull of sorrow!
(*OC* 1.555)[57]

Most likely, he was thinking of the city which lay ahead of him and of the faces of the people he knew there, friends and enemies. In leaving Madrid for Granada, Lorca was leaving sunlight for moonlight—to use the terms he himself employed in describing the dance between toro and torero. Lorca's favorite style of bullfighting was not that of Lagartijo, who achieved bullfights "where there was only sun...the shade...pure simulation." Lagartijo, Lorca wrote, "loved the nude and the concrete line, he loved the circumference of the sun and suppressed the infinite corner of the shade, terrible projected corner where wide rivers sound under the silent branches" (*OC* 1.1161; CM57).

Neither was Lorca a follower of Bombita, who "learned to jump from one half of the ring to the other without catching cold" (*OC* 1.1161; CM 57). Nor of the madly heroic Machaquito, who "used to bang terribly into the dense wall of the shade." Lorca was deeply aware of the literal and metaphorical danger of ignoring the shadow and its tricky blindspots. He wrote:

> Bullfighters die in the ring because of these antagonistic halves...Between the yellow and the black is a dangerous play of distances; the air fills with concave and convex lens, and the bull swells and wanes, agile, dazzling, and uncertain like a torch in the tower. (*OC*, Ibid.)

Here, in Lorca's penetrating insight into the metaphor of the *corrida*, the shadow side of Dionysos is paradoxically not found simply in the shadow but in the ambiguity of the shadow.

> The bullfighter who does not know how to cross the line dividing the ring in two can fall down the stairs or lose his slippers for all time while passing from the brusque, stubborn sand that is hard as the gold coins of Carlos III

121

to the other sand that is soft and difficult as the desert at night. (*OC*, Ibid.)

He also knew that it is nigh fatal to fight the bull in the shade. He says:

> It has always frightened me to see bullfighters in the shade drawing themselves erect for the kill. The shade is closed like a vertex and does not help them flee with precision. It gets in the way, as inert and heavy as a dead whale on the ocean. (*OC*, Ibid.)

Lorca's favorite bullfighter was Belmonte: "dressed in green, ecstatic and full of the curved emotion of the tense bow." Belmonte's extraordinary genius was to "theoretically suppress...the violent light of sun and shade." Belmonte that "inspired draftsman, tamer of headless rhythms," succeeded "in fighting by moonlight." When Belmonte came into the ring, "the bullfight" turned "a perfect olive color...dim and splendidly drawn."

> Some of the spectators are wearing sandpaper suits, and when the man from Triana wheels around on his plinth, his chin nailed to his left nipple, their ovations are as furious and melancholy as a big rainstorm. Our heart feels the light of a cold moon. A cold moon shining on dying birds. Belmonte stands apart. (*OC*, Ibid.)

Returning to Granada, Lorca was Belmonte fighting bulls by moonlight.

The Moment of Truth

All Granada knew of the poet's return to the city. Three newspapers announced his arrival, *El Defensor* by a spread in the center of the front page. And four days after his arrival, on the 18th of July, news came that Franco's putsch had begun and

Civil War was upon Spain. The 18th of July was St. Frederick's Day, usually a day of celebration in Lorca's family because both the poet and his father were named after the martyr. And so, on the day of San Federico the heart of Spain burst like a fallen pomegranate. By the 23rd, Granada had fallen to the army under Nationalist direction. Wartime laws were announced, though chaos continued for months. Republicans and left-wing subversives were rounded up and shot by the hundreds. Black squads and self-appointed thugs hunted down anyone even remotely connected with the Left. Lorca's parents' home, the Huerte de San Vicente, was visited several times by groups of men who interrogated the poet and beat him up.

Finally, Federico telephoned a friend and fellow poet in town, and that day, at Luis Rosales' invitation, Federico moved secretly into the Rosales' house on Angulo Street. That was the 9th of August. Although Luis' father was a well-known merchant and decidedly anti-Falangist, two of his sons were already in Falangist uniform. Luis, however, was a poet and admired Lorca's work.

The family agreed to hide Federico. As the sons either lived away or were at the front, and their father was away at his shop, Lorca spent his days with the three women relatives of the house and their cook and a one-eyed servant, these two also women. The servant told later interviewers that the poet spent much of his time playing the piano and writing, when not listening to the news on the wireless.

Federico was trapped and he knew it. It could have been then that he composed some of the last poems we have from his hand, the bittersweet masterpieces called *Sonnets of Dark Love:*

> You'll never understand how much I love you
> because you sleep and stay asleep inside me.
> Weeping, I hide you, hunted down
> by a voice of penetrating steel.
> Hordes of people leap through the gardens
> waiting for your body and my death throes
> on green-maned horses of light.[58]

With the publication of these sonnets in 1984 in Madrid, we at last have some idea of Lorca's imaginal reality during his last nine months. The poems speak of a terrible sense of isolation from the beloved. In one poem he speaks to his beloved on the telephone: "Voice, sweet and far away, poured out for me, / Voice, sweet and far away, savored by me." But mainly there is an omnipresent foreboding and premonition of death. None of that was apparent to the women of the house. Esperanza Rosales remembered the poet trying to cheer their flagging spirits, playing folk songs on the piano, telling stories from his travels and reciting his poems.

But the enemy hadn't forgotten him. According to Gibson, Lorca's sister, Concha, after seeing her father beaten up, told the thugs who had come to the Huerta de San Vicente that her brother wasn't in hiding, but had merely gone to a friend's to read poetry. This clue was enough for them to track him down. On the 16th of August, a party of men backed up by armed troops knocked at the door of the Rosales' house with a signed accusation against Federico. The grounds were that he was suspected of being a Russian agent.

After two nights in a cell in the Civil Government Building, Federico was taken at dawn up to Viznar above Granada in the hills and shot, without a trial together with two banderilleros and a crippled schoolteacher. A Gypsy was made to dig their graves.

Between two old olive trees in the shadow of a pine forest, not far from an ancient Moorish spring called *Ainadamar*—The Fountain of Tears—the man who carried the deep soul of Spanish poetry was murdered in the name of national unity.

How far he plumbed the depths of his Dionysian experience we will never know. But certainly the work which survives gives an unmatched richness of Dionysian expression, coupled with an intense awareness of its vigorous repression. Remember that he had just finished writing *The House of Bernarda Alba* on the day he left Madrid for Granada.

There is a point at which bullfighting becomes lethal. Bullfighters know that when a bull has been too long in the arena, he learns to go for the man and not for the muleta. At this point, if the corrida continues, the roles are reversed and the bull-fighter himself becomes the sacrificial offering— "horn of the lily through green groins." Dionysian ambiguity until the last. As it is said in the *Bacchae* of Euripides, "He who leads the troupe becomes Dionysos" (*Bacchae*, line 115).

Rafael Lopez-Pedraza sees in Lorca's death "a scene on the stage of the World Theatre, the place where reflection is made possible from within its archetypal valuations." This means seeing it as a "historical re-actualization of a timeless mythol-ogem: the persecution and death of Dionysos by the Titans, is center stage, *a primordial image*. Garcia Lorca's death…was Di-onysian with all religiosity that the Dionysian signifies."[59]

We also see Dionysos at work in Lorca's life and death if we understand Federico as a torero of the imagination, metaphor-ically dedicated to the death of the bull ego. And now we can tie up many of the loose ends in this pluralistic presentation: the agrarian complex, *duende*, the bisexual consciousness of the Dionysian, its communal eros and love of what is weak, a low-ering of the brilliance of the analytical mind and the cultiva-tion of a new aesthetic based on a combination of accuracy and precision with intoxication and playful spontaneity. Outrage against the repression of the feminine. A serious play with death in the moonlight. A passion for images, a love of meta-phor and the ambiguous. A love of deep song and of those arts which can transmute death into themselves.

The only real enemy here is the animus-ego of heroic, single-visioned consciousness. *This* was the bull that confronted Lorca over and over again, in so many disguises. It is not identifiable as any literal party, organization or person. Yes, Lorca was lit-erally killed. But this in no way invalidates his spirit, his art or his profound contribution to the revisioning of the Dionysian.

Lopez-Pedraza claims that, archetypally, Dionysos will al-ways be persecuted and dismembered; he was the most re-pressed of all the Gods (Euripides says that he was even repressed in Thebes, the city where he was born), and it does not seem to matter in which political regime he lives—it all be-longs to his essence.[60]

In a conversation during the time this chapter was written for presentation as a paper, I learned from Pepe de Trevellez, a schoolteacher from Granada, that all through the years after the war, Lorca's place of execution and burial was secretly visited by a group of Gypsies each summer on the anniversary night of his murder. There they played, danced and sang his poems in the light of torches and candles. This burial place above Viznar near the Fountain of Tears was held to be sacred ground; and after Franco's death Lorca's grave has finally been marked with a block of inscribed granite and the area turned into an official (and rather unfriendly) shrine. This does more to blur one's experience of the place than to deepen it. But this spring I did notice that previous visitors had found the stone outside the shrine and had hung chamomile flowers in the branches of the remaining olive tree.

In a talk given in Lorca's honor in Sao Paolo in 1968, Pablo Neruda mourned this life which was cut off in its prime and the beauty of which the world had been deprived. But he saw through this literal end into something archetypal: the Dionysian mythologem still at work in Lorca's own myth:

There are two Federicos: the real and the legendary. And the two are one. There are three Federicos—the poet, the man who lived, and the man who died. And the three are a single being. There are a hundred Federicos, each of them singing. There are Federicos for the entire world. His poetry, his life, and his death have spread across the earth. His song and his blood are multiplied in every human being. His brief life is not ended. His shattered heart was bursting with seed: those who murdered him could not have known that they were sowing the seed, that it would send forth roots, that it would sing and blossom everywhere, in every language, ever more resonant, ever more vivid.[61]

Or as Federico himself wrote about that other great Dionysian genius of his time, the great torero, Ignacio Sachez Mejias:

126

Nobody knows you. No, I sing of you.
For posterity I sing of your profile and grace.
Of the signal maturity of your understanding.
Of your appetite for death and the taste of its mouth.
Of the sadness of your once valiant gaiety.
It will be a long time, if ever, before there is born
an Andalusian so true, so rich in adventure.
I sing of his elegance with words that groan,
and I remember a sad breeze through the olive trees.

(*OC* 1.558)[62]

4

THE CAST OF MASKS IN THE LIFE AND WORK OF ROBERT SCHUMANN

PART I

The Genius of Culture and the Culture of Genius

Tuning Up

Therapy, we are often told—by those who do not believe that therapy is the problem and that therapy itself needs therapy—has to do with patients, clients, analysands and their personal pathologies. Therapy deals with personal betrayals and break-downs, personal fictions and fixations, personal obsessions and personal repressions, personal panics and personal guilts, denials, evasions and projections and the personal treatment of all this, and more, for the purpose of a personal cure. It is my analysis, my therapy, my individuation.

Archetypal psychology has criticized this single-visioned, self-identified preoccupation with the personal as being an activity largely in the service of the heroic ego, monotheistic and monomaniacal in its exploitation and subjugation of images,

This chapter was first given as a paper at the 4th Annual Conference of The London Convivium for Archetypal Studies in London, June, 1990.

animals, myths, angels, daimones—the whole "incomprehensible mystery" (Lorca) of the soul in its divine diversity and glorious polycentricity.

Archetypal psychology aims instead at evoking an imaginal ego, offering an "image-focussed" therapy, a therapy that is a soulmaking and an imagining, in which

> imagination is recognized as an engagement at the borders of the human and a work in relation with mythic dominants...its intention the realization of the images— for they are the psyche—and not merely the human subject. As Corbin has said: "It is their individuation, not ours," suggesting that soulmaking can be most succinctly defined as the individuation of imaginal reality.[1]

It may thus come as a surprise that I am so concerned with the particularity of individuals. In the preceding chapters I have focussed on individuals—individuals whose lives were pure *pathologizing*, shot through with suffering and pain, but whose genius created works which will remain sources for soulmaking as long as they survive and there are people to experience them.

I have examined the life and work of the Norwegian painter Edvard Munch and the Spanish poet Federico García Lorca. And I have reviewed in depth one work—the film *Andrei Rublev*—by Russian filmmaker Andrei Tarkofsky. Here I will look even deeper into the relation between genius and culture, with particular reference to the German composer Robert Schumann. I begin at the interface of genius and culture.

First, from the side of culture: Developing a psychology of culture means seeing that a) culture always has a *local habitation and a name*, given largely through the poetic efforts (*poiesis*) of its artists and artisans, and that b) *individual experience and expression of soul is always conditioned by the surrounding medium of the culture in which it appears.* I am defining culture as *a living dialogue between heart and world.* Culture is seldom what is uppermost in society. It is not the prerogative of those who stuff their bank vaults with Van Goghs and doze in their boxes at the opera; it is not precluded from the lives of the materially poor. In its finest essence it is invisible, only becoming part of the world through the efforts of individual artists. Bennetons chain stores and MacDonalds fast food halls are not part of our culture. But they are part of our civilization. The ruling spirit of the times, the *Zeitgeist*, is perhaps after all not so much culture as civilization. Culture, I suspect, is probably closer to the uncanny, underside of the *Zeitgeist*—its *Ungeist*, as Alfred Ziegler calls it.

Second, from the side of genius: Following Jung's claim that creativity is as much an instinct in human beings as hunger, sexuality, the drive to activity, and reflection, James Hillman writes:

> If the creative instinct is given to each of us, and its modification through psyche is given to each, then we can no longer maintain a rift and split between man and genius.
>
> Why must the person who lives largely in terms of the creative instinct be damned out of common humanity? And the reverse: why can't the common man change his...concept of genius, so charged with ambition and envy, and be done with this fantasy of the extraordinary personality? Has not each of us a genius and has not each genius a human soul?[2]

Genius, which is the Roman form of the Greek *daimon*, has ancestors as far back as ancient Persian Mazdaism and its magnificent angelologies. As we noted in our discussion of Lorca, *daimones*, according to Socrates' teacher, Diotima, are beings halfway between men and Gods, their faithful translators and go-betweens, mediating and intermediate. Today, the notion of genius has all but lost this connection with soul and divinity. All that remains of genius is a mental factor on a scale of measurement, an Intelligence Quotient computed from a standardized test.

But what if, as Novalis said, "to become a human being is an art" (Pollen), and genius is Everyman's brilliant guide and teacher of that art? Then we are in trouble. Novalis also said that "without genius none of us exist at all. Genius," he said, "is necessary for everything" (Fragments II, 420.10). Thus there is hope for a true communion between humanity and divinity as long as the human soul of genius is alive and free.

Culture seems to emerge as a blossoming of genius—genius seems to flower with the flowering of culture. Living culture though is often subversive, radical and inimical to the status quo. Culture, as we have said, is not another word for civilization.

Romanticism and the Old Position

Robert Bly considers that the eighteenth century was the peak of human arrogance. "Bushes were clipped to resemble carriages, poets dismissed the intensity and detail of nature...empires were breeding, the pride in human reason deformed all poetry and culture."[3] Bly calls the conviction that nature is defective because it lacks reason the "Old Position." Those who clung soporifically to the Old Position the romantics called "Philistines."

By the end of the eighteenth century, Bly says, "an explosive reaction had taken shape." He speaks of the "angry attack" on the "pride in single consciousness, the smugness of human reason." This storm of anger, oddly, was later called "Romanticism." Romanticism, he says, implies too much gentleness for this kind of outburst. There was a fierceness and a wildness in the attack on the Old Position, particularly in Germany—in the early Goethe, in Hölderlin, and in Novalis. The energy in these men's ideas is immense and exciting. Bly imagines this response to the Old Position as an enormous upwelling of water—water which is "still fresh and drinkable."[4]

It was into the second generation of Romantics that Robert Schumann was born in 1810. Inferior forms of Romanticism were already then emerging, but I want to concentrate on its potent essence. Wallace Stevens stresses that:

> although the romantic is referred to, most often, in a pejorative sense, this sense attaches, or should attach, not to the

romantic in general but to some phase of the romantic that has become stale. Just as there is always a romantic that is potent, so there is always a romantic that is impotent.[5]

Certain characteristics attributed to Romanticism—that it is nebulous, chaotic, sentimental and escapist—might better be seen as aspects of the *impotent* Romantic.

One characteristic of the *potent* Romantic is the invocation of the vertical dimension of experience, as distinct from the horizontally flattened perspective of the heroic ego. Seeking depths as well as heights, the potent Romantic calls new forms of aesthetic imagination into being[6] and revitalizes old ones. In order to see how the Romantic does this, and in order to deepen our sense of the Romantic genius, we must make certain inherent connections more apparent. There is a cluster of five notions in Romanticism, notions which are so interwoven as to seem virtually inseparable. But let us look at them one by one.

1) First, there is that quality (Greek *ethos*, or Sanscrit *Rasa*, meaning "taste") by which we feel we recognize the Romantic, whether in poetry, prose, painting or music—that indefinable longing for the unattainable, the soul's yearning for its origins, called in German *Sehnsucht*. We cannot simply translate this as "nostalgia," because it is not a longing for any literal time, place or home. According to James Hillman, the Greek word for this specific erotic feeling of nostalgic desire was pothos. Plato defines it in the Cratylus (420a) as a yearning desire for a distant object...

> There are three portions or persons of Eros that have been classically differentiated: *himeros* or physical desire for the immediately present to be grasped in the heat of the moment; *anteros* or answering love; and *pothos*, the longing towards the unattainable, the ungraspable, the incomprehensible, that idealization which is attendant upon all love and which is always beyond capture. If *himeros* is the material and physical desire of eros, and *anteros* the relational mutuality and exchange, *pothos* is

132

love's spiritual portion…It is the fantasy factor that pulls the chariot beyond immediacy, like the seizures that took Alexander and like Ulysses' desire for "home."

Pothos here is the blue flower of love that idealizes and drives our wandering; or as the Romantics put it: we are defined not by what we are or what we do, but by our *Sehnsucht:* Tell me for what you yearn and I shall tell you who you are. We are what we reach for, the idealized image that drives our wandering.[7]

One of the purest expressions of this *pothos* in early German Romanticism is a poem by Goethe called "Selige Sehnsucht." Here it is in Robert Bly's translation:

Holy Longing

Tell a wise man, or else keep silent,
because the massman will mock it right away.
I praise what is truly alive,
what longs to be burned to death.

In the calm water of the love-nights,
where you were begotten, where you have begotten,
a strange feeling comes over you
when you see the silent candle burning.

Now you are no longer caught
in the obsession with darkness,
and a desire for higher love-making
sweeps you upward.

Distance does not make you falter,
now, arriving in magic, flying,
and, finally, insane for the light,
you are the butterfly and you are gone.

And so long as you haven't experienced
this: to die and so to grow,

133

you are only a troubled guest
on the dark earth.[8]

One can understand that Franz Schubert would want to set this to music, with all the *Sehnsucht* he could command, and that it would be sung when musical friends gathered for an evening's *Schubertiade*. This is probably how Schumann would have heard it on his first summer in Leipzig at the age of eighteen, in 1828, the year Schubert died.

2) The second vital notion within Romanticism is *doubleness*. The mysterious *Doppelganger*, the double, was a theme which fascinated the Romantics, and it appears again and again in their works, from Jean Paul through Kleist and E.T.A. Hoffmann to Grillparzer and Heine. Doubleness is intimately related to *Sehnsucht*. With *Sehnsucht* we discover, at the heart of Romanticism, a metaphorical nostalgia, a Platonic memory of our placeless origins.[9] And what is at the root of this "nostalgic longing and wandering in search of the lost or missing other" is, as we have seen, the *essentially double nature of consciousness*.

In his short but brilliant essay on *pothos*, Hillman refers to the ancient Greek initiations of the Kabiroi on the island of Samothraki, "perhaps the most important, after Eleusis, of all mystery initiations of the ancient world,"[10] suggesting that this initiation transmitted "an awareness that individuality is not essentially unity but a doubleness, even a duplicity, and our being is metaphorical, always on two levels at once."[11] Implicit in this point of view is the idea that we are, all of us, in the unconscious precondition of oneness before some experience in life initiates us into the awareness of our double nature.

> This initiation does not make us whole; rather it makes us aware of always being in tandem with another figure, always in a dance, always a reflection of an invisible other, in whatever form the other is constellated from moment to moment. It is beyond reach; the other is an image that is attainable only through imagination.

It is clear then, as Hillman continues, that

> our wandering and our longing is for the very arche-
> typal figure that instigates the longing, the puer eturnus
> in his personification as Pothos. Our desire is towards
> the image that initiates the desire; it is an *epistrophé*, a de-
> sire that would return desire to its source in the arche-
> type. And this archetype of the puer eternus is, as Henry
> Corbin has often said, the figure of the angel, the wholly
> imaginal reflection of ourselves—an image who makes
> us realize that we are metaphors of him...Ultimately,
> then, our *pothos* refers to our angelic nature.[12]

3) The third notion vital to Romanticism is *metaphor*. Novalis,
who along with Goethe stood at the fountainhead of German
Romanticism, explicitly considered mankind as synonymous
with metaphor: "What is a human being? A perfect spiritual
metaphor. All true communication thus takes place in images"
(Pollen).

Archetypal psychology emphasizes the difference between
an awareness initiated into doubleness and its precondition, a
onesidedness or unity of personality before initiation: "Metaphorical man, unlike literal man fixed in his certainties, is always
at sea, always en route between, always in two places at once."[13]
Henry Corbin calls these two places the celestial and the terres-
tial poles of our being. The angel is our celestial twin or double
"who makes us realize that we are metaphors of him."

Through its concern with metaphor and the metaphorical
perspective, Romanticism countered the self-satisfied single-
mindedness of Philistinism and the salvationist programs of scientific rationalism by delivering all things to their shadows,
undermining the very notion of progress and bringing about the
death of naïve realism, naturalism and literal understanding.[14]
Throughout the dark ages of the Enlightenment early Romantics honored soul and gave it a home.

4) The fourth notion vital to the Romantics is that of the *romanticizing* activity itself. Turning the noun into a verb, they

turned awareness into activity, into the creative activity which Keats, in England, was to call *soulmaking*. Novalis stated this theme first, articulating a method which would become a touchstone for all Romantic artists to come:

> The world must be romanticized. In this way one recovers its original meaning...When I give to the common an elevated meaning, to the usual a mysterious appearance, to the known the dignity of the unknown, to the finite an infinite lustre, I am romanticizing it. (Pollen)

One very strong element in the psychology of Jung is the notion of *mythologizing*, which he inherited from the Romantics. Jung was, of course, steeped in the philosophy of the German Romantics. In his later years he wrote: "To the intellect, all my mythologizing is futile speculation. To the emotions, however, it is a healing and valid activity; it gives existence a glamour which we would not like to do without. Nor is there any good reason why we should."[15]

Archetypal psychology is much indebted to the Romantics. Hillman writes that "the word 'archetypal'...rather than pointing *at* something archetypal points *to* something, and this is *value*...by archetypal psychology we mean a psychology of value. 'Archetypal' here refers to a move one makes rather than a thing that is."[16] For Hillman,

> archetypal psychology "sees through" itself as strictly a psychology of archetypes, a mere analysis of structures of being (Gods in myths), and, by emphasizing the valuative function of the adjective "archetypal" is immediately valued as universal, trans-historical, basically profound, generative, highly intentional, and necessary.[17]

A modern way of "romanticizing the world"?

5) I have considered the notions of *Sehnsucht* and doubleness; and I have considered metaphor and the romanticizing

activity. The last notion, the fifth—and it is like a musical fifth in the way it harmonizes with the first notion and makes strangely meaningful chords with the others—is the notion of *the mask.*

The romanticizing quality of the mask is immediately apparent—as is its metaphorical nature. Its deep connection to *pothos,* or to *Sehnsucht,* is less obvious though equally inherent. But it is in its vivid annunciation of the double that the mask is often so startling. Gaston Bachelard writes that "the mask, in short, makes possible the exercise of that right we grant ourselves to have a double. It opens up an avenue of being for this potential double to whom we have not as yet learned how to grant the right to exist."[18]

Dionysos is, of course, the God of Masks, of Masquerades and Carnivals. The mask does not have to be of Dionysos; but there is a divinity in the mask that recalls us to that mysterious other, that makes us realize our metaphorical nature and, ultimately, the angel of our being.

The puritanical idea, of modern monotheistic psychologies, that masks are synonymous with subterfuge, deception and the false self and that masks are only something to be aggressively confronted and torn away to reveal the true self, is an expression of the hopelessly literal attitude of ego bereft of all imagination. As Ginette Paris says, "This negative definition of the mask as something behind which one hides is just the opposite of the ancient concept of mask as a link between the person and the archetypal animal, ancestor, or divinity embodied."[19]

The Romantic era inherited the masked ball from the age of Rococo, in which a certain frivolity masked a deeper anguish. The masquerade, like the carnival, does have roots as far back as pagan Greece, but the particular metaphorical form that the Romantics inherited seems to have been created by Lorenzo de Medici and Marsilio Ficino in the last decades of the fifteenth century in Florence. Those prolific and elaborate city carnivals in which pagan deities and myths were reinvoked—through pageants, costumes, floats and masks—were just one more form

in which the imagination of the Renaissance celebrated its redis-
covery of pagan polytheism. The masquerade was another.

In 1533 the fourteen-year-old princess, Catherine de Medici,
left Florence to marry Henry II of France, becoming, with her
active mind and lively interest in the arts, the most powerful
figure in France for the next fifty years. Court entertainments—
sophisticated and elaborate masquerades based on classical
mythology like those initiated by Ficino and Lorenzo—soon
spread through all the courts of Europe. In the following centuries the custom of the masked ball spread from the court into
the general population.

It was in the time of the Romantics that the theme of the
masked ball entered literature as a dominant motif. The masquerade became, for the Romantic writer, a kind of crystal ball
which focussed the mythology of everyday life. Novalis writes
that "the novel deals with life, depicts life. It would be a mime
only in respect of the poet. It frequently contains events of a
masquerade—a masked event among masked people. Remove
the masks—there are well-known events—well-known people"
(Fragments).

"For the Romantics," writes Marcel Brion, "the masked
ball was always the symbol of illusion and aspiration. The
mask itself was a sort of prison, but it was also a magic instrument, a talisman, changing the wearer into the character of his
disguise."[20]

Jean Paul, that most loved novelist of the German Romantics, who gave a central place in each of his novels to one of
these fantastic masked balls, writes:

A masquerade is perhaps the most perfect medium
through which poetry can interpret life. In the same way
that the poet conceives all conditions and seasons as being of equal worth, all outer phenomena as mere trap-
pings but all inner qualities as air and sound, the human
being seeks in the masked ball to poeticize both his very
self and life as a whole.[21]

138

PART II

Butterflies and Sphinxes

The Chrysalis of Genius

We have considered the genius of culture, in particular, of the culture of German Romanticism. Now we shall turn to the other side of our chiasmus: the culture of genius.

In 1981 a book by twelve musicologists appeared in Germany celebrating "The Composer, Music Critic, Journal Editor, Conductor and Poet, Robert Schumann." It was called *Robert Schumann, Universal Spirit of Romanticism.*[1] One hundred twenty-five years after the death of this man, the real extent of his contribution to the Romantic tradition and the musical imagination of the Western world at last began to be recognized. In particular need of recognition have been the works of his later years, so stupidly written off by critics as enfeebled products of an exhausted, disintegrating mind.

Schumann always had his admirers, individuals who, like initiates into a secret brotherhood, treasured his exquisite masterpieces and would brook no aspersions on his work. Marcel Brion, the French art historian, was very outspoken on Schumann's significance:

> Nourished by the poets of that wonderful period, Schumann's work might well be regarded as a musical transcription of their work; but it went just so much further, to become *the supreme product of the German romantic soul*, revealing its genius at its most intense and perfect. [emphasis mine][2]

That Schumann's music should be "the supreme product of the German romantic soul" takes on a special poignancy when we recall Hegel's remark that the "basic tone" of romantic art was "musical." Schumann's genius then is linked to the genius of

Romantic literature—of this there is no doubt. In him there was a deep and secret harmony between literature and music. Perhaps this is what gives his work such originality. As Hans Pfitzner commented, "Not Beethoven and not Mozart and not Wagner nor any other composer started his creative work with such originality, such self-contained perfection, as Robert Schumann."[3]

It was usual among the romantics to distinguish between genius and talent. Here is Novalis:

> Genius is the capacity to treat objects of the imagination as real, and even to manipulate them as such. The talent of describing, of observing exactly—appropriate for describing one's observations—is distinct from genius. Without this talent, however, one sees only half, and is only half genius; one can have a capacity for genius which never comes to be developed due to a deficiency of those talents. (Pollen)

Perhaps one should speak of a necessary *devotion to* the genius— a labor in its service—the painstaking work of embodying its inspirations: Novalis's "talent." The materialization of spirit is, after all, just as important as the spiritualizing of matter.

In Schumann's case this talent, without which "one sees only half," had to do with the musical transcription of ideas and images thrown up out of the vortex of Romantic feeling and thought.

Novalis once told Jean Paul that he translated musical improvisations into poetry. And Jean Paul himself played the violin. His novels are steeped in music, and at least half of his heroes are musicians. E.T.A. Hoffmann, that other great Romantic author and also one of Schumann's favorites, was not only one of the most seminal writers on music in the entire nineteenth century but also a composer of operas and teacher of music. But neither Novalis, Jean Paul nor Hoffmann created any music to compare with Schumann's. Schumann was both a good wordsmith and a great composer.

We approach that particular characteristic of Schumann's genius which makes it so unique. Eric Sams writes that "music is for [Schumann] another form of ideas, as steam is another form of water...the musical stage is of course the higher of the two; more ethereal, less tangible and composed of small separate entities or droplets of sound."[4]

Schumann's gift for transcribing ideas into music was related to his ability to see correspondences. William James maintained that genius was the power of seeing analogies.[5] Schumann's capacity in this regard was prodigious.

This is how we must understand Schumann when he describes Schubert's music as "the tonal equivalent of a blend of Jean Paul, Novalis and E.T.A. Hoffmann"[6] or when, in a letter written when he was nineteen, he says that to play Schubert is "like reading one of Jean Paul's novels." That letter continues:

> There is no other music which presents so bewildering a psychological problem in its train of ideas, its apparently abrupt transitions. It is rare to find a composer who can stamp his individuality plainly on such a heterogeneous collection of tone-pictures, and still rarer are those who write, as Schubert did, as their hearts prompt them...He wrote notes where others use words—so, at least I venture to think.[7]

Schumann is not speaking of program music, which he intensely disliked. To think this is to do him a gross injustice. His thinking is far more subtle. Writing on Berlioz' "Symfonie Fantastique," which he praised in many respects, he takes the composer to task for being too explicit in his program notes. "There is," he writes, "something unseemly and charlatan-like about such guideposts. He [Berlioz] might at least have confined himself to the headings for each of the five sections."[8] What Schumann is after is the *analogue* of image in the realm of music and its soulmaking, metaphorical power. In his critique he continues:

141

Alongside the purely musical fantasy there is often, all unwitting, an idea at work...amidst the sound, certain contours and outlines, which, as the music itself takes shape, crystallize and develop into distinct images. When music-related elements contain within themselves thoughts and images tonally produced, the expressive character of the composition will be the more poetic or the more plastic as the case may be the more keen and imaginative the composer's perception, the more gripping and elevating the work.[9]

Perhaps we should add to all its other definitions that genius is *a specially developed sense for the extremely subtle*. Coleridge, writing in 1815, described this sense exactly:

They and they only can acquire the philosophic imagination, the sacred power of self-intuition, who within themselves can interpret and understand the symbol that *the wings of the air-sylph are forming within the skin of the caterpillar;* those only who feel in their own spirits the same instinct which impels the chrysalis of the horned fly to leave room in its involucrum for the antennae yet to come. They know and feel that the potential works in them, even as the actual works on them! [emphasis mine][10]

A popular story about Schumann, and one published anonymously in his lifetime,[11] tells how as a boy he had a special knack for painting feelings and characteristics in tones. It was said that he was able by certain figures and passages to depict on the piano so exactly and comically the various personalities of the comrades there beside him that they doubled up with howls of laughter on recognizing the accuracy of the musical portraits.

Literally true or not, this story depicts a certain gift, nascent and largely potential, but nevertheless indubitably there. As a man, Schumann conceived of tone as a "purely spiritual essence"—perhaps as the perfume of honeysuckle or jasmine seems to be the pure essence of the flower's character. Schumann said about tones that they

> are the finest matter which our spirit contains... they alone are the greatest gift of the deity, because they can so easily be understood and universally comprehended...Music...is the spiritual language of emotion, which is hidden more secretly than the soul...just as at the clavier the keys must be touched before they sound; it is only then that the emotion communicates with the slumbering realm of tones. Thus, music is the spiritual dissolution of our sensations...Whoever possesses tones, does not need tears, both are equivalent—dissolved sensations of the soul.[12]

I believe that Schumann's gift of characterizing or personifying in music is a development of his grasp of music as the "spiritual language of emotion."

The Birth of a Butterfly and the First Masked Dance

There is a resonance between music and experience. Experience is not an objective fact. There is a danger, particularly in psychology, to the soul's very existence when experience is subjected to "the objective look." The late R.D. Laing, certainly the most cultured psychiatrist I have known, wrote that

> we have to clear a space for the discussion of experience as such, because the methods used to investigate the objective world, applied to us, are blind to our experience, necessarily so, and cannot relate to our experience. Such blind method, applied blindly to us, is liable to destroy us in practice, as it has done already in theory...Experience is not objective and is not conveyed to objects. The way it is communicated or conveyed is different from the transfer of objective information...Experience takes

on dramatic forms more akin to music unfolding diach-
ronically through time than a pictorial depiction syn-
chronously present, unchanging through time.[13]

Listening to music we are led primarily to the contemplation of
the qualities of time. Thomas Moore, in his book on Marsilio Ficino, claims that music provides a way of helping imagination
sort out and find order or pattern in experience:

> The terms used in music could fairly easily be applied to
> the soul, to the extent that music theory is itself a poten-
> tial archetypal image-system for the psyche. Like music,
> life is built up of episodes and motifs, these are based on
> more universal scales and modes; counterpoints and
> harmonies fill life as do climaxes and cadences, and fi-
> nally melodies correspond to our unique personal histo-
> ries—what Jung would call a process of individuation
> built upon collective materials. It is difficult to say then
> which comes first: music of the soul or music in sound.[14]

Melody—or the melodic motif or motto—is one of the more basic dramatic forms of music akin to experience. The funny
thing about melodies, as Moore has noted, is that although
they may correspond to our unique personal histories, they are
also built upon collective materials. Melody is always intimately part of the culture or subculture out of which it
emerges. The archetypal nature of melody is very apparent in
the following exposition by Laing, who was himself a superb
pianist and an accomplished improvisor:

> A melody is a patterned sequence of notes of different
> pitches. The absolute pitches of the notes are their quan-
> tity, their relative positions; and the parts they play in the
> dramatic dynamic structure of the melody are their qual-
> ities. The melody does not consist of the notes separately
> or alone, but in the form generated by the sequence of the
> ratios of the pitches of the notes. These ratios are not

themselves notes. They are the differences between the notes. They do not themselves make a sound. If the music gets to us, there is an instant sympathetic vibration through which we resonate and commune with it. This resonant communion is not the way objective facts are communicated.

There is a resonance between the singer, the song, sung and heard, and the listener. A melody reverberates and regenerates feeling, mood, atmosphere, nuances of pathos, that no scientific discourse can convey, let alone scientific method begin to study, across widely different people, cultures, times and places.[15]

Although I can only begin to justify my evaluation here, I would say that the essence of Schumann's genius and, simultaneously, of his contribution to the Romantic imagination is to be found in his deep penetration into the mysteries of melody and the enormous exuberance he felt and communicated in his ability to discover and liberate melodies from their sonic cocoons.

The story begins with Opus 1: *Theme on the Name Abegg with Variations for the Pianoforte, dedicated to Mademoiselle Pauline, Countess d'Abegg,* composed by Schumann in Heidelberg in 1830 at the age of twenty. He shouldn't have been writing music, but studying law, that "cold subject, depressing from the beginning with its soulless definitions," as he wrote in a letter home. There is nothing particularly outstanding in this first piece of music for solo piano, except its cryptic title and the manner in which the letters of the name of the person referred to in the title appear as the sequence of notes, A-B-E-G-G, which in waltz tempo, make up the theme and its variations. There was nothing new in basing a composition on the letters of a proper name—Bach had done it already in *The Art of the Fugue,* using the letters of his own name. Schumann, however, adds an ingenious twist to the forwards and backwards variations by using the notes in vertical combination, turning the theme into a chord, standing it on end, as it were.

"The music is vividly expressive. The elated outgoing arpeggios of the theme in waltz time clearly embody the feeling of dancing at a masquerade."[16] The lady in question is said to have been met at masked ball, though it has never been discovered whether she existed outside of this piece. Her title of "Countess" is a disguise. "Just what kind of theme is this?" asks Eric Sams, in his paper on "Schumann and the Tonal Analogue." It is a theme, he answers, "composed of arbitrary notes, yet symbolizing a person, and a scene, and a state of mind, and also developed purely technically as music in some rather unexpected ways."[17] Schumann's own word for this theme was *papillon,* a word he often used in connection with his works and parts of works and which had a very special meaning for him.

Masks Into Butterflies

Schumann actually referred to the "Abegg Variations" as "Papillons," and the original title of his Op. 2 was *Papillons musicals* [sic]. He referred to his *Intermezzi,* Op. 4, as "Papillons on a larger scale," and he offered the *Impromptus,* Op. 5, to a publisher as "a second set of Papillons." He also gave that title to one of the pieces in *Carnaval,* Op. 9. Eric Sams suggests that "by 'Papillons' Schumann means motifs that can appear or disappear, fly forward or backward, and assume an infinite variety of shapes and colors."[18]

There is more. And what an insight into the extraordinary unfolding of psyche is blindly passed over when we fall for the smug clichés that would discount Schumann's Papillons as "all fluff and tinsel," "pure flightiness," or as one biographer described them, "fanciful changes of mood and direction as the music...flits from one scene to the next."[19] We would do better to meditate on Coleridge's air sylph whose wings are forming within the skin of the caterpillar.

"Music," for Schumann, "was the word given a new freedom by a change of existence from one mode to another, as a chrysalis changes into a butterfly."[20] The young composer once compared himself in an unproductive mood to a chrysalis awaiting change. And here we come to a really startling find. Sams points out that

> the German word for the larval state, "Larve," like its Latin and French equivalents, also means mask... "Larventanz," or masked ball, is the actual name of the chapter in Jean Paul from a reading of which there emerged, according to Schumann, one "Papillon" after another. This play on words is Schumann's own; he writes those words, "Larventanz" and "Papillon," in the same line of a letter home excitedly explaining that there is a direct musical transformation from the one to the other, from masks or larvae, to butterflies. And indeed his musico-verbal ideas kept on and on, for years after, emerging from just such masquerades.[21]

This is an amazing idea: mask into melody, or, put in another way, persona into psyche. With this insight we have turned a corner and are standing suddenly in the imaginal workshop of the Theophanic Imagination. For this is where—in the sweating chamber of the soul's alembic—the archetypal images of the celestial double begin to appear.

Twins at a Masked Ball

We have noted the importance of the mask and the masquerade for the Romantic imagination, and we have looked at the mask as metaphor of the essential doubleness of individuality and as an expression of *pothos*, or *Sehnsucht*, that archetypal longing that drives our wandering and searching. There is no doubt that the masked ball, that Romantic metaphor of divine hide and seek, was an image which captivated Schumann all his life. In that archetypal arena of cosmetic ambiguity where reality becomes poetry, and vice versa, conventional distinctions are ritually abandoned. A beautiful nymph appears in the guise of an old witch; the God Aesclepius turns out to be the local undertaker; a wealthy heiress enters as a match girl; goatish Pan may be shy Matilde and the sultry Queen of the Night that polite gentleman from the city. As in a fairy-tale bazaar all manner of legendary figures, historical personages, Gods and Goddesses jostle side by side with shepherdesses, pirates, counts, court jesters and macabre beings from the underworld.

Not only are the *Abegg Variations*, Op. 1, and *Papillons*, Op. 2, connected to the masked ball; many of Schumann's other works are inspired by the ball's archetypal magic: *Carnaval*, Op. 9, *Faschingsschwank aus Wien*, Op. 26, *Ballszenen*, Op. 109, and *Kinderball*, Op. 130.

The genesis of his idea of the musical metamorphosis of masks into melodies (larvae into *papillons*), as we have mentioned, coincided with his meditations on a novel by his favorite writer, Jean Paul, called *Flegeljahre*, known in English as *Salad Days*, or simply *Walt and Vult* or *The Twins*.

For Schumann, Jean Paul Richter was as sacred as Bach, and *Flegeljahre* was "like the Bible." He always maintained that he had learned more counterpoint from Jean Paul than from any music teacher. It is said that Schumann knew the whole of Goethe's *Faust* by heart, but it is also clear that he was so familiar with *Flegeljahre* as to have been one of its characters. At the end of his life, alone and dying in the asylum at Endenich, he asked for this book and reread it intensely.

He had begun reading Jean Paul early. He didn't have to go far. His father was a bookseller, publisher, author, translator and book collector. By the time Schumann was composing his first music and straining under the imposition of the law studies into which his family had pushed him, he knew the scenes of *Flegeljahre* thoroughly. His own copy is marked in many places which correspond with sections of his Papillons.

Flegeljahre seems to have been written for Schumann. It treats of the relationship between the twin brothers Walt and Vult Harnisch. The more independent and aggressive Vult runs away from home while his shy and dreamy brother Walt attends law school and prepares to manage their father's estate. When Walt is in serious difficulties over his final exams,

Vult miraculously reappears and helps him. They agree to stay together, travelling and writing books. Walt is to do the poetry and Vult the satire.

On one of their adventures, they meet a beautiful Polish heiress, Wina Zablocki. Walt falls deeply in love but is too shy to court the young lady. The opportunity arises at a masked ball at which all three independently appear. Walt, masked and dressed as a miner from the Hartz mountains, at first cannot locate Wina among the bewildering crowd. Finally, recognizing a beautiful pair of lips beneath the half-mask of a nun, he asks if it is she. The nun whispers yes and accepts his invitation to dance. Out on the dance floor Walt is so intoxicated by her nearness that he extemporizes, wildly poetic, meanwhile, entirely forgetting to move his feet. His delirium is rudely interrupted by a flower-crowned nymph dressed as the Roman Goddess of Hope, *Spes*. Commanding Walt to follow her, the figure leads him into a room away from the ball and reveals herself to be Vult, who insistently demands that they instantly exchange clothes and masks. The reason, Vult roughly explains, is that Walt is a hopeless dancer—he moves like a mule driver. If Vult, who is a musician and a great dancer, can dance with Wina, it is sure that he will win her heart for Walt. As it turns out, Wina *is* very impressed with Vult's elegant performance. She makes it clear that she does return his love. For a moment Vult, masked as Walt, takes on all the poetic qualities of his brother, but in the end he realizes that he has lost both to each other and so abruptly leaves. Vult returns to the shared room, packs his bags and writes a hurt, angry letter to his brother. The novel ends the next morning as Vult slips out of the house and, playing his flute, walks away. The last words of the book tell of Walt's hearing "the vanishing tones with delight, never imagining that his brother was vanishing with them."

Papillons, a sequence of twelve miniatures, was given its final form in 1831. In a letter to his brothers (April 17, 1832) accompanying the score of the finished work, Schumann asks them to "carry off the *Papillons*" to his three sisters-in-law to whom he had dedicated the work, to ask them "to read the closing scene of Jean Paul's *Flegeljahre,* and to tell them that *Papillons* was intended to turn this masked ball into music. Then ask them," he writes, "if they do not perhaps find faithfully reflected there something of Wina's angelic love, Walt's poetic nature and Vult's swift-flashing soul." Several of the Op. 2 pieces in waltz rhythm were taken from a series of waltzes written in 1829; two others are revisions of four-handed polonaises from 1828. All of these are inspired by dance music by Schubert, whose polonaises and waltzes Schumann often played.[22] To a friend in 1834 Schumann wrote that he "fitted the words [of the novel] to the music and not vice versa...Only the last number," he writes, "by a freak of fortune, similar to the first, was inspired by Jean Paul."[23] What Schumann is referring to here is the bold, intrusive theme which is introduced in the first miniature and which reappears in the last section and then is made to dwindle, note by note, finally vanishing altogether. That the theme was meant to be a musical image of Vult there can be no doubt. But in another letter, Schumann writes:

> I feel I must add a few words about the origin of the Papillons, for the thread that is meant to bind them together is scarcely visible. You will remember the final scene of Jean Paul's Flegeljahre: fancy dress ball—Walt—Vult— masks — Wina— exchange of masks —Vult's dancing— confessions — rage — revelations — hurry away — concluding scene, then the departing brother. Again and again I turned over the last page, for the end seemed to me but a new beginning.

Almost without knowing, I found myself sitting at the piano, and one Papillon after another came into being.[24]

The contradictory statements in these two letters indicate how for Schumann the poetic imagery of the novel and its musical metamorphosis were at first indistinguishable. My guess is that he only gradually became aware of what he had been quite naturally doing all along. It was when he began to see the real possibilities of his metaphor that he began to develop it more as a musical method. As Sams argues, "We need not infer that Schumann consciously needed ideas and images to compose; rather that his music is no other thing than the diffusion of those ideas and images into a more rarified form."[25] The idea of a melodic motif, a *papillon*, arising out of a poetic image or mask (a larva) was Schumann's own, but the immediate source of the idea that thought itself resembles a butterfly was probably Jean Paul, who "makes a very interesting distinction between two classes of thoughts: daytime ideas, the dayflyers or genus *Papilio*, and the night thoughts or night flyers, otherwise known as 'Sphinxes.'"[26]

Schumann, of course, did title one of the pieces of *Carnaval*, Op. 9, "Sphinxes." Sams continues:

> We have probably all been puzzled by the appearance of "Sphinxes" in *Carnaval*. We think first of Greek or Egyptian myth. But those Sphinxes asked riddles or kept secrets; whereas Schumann's, on the contrary, answer riddles and disclose secrets; his Sphinxes are not so much myths as moths, or *Papillons de nuit*. And that is what a Sphinx actually is, in its dictionary sense. In English or German, even in French, it means a moth or "Papillon." And in *Carnaval* it means a meaningful musical idea.[27]

Schumann was not yet twenty-one. But with the creation of Op. 2, *Papillons*, he had established a unique, alchemical form of musical composition and a style which would permeate his life's work. And he would certainly have given much of the credit for this to Jean Paul and his *Flegeljahre*.[28] Eric Sams, whose brilliant and sensitive work on Schumann is, I feel, unmatched, clearly demonstrates that the *papillon* method became Schumann's lifelong mode of composition, that through all of Schumann's output of symphonies, choral and chamber music, piano cycles and songs there is the presence of motifs which are "unifying, expressive, structural, reversible—in short, 'Papillons.'"[29]

If we recall that in his first ten years of composing Schumann wrote almost entirely for the piano, we may more easily understand that baffling explosion of songs (130 of them) in 1840—songs which showed such mastery and dazzling melodic beauty that they immediately made him, after Schubert, the greatest living songwriter in the world. Far from being a sign of limitation, Schumann's single-minded concentration on the capacity of the piano as an instrument for expressing soul states is rather a sign of his genius. Brion goes so far as to say that

> Schumann's piano works written between 1834 and 1840 show an intensity of feeling which has perhaps never been equalled in music composed for that instrument... As the years advanced, Schumann's musical language was enriched by many subtleties, shades and half-tones, which translated with equal suppleness and precision the passage from one emotion to the next...Schumann's palette had more colors than any other musician and an infinite scale of shades.[30]

Another Octave

"It's too bad for the wood which finds itself a violin."
—ARTHUR RIMBAUD

Schumann's first major work after *Papillons* was *Carnaval*, Op. 9. But between 1831 and 1834, the date of its composition, a great deal was to happen in his life. Already on the Easter of 1830, after witnessing a performance of the legendary Paganini, Schumann seems to have decided to begin the torturous process of extricating himself from his law studies—of course, against family wishes. By October 1830 he had finally left Heidelberg for Leipzig where he had the promise of the music teacher, Friedrich Wieck, to take him on as a pupil for a trial period of six months. Yet by the spring of 1831 his position as a pupil was still not at all clear. He moved lodgings frequently, unable to settle. He had taken the plunge into a career of music, but so far there was no reinforcing echo coming back from his voiced decision. Although he had drinking companions and even a girlfriend or two, he was basically very isolated. One of the entries from his diaries from this time reads, "Solitude is the nurse of all great spirits, the mother of heroes, the companion of poets, the friend of artists."[31]

He started work on a play based on the tragic medieval history of *Abelard and Heloise*. The choice is strange. It was a theme apparently very far removed from Schumann both in experience and setting. Abelard was a brilliant scholar who became a priest. After taking vows of celibacy, he entered a passionate secret relationship with Heloise, the beautiful niece of Canon Fulbert. She bore him a child, they were secretly married and Heloise, for his protection, left him to live in a convent. Even so, her uncle discovered their relationship and its outcome. He had Abelard captured and then brutally castrated. The story held Schumann, but he could not work it into a play; he felt blocked, could not find a "poetic" ending and gave up.

There is one possibility which would make entire sense out of this peculiar choice for a first play. Robert had met Clara, the nine-year-old daughter of Wieck, already in 1828. Clara, destined to become Robert's wife and to share with him one of history's most moving love stories, was now twelve. Although there is no record that they declared their love for each other until she was sixteen, four years later, it is abundantly clear that they were drawn to each other already from the start. Apart from there being anything between them at this stage, Schumann's psyche had a great propensity for mythologizing on themes long before they were actual in his life. Clara's father, on discovering their love, did prevent them coming together for some five years, until Clara was of age and she could marry without his consent. Wieck, it could be said, did everything in his power to "castrate" Schumann, psychologically, socially and professionally.

By June 1831, Schumann was in a very miserable state. In his diaries from this time he expresses a deep dissatisfaction with himself. He is unhappy, uncertain about his future and his present. In angry despair he even lashes out against his beloved art: "Music, how you disgust me and repel me to death."[32]

The musical genius which had produced *Papillons* required another metamorphosis. Something in Schumann knew that the art had to become more interior. There had to be a qualitative leap. Another octave needed to be sounded. He had touched something fundamental in Jean Paul's Walt and Vult. But the novelist's twins were too static, too fixed, too external. Schumann could not find a way of proceeding in music, so he tried literature. But here too he was stymied. Intensely lonely, desperately insecure and unsupported by his family, he felt estranged from everything.

On the day of his twenty-first birthday, June 8, 1831, he woke up from "a deep sleep as from before birth." In his diary he wrote:

> At times it is as though my objective being is entirely split from my subjective being—it seems as if I stood between my appearance and my being—between form and shadow. My genius are you abandoning me?[33]

His genius did not abandon him, but the fear was there. As Henry Corbin tells us, in his reading of the visionary recitals of Avicenna and Shaikh Sohrawardi, it is at the time of greatest estrangement that the angel of our being appears:

> At the moment when the soul discovers itself to be a stranger and alone in a world formerly familiar, a personal figure appears on its horizon, a figure that announces itself to the soul personally because it symbolizes with the soul's most intimate depths. In other words, the soul discovers itself to be the earthly counterpoint of another being with which it forms a totality that is dual in structure.[34]

A few days later, returning to Leipzig from his "coming of age day" in his home town of Zwickau, he conceived the idea of a novel in which most of the characters would be modelled on people in his circle—Wieck was to become Meister Raro; his lovely and precocious daughter Clara, Zilia; Christel, a recent girlfriend, Charitas. He also added characters like Paganini and Hummel "to connect the threads" of the plot. However, there was one person who was entirely imaginal—Florestan, the Improvisor. Florestan is, of course, the hero of Beethoven's opera, *Fidelio*. In the opera he is chained to a rock in a dungeon, starving and about to be killed by the villain Pizarro, when he is rescued by his wife Leonora, disguised as a man called Fidelio.

Schumann was soon calling Florestan "my bosom friend." Florestan was rash, impetuous, intuitive, extravagant, passionate, bold and flamboyant.

One month after the birth of Florestan, a second imaginal character appeared. He was called Eusebius. Schumann had at last found a way of personifying his own dyadic unity, a way which allowed these twins a creative autonomy previously constricted in the figures of Walt and Vult. Eusebius, like Walt, was dreamy, reflective, retiring, nostalgic, poetic, melancholy, lonely and introverted. Eusebius was the name of a fourth century saint whose name day fell on the fourteenth of September, just two days after Clara's.

Schumann did not write the novel, which was perhaps just as well. The main thing was that Florestan and Eusebius were now in the world. Soon Schumann was calling them "two of my best friends" and saying that "they cheer me up greatly."

For the next ten years Florestan and Eusebius were his constant companions—holding dialogues in the pages of his diaries, contributing ideas for his musical writings, inspiring new compositions and even appearing themselves in the music, as differentiated states of soul in melodic forms.

Psychiatry has always gotten this wrong. One of the latest in a long series of psychiatric diagnoses (including that of Bleuler, Jung's senior at the Burckholzi, who cited Schumann as a textbook example of schizophrenia), by psychiatrist Peter Ostwald, has it that Schumann had a "schizo-affective disorder" and that he was beset by "morbid, nihilistic fantasies that often interfered with orderly thinking" combined with "a regressive pull toward states of terror and confusion [which] held him back and contaminated his interactions with other people."[35]

Regarding Schumann's personifying, Ostwald writes that "it is not unusual for children or even adolescents to create imaginary characters who provide solace and companionship—*but when an adult does so, it is a sign of either a very vivid imagination or a psychotic tendency. In Schumann's case it indicated both.*" [emphasis mine][36]

Joan Chisell, otherwise one of the most sympathetic and sensitive writers on Schumann, falls unconsciously into the same clinicalizing perspective when she writes: "But Schumann's subdivision of his own personality was no mere romantic extravagance, but *rather a downright recognition of a very real form of schizophrenia.*"[emphasis mine][37]

Diagnostic language, applied to the soul, is a smokescreen for ignorance, a smokescreen for a lack of respect for soul and for our experience of it. Diagnostic language is the outcome of centuries of staring at phenomena with the "objective look," that "ethically blank, heartless scientific gaze," as Laing calls it, at which the entire Romantic movement was in uproar: a gaze which "does not see or hear *us*—we who desire, who speak and act." To this gaze "there are no intentions and deeds. There are units, constants, and changing patterns of verbal and bodily behavior. Gone are conduct and destiny."[38]

How different is the image-oriented thought of Carl Jung, who said, "Perhaps—who knows, these eternal images are what men mean by fate" (*CW* 7.183). Or Heraclitus, who said, "A man's character is his daimon" (*Ethos anthropo daimon*, Frag. CXXI).

The diagnostic look is no less destructive to the landscape of the soul than chain saws and bulldozers are to the Amazonian rain forests. Again, as Laing reminds us, "such blind

156

method applied blindly to us, is liable to destroy us in practice, as it has done already in theory."[39] As Hillman makes the point, "our desire is to save the phenomena of the imaginal psyche."[40] Diagnosis and understanding are as far apart as microchip and microcosm. Again to quote Bachelard quoting the French poet Paul Eluard, "I can understand another soul only by transforming my own, 'as one transforms one's hand by placing it in another's.'"[41]

Personifying: A "Mythod"

"In the world we search for a design—this design is we ourselves. What are we? Personifyings, omnipotent points."
—NOVALIS

To place our hand in Schumann's would be to recognize and commune with his gift of personifying. In this way we might even see him, as Jung saw the alchemists for his psychology, as a precursor and an exemplar of our psychology. Imaginal friend and teacher, not clinical object or textbook case.

For archetypal psychology personifying is, along with pathologizing, psychologizing and dehumanizing, one of the main methods for undoing culture's greatest enemy—the too narrow identification of psyche with the ego personality.[42] By actively imagining the psyche into multiple persons, we prevent the ego from identifying with...each and every impulse and voice," says Hillman. "The purpose of personifying is always to save the diversity and autonomy of the psyche from domination by any single power."[43] Personifying, let us remember, is not a projecting of soul into things; it is a "spontaneous experiencing, envisioning and speaking of the configurations of existence as psychic presences."[44] Early in this century Jung identified these configurations as "complexes" or "splinter psyches"—"the little people" of the psyche.

Florestan and Eusebius are, then, complexes. But what a difference it makes to change the rhetoric by naming them and giving them faces. Hillman writes:

157

When a complex is imagined as a distinctly separated entity, a full "person," equal to my notion of ego in intentions, mood, and willfulness, then my relations to my complexes will be as in a dream where they are no more or less real than the dream "I." When the complex is fully personified...I am able to love it. What was once an affect, a symptom, an obsession, is now a figure with whom I can talk. In Jung's sense we are reversing history in our souls, for by personifying I restore the disease to its God and give the God its due. "To serve a mania is detestable and undignified, but to serve a God is full of meaning."[45]

Our conditioned inhibition often prevents us from acknowledging the autonomy of those psychic persons and becoming enriched by their presences. Personifying then becomes a timid therapeutic accessory. Schumann did not have the qualms of ego psychology—though the monotheistic thrust of the Lutheran Church would have been pressure enough. And of course, in some ways, Schumann was even ahead of us—for example, in his way of "hearing" persons as *papillons* born from their masks, awaiting transformation by transcription into musical notation.

In December 1831 Schumann made his debut as a writer in the *Popular Musical Gazette* with an appraisal of Chopin's Op. 2, "Variations on a theme from Mozart's *Don Gionvanni.*" It was a remarkably perceptive recognition of the as yet unknown Polish composer's genius. In Schumann's appraisal Florestan and Eusebius make their first public appearance.

The other day Eusebius came quietly into the room. His pale features wore the enigmatic smile with which, as you know, he seeks to arouse curiosity. I was sitting with Florestan at the piano: He is one of those rare musicians who seem to sense strange, new forces that lie in store. But this time even he was about to be surprised.

With the words: "Hats off, gentlemen, a genius!" Eusebius spread a piece of music out in front of us. We were not allowed to see the title. I turned the pages idly—there is something magical about the secret enjoyment of music unheard. Moreover, every composer seems to have his own musical handwriting— Beethoven's looks different from Goethe's. Here it was as though I were the object of strange stares coming from the eyes of flowers, serpents, peacocks and maidens. Now and again it became clearer, and I thought I could detect Mozart's "La Ci Darem La Mano" threading its way through a hundred chords. Leporello seemed to cast secret glances at me, and the Don hurried past in a white cloak.[46]

Encouraged by Chopin's bravado Schumann returned to developing his idea of *papillons*. In 1832 he wrote his Op. 4, *Intermezzi*, first called "Papillons on a large scale," and in the same year he offered a publisher his Op. 5, *Impromptus*, as a "second set of Papillons."

The Davidsbundler: Imaginal Academy at The Kaffebaum

We have said little so far about Leipzig, the city where most of these events of the 1830s took place. Since becoming the home of J.S. Bach after he was made cantor of Thomaskirche in 1723, Leipzig had been renowned for its music. The third most prosperous city in Germany and already for half a century considered to be its intellectual capital, Leipzig was nicknamed "Little Paris." When Goethe arrived there in 1765 from his native Frankfurt, he found that his fine new clothes were out of date. The city sported a breezy elegance. Leipzig was already then, according to Goethe, also a "source of syphilitic infection."[47] Schumann's favorite public place in Leipzig was a famous old restaurant, *The Kaffebaum*, a coffee house since 1694 and a popular haunt for Goethe, Lessing, Liszt and many others from the world of arts. This coffee house with its baroque motif of a coffee tree over the entrance, now became the birthplace of a new brotherhood, a small circle of like-minded friends who met there in the evenings and pledged themselves "to break the paralyzing grip of the cultural Philistines, especially those who took virtuosity for genius and technical skill for profundity."[48] By the summer of 1833 Schumann had the idea of gathering these literary and musical forces to create a review "to champion the cause of poetry" and "relentlessly attack her detractors."[49] Searching for a suitable patron, Schumann hit upon the idea of David, the Biblical musician-king who slew the Philistines. The choice was a good one, and it stuck. That December and January Schumann described this mysterious new organization in the Leipzig *Komet*, disclosing that Florestan, Eusebius and Meister Raro were its founder members. Thus, the League of David, *The Davidsbund*, was born.

The major influence on Schumann at this time was E.T.A. Hoffman, a writer of mesmeric, daimonic power, who was, perhaps more than any of his contemporaries, in touch with the darker, wilder side of the romantic *Ungeist*. The uncanny, the grotesque, the illogical and the fantastic were for Hoffman also gateways to the supernatural and, of course, creative genius. Nowhere else is the countercultural aspect of Romanticism so much in evidence. Hoffman raged with savage articulation against the mediocrity and self-satisfaction of the Philistines. And his voice reverberated in all its macabre intensity far beyond his time—in Poe, Baudelaire and Dostoyevski, all deep in his debt.

Hoffman's strange novel, *The Serapion Brotherhood*, written fourteen years earlier, provided Schumann with a romantic version of the archetypal idea of the academy. In the novel, a company of literary and musical friends meet again after twelve years' separation to share their experiences and to form a group. They take their name from a poet-hermit, whom one of them has met on his travels—a man who was considered quite mad by society but who seemed to live in perfect attunement to Nature. This hermit believed with unshakable conviction in the reality of his imagination; he was a true seer. The Brotherhood agree that it is useless "for a poet to set to work to make us believe in a thing which he does not believe in himself, cannot believe in, because he has never really seen it." The greatest stress is placed upon the "clear grasp" of the image in the creation of a work of art. Hoffman called this the Serapiontic Principle. The characters adherence to this principle was an assurance that they would not "drift into Philistinism."[50]

The conviction that a review must be founded took fire and in April, 1834, the first issue of the *Neue Zeitschrift für Musik* (The New Review for Music) appeared, with Robert Schumann as chief editor. He was to remain editor for the next ten years, bringing out two issues every week. And here Florestan and Eusebius and Raro were not only regular contributors but actual friends as well. There was Schumann's friend and coeditor Ludwig Schunke, Karl Banck (whose pen name became "Serpentin"), Stephen Keller (known in the review as "Jean Quirit"), Theodore Töpken, Julius Knorr, and Anton Florentin Zuccalmaglio (St. Diamond). Most of Schumann's friends appeared in the pages of the new review: Felix Mendelssohn (as "Meritis"), Clara Wieck (as Chiara) and the young Richard Wagner. Mozart, Berlioz and Chopin were made honorary members of the Davidsbund. The most regular contributors to the review, however, were the incisive and stormy Florestan, the sensitive, melancholy Eusebius and the disciplined Raro.

Any new composition of interest was reviewed, but articles also appeared on Bach, Beethoven and Schubert. A completely new way of writing about music appeared in the world, inspired by Hoffman's *Kreisleriana* and his writings on Gluck and Beethoven. A new language was being created which, according to Schumann, would be as aesthetically close to the music it was discussing as possible. "Instead of contemplating a work externally, the romantic critic would plunge into it, breathe it, commune with it."[51] They established musical criticism as we now know it.

During the 1830s the Davidsbund was an imaginal world for Schumann, informing virtually every area of his creative life, in literature as well as in music. In 1834 Robert began working on a composition, which was to be published in 1836 as his "Sonata No. 1 in F Sharp Minor, Op. 11." It was dedicated to Clara—by Florestan and Eusebius. He also began a series of miniatures called "Twelve *Davidsbundler* Etudes," later published as simply "Etudes, Op. 13."

Alongside his ever-deepening exploration of archetypal essences in sound—the discovery of more and more species of *papillons*—Schumann was simultaneously exploring possibilities of giving "voice" to the imaginal persons of his psyche—in the sense of allowing them to compose whole movements of his works.

This direction of Schumann's exploration first becomes apparent in Op. 9, *Carnaval*, a masquerade filled with Papillons. It began as a set of variations[52] on Schubert's "Waltz of Longing," the *Sehnsuchtswalzer*, part of which is left showing in *Carnaval* as a direct quotation for everyone to hear, in the same key and at the same place.[53] By introducing this Papillon from his beloved Schubert, Schumann invokes the spirit of the other composer, and by composing his own variations thereon, he celebrates the other's genius with a salute from his own. In the *Préambule* we sense all the confederates of the "League of David" gathering, and in the following sections various old and new faces appear. The way in which the various masks present themselves is rather like persons in a theatrical masquerade who disentangle themselves from the milling crowd, take a bow center stage, then turn and disappear again. We meet Pierrot, Arlequin, Eusebius, Florestan, Chiarina (Clara), Estrella (Ernestine von Fricken)—even Chopin and Paganini. It is like a snowstorm of butterflies over the Argentinian pampas.

Listening to the piece called "Florestan," we hear a familiar theme drifting in without comment, "adagio" in the ninth bar—then reappearing later marked by Schumann with the singular word, "Papillon." The "Papillon" in question is, of course, the one which begins and ends Op. 2, the melodic motif of Vult Harnisch, the forceful twin from Jean Paul's *Flegeljahre*.

Carnaval ends with a brilliant and fiery piece called "The March of the League of David Against the Philistines," in which the keyboard virtually explodes in cross-rhythmic, contrapuntal fireworks as the notes come flying out and the *Davidsbundler*

162

rally for their rout of the Philistines, symbolized by a seven-teenth-century folk tune known as the "Grossvater Tanz."

The mythic figure of David, the warrior-king and giant-killer who was renowned for his Orpheus-like abilities as a musician, was indeed an appropriate choice as patron for Schumann's imaginal company of artist friends. David is a fig-ure who combines both Florestan's exuberance and Eusebius's lyrical sensitivity.

Robert Schumann: *Carnaval*, Op. 9, " Florestan "

Robert Schumann:
Davidsbundler, Op. 6, 2
" Eusebius " Tänze

Schumann continued, however, to explore the twins' natures separately. In several works of the 1830s he placed the initial "E" or the initial "F" at the end of a movement in order to indicate its authorship. This is true of each of the eighteen movements of

Op. 6, the *Davidsbundlertanze*, "Dances of the League of David" (1837), and of Op. 12, *Phantasiestucke* (1837), which has eight movements distributed evenly between the two characters and four movements shared: *Des Abends*—E; *In der Nacht*—F; *Aufschwung*—F; *Fabel*—E and F; *Warum?*—E; *Traumesvirren*—F and E; *Grillen*—F and E; *Ende vom Lied*—E and F.

These piano works do not adhere to any classical sonata form. They belong to the world of Romantic miniatures, like Beethoven's *Bagatelles*, Schubert's *Moments Musicaux* and Mendelssohn's *Songs Without Words*, with which they stand as incomparable examples of the genre.

In 1840 when Schumann turned to writing songs, he left the outward show of the Davidsbund behind. The last mention of Florestan and Eusebius in the *New Musical Review* was in 1843. Soon after that, Schumann left the editorship to a colleague. But in 1841 the *Review* carried the text of Schumann's address to the Seventh Annual Meeting of the Davidsbund, an address with the tone of a farewell speech. In it Schumann invokes David, the slayer of Philistines, but declares that the name of this king should above all remind his listeners of the "holy marriage of poetry and music." He states the need to dissociate music from fashion and urges the confederates to see themselves as "caretakers of the temple of art." They should not onesidedly defend the old and attack the new but "recognize all worthy endeavors and appreciate every merit," because "something noble and beautiful can mature in every latitude and location."

Epistrophé and a Look Into the Star Mirror

We have noted the similarities of Schumann's ideas to those of archetypal psychology. In particular we have seen how Schumann, through personifying complexes, transformed them into friends with whom he could speak and how these friends in turn greatly enriched his musical and literary creativity. Archetypal psychology also holds that within every complex there is an archetype and that within every archetype there is a God.

If we were to ask to which archetypal sources we could lead back or "revert" the characters of Florestan and Eusebius, for example, we might begin by reviewing their qualities. Florestan is stormy, fierce, audacious, wild, fiery, noble, lucid, radiant, brilliant, golden. Eusebius is melancholy, solitary, sensitive, subtle, dreamy, poetic, visionary, aesthetic, mild, watery, contemplative, gentle, murky and obscure.

These words are a carefully considered selection which I have compiled from three sources: they are adjectives used by many writers on Schumann, and they are adjectives born from my own listening to the music associated with Florestan and Eusebius and adjectives that occurred to me on reading articles signed by Florestan and Eusebius in the *New Musical Review*. I am here following the Renaissance style of thinking about phenomena developed by Ficino in his treatise *De Vita Coelitus Comparanda*, "How Life Should Be Arranged According to the Heavens" (Book Three of *Libri de Vita Tres*, "The Book of Life"). I am greatly aided in this by Thomas Moore's excellent study of Ficino's astro-musico psychotherapy, *The Planets Within* (see note 14).

Ficino is, of course, intensely concerned with the question of attunement to the spectrum of planetary influxes, or "rays," in our lives. For Ficino all experienced phenomena are referable to planetary deities. An understanding of these sources, according to him, can help us differentiate the powers that play in our lives, enabling us to enter into a meaningful and creative rapport with them.

Astrology, central to Ficino and his grasp of music, does not seem to be an analogy with which Schumann was familiar. Nevertheless, I want to include a consideration of this subject because it makes a link between Schumann's intuitive "mythod" and the Ficinian understanding of there being different musics characteristic of different planets. I think that this link is readily perceptible in Schumann's music, given a willingness to listen.

In Ficino's way of thinking the brilliance of Florestan would be an attribute of Apollo, the Sun God, also the God of Music.

This brilliance is the *ratio lucis,* or reason of light, not the light of reason. This light gives us a "vision of the interior of things," a vision which establishes "a relationship between ourselves and our world whereby we perceive our place and sense the connection between human ego-mentality and far deeper sources of understanding. The quality of this intelligence, far beyond rationality, appears in Ficino's description of light. The light of the heaven, he says, is an image of all the following: the fruitfulness of life, the perspicacity of our senses, the certitude of our intelligence and the bountifulness of grace. These are all qualities of intelligence, the way understanding is perceived."[54]

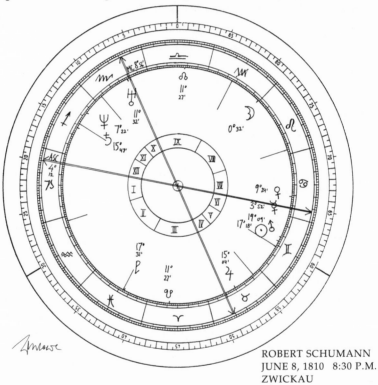

ROBERT SCHUMANN
JUNE 8, 1810   8:30 P.M.
ZWICKAU

Robert Schumann was born with the sun in 17° Gemini 18 in the Sixth House. His involvement with twinship finds an archetypal resonance already here. Schumann's intelligence, in Ficino's sense, is archetypally informed by a twofold vision

166

from the start. And that vision is displayed in the style of his imagination and of his music.

However, not all of our Florestanian adjectives can be said to be solar-Apollonian. Florestan is not only golden, brilliant and lucid; he is also stormy, fierce and audacious. For Ficino these latter qualities are associated with Mars, the hottest planet in the paradigm. "This red hot spirit not only provides directly for an attitude of militancy, overcoming timidity and passivity, it also intensifies the spirits of other planets."[55] Ficino claims that "Mars warms the coldest things and energizes the sluggish."[56] He also ascribes to Mars the power to "excite the winds."[57]

Mars in Schumann's birthchart is placed at 19° Gemini 9', less than two degrees away from his Sun. This conjunction can be regarded as another analogue of Florestan. Thus we find the conjoined divinities of Sun and Mars at the core of the Florestanian image.

But what about Eusebius? His melancholy, his solitariness, his contemplative nature are considered by Ficino as qualities associated with the planet Saturn. But this planet of melancholy, in his own way, "brings us out of the world of the literal, away from plain life experience, into the realm of eternal patterns, the true home of the soul, or more plainly, to a state of consciousness in which the psychological dimension in its purest can be perceived and appreciated."[58] Saturn in Schumann's birthchart is placed at 15° Sagittarius 47' in the Twelfth House. It is thus almost directly opposite the Sun-Mars conjunction in the Sixth with which it forms a tandem.

Now, though, what about those other qualities of Eusebius's nature—the dreaminess, the poetic and visionary sensitivity, the mildness, the wateriness? Saturn is hardly watery. Here we are in a different position than Ficino because we operate astrologically with the three "outer" planets, which were unknown to him. And contemporary astrology sees qualities like "watery," "dreamy," "poetic," "visionary" and "aesthetic" as associated with the planet Neptune. In Schumann's chart, Neptune is placed at 7° Sagittarius 22', conjunct his Saturn at 13°; it is thus also opposite the Sun-Mars conjunction in Gemini.

Already a definite polarity is visible between these two sets of paired planets on opposite sides of the zodiac. I do not consider this to be an explanation of Schumann's life, but rather a mirroring, an analogy on another octave. And there is much more to it. We would have to speak of how Pluto squares this opposition, creating all the dynamism of the T square. And how the Venus-Mercury conjunction astride the descendent is mirrored in the incredible sweetness and tenderness of his music. Or how the Jupiter-Uranus opposition astride the M.C./I.C. axis is mirrored in the radical and intuitive bursts of insight, colored by impatience with a world which could not see so far ahead as he.

It should be clear that Schumann was not simply living out his chart. Had he been doing so, the oppositions could have meant nothing but conflict and perhaps little or no creativity. His genius was the musical working out of the twin-relationship in terms of *counterpoint*, not embattled opposition.

It is the creative genius manifest in the life of Schumann that points the way to what Hillman calls the "imaginal ego," one that is at home in the imaginal realm, an ego that can undertake the major task now confronting psychology—*the differentiation of the imaginal*, the discovery of *its* laws, *its* configurations and moods of discourse, *its* psychological necessities. "Until we know these laws and necessities," Hillman maintains, and I agree, "we are caught in calling its [the imaginal's] activities 'pathology,' thereby condemning the imagination to sickness and the persons of it to making their appearances mainly through psychological manifestation...But...differentiating the imaginal begins only when we allow it to speak as it appears, as personified. Personifying is thus both a way of psychological experience and a method for grasping that experience."[59]

5

THE FIRES OF EROS AND
THE ALCHEMY OF SEDUCTION

Notes Toward
a Poetics of Love

A Sonata in Five Movements

"Love runs to meet us even before we start looking."
—MARSILIO FICINO in *de Amore*.[1]

1. Introduction (Allegro vivace)

In this chapter I entertain a claim implicit in archetypal psychology's way of moving into the world—that at least some of
us desire a psychology that starts in the processes of imagination and that rests upon a poetic basis of mind,[2] that "find[s] its
way into poetic speech."[3]

If we are going to speak of love—and psychology assumes
this capability—we should first of all imagine a *poetics of love,*
for which we must turn to the poets. Not to just any poets, but
particularly to those of whom it could truly be said that they
belonged to that transhistorical society called by Dante and his
companions the *Fedeli d'amore,* the faithful followers, or servants, of Love. Not the masters of Love, but the *servants* of
Love. Our first and last words will be given to these poets:

This chapter was first given as a paper at the 3rd Annual Conference of The
London Convivium for Archetypal Studies, "The Lunatic, The Lover and The
Poet," in London, June, 1989, and published in *Sphinx 3,* 1990.

Irresistible
and bitter-sweet

once again

that loosener
of limbs, love

Snakily
strikes me down[4]

says Lady Sappho, who shares with Orpheus[5] the legendary
distinction of being the first to give Eros his nickname—*glucop-
ichron*, meaning "sweetlybitter," or, as we say, "bittersweet."
The poetess thus gives us the opening chords as well as the
tonic key of this whole sonata: Eros is irresistible and bitter-
sweet. Definitely not simply the key of C Major; probably neither major nor minor, but something far more archaic and
Orphic, a mode on the lyre which is sweetly seductive, bitingly
bitter, a mode ambiguous in the extreme. Profound, fateful,
theophanic and incomprehensible! I am powerless when he
strikes me down, weak in the knees, fluid, loosened from the
cramped style of ego and its tight-knit, muscular defenses,
floored, struck by an arrow dipped in the metaphorical toxins
of archetypal longing.

The key, then, of this Geminian sonata in erotic poetics is a
scale, or ladder, which ascends from its darkest, most basic
tone, through subtle and rhapsodic oscillations to its highest
and most celestial, to that which reveals itself to be the same
but different, transformed into a dimension of another order—
a mirror image whichever way you happen to look at it. As
above, so below.[6]

In other words, an octave may be played beginning at either
end. With an exquisite sense of paradox the Greeks expressed
this in their word for the highest-sounding string on the lyre—
nete—which means "lowest." And mirroring this reversal, they
named their lowest-sounding string *hypate*, which means "the
highest." Why? The high note, *nete*, was the string closest to the

170

performer. The bass note of the lyre, the lowest, was furthest away from the performer and therefore the "highest." In a classic move of archetypal epistrophé, *nete* was given to the Moon, *hypate* to Saturn.[7]

We may begin with either the Lunatic or the Saturnian, the bitter or the sweet, the agony or the ecstasy, the earthly or the heavenly. In the end it doesn't matter. *Gloria duplex!* What matters is what kind of music we make.

By invoking the poets of the *Fedeli d'amore* we are not looking for a prescription: *these* are the rules, *this* is how you do it (Saturn). Nor are we merely looking for a Romantic defense of the madness of love (Luna). No. Rather, we are looking for *at least* a conjunction, an imagination of love and a language for that imagination, an eloquence, a rhetoric—what the Renaissance called *loquenza*. For example, to improvise on my opening, we could imagine a poetics of love which is *both* Saturnian and Lunatic. In his poem "The New Rule" Rumi says:

> It's the old rule that drunks have to argue
> and get into fights.
> The lover is just as bad: He falls into a hole.
> But down in that hole he finds something shining
> worth more than any amount of money or power.

> Last night the moon came dropping its clothes in
> the street.
> I took it as a sign to start singing,
> falling up into the bowl of sky.
> The bowl breaks. Everywhere is falling everywhere
> Nothing else to do.

> Here's the new rule: Break the wineglass,
> and fall toward the glassblower's breath.[8]

How Rumi images love! We—fall—toward—the glassblower's breath! This, he says, is the new rule. The blind night of Eros, that black hole of initiation, is always a *vita nuova*, with

171

its command that I change my life. Falling into this hole is falling up into the bowl of sky. The bowl breaks and everywhere is falling everywhere. But, "down there" the lover finds something shining.

We could say that falling in love stands everything on its head. The new rule evokes a new order in which value is in neither money nor power but appreciation. Love teaches aesthetics. We come to see differently, so differently that Love has often been depicted as blind.

Shakespeare, in the character of the Sufi-like poet Berowne, created his finest spokesman for the passionate Renaissance imagination of the *Fedeli d'amore*. Berowne, a lover of beauty and a poet inspired by the anima, chides his comrades over the vow they've all taken to ignore women in order to cultivate high learning, and in so doing he gives one of literature's greatest declarations of love's power to transform perception:

> O, we have made a vow to study, lords,
> And in that vow we have forsworn our books.
> For when would you, my liege, or you, or you,
> In leaden contemplation have found out
> Such fiery numbers as the prompting eyes
> Of beauty's tutors have enrich'd you with?
> Other slow arts entirely keep the brain;
> And therefore, finding barren practicers,
> Scarce show a harvest of their heavy toil;
> But love, first learned in a lady's eyes,
> Lives not alone immured in the brain,
> But with the motion of all elements
> Courses as swift as thought in every power,
> And gives to every power a double power,
> Above their functions and their offices.
> It adds a precious seeing to the eye:
> A lover's eyes will gaze an eagle blind.
> A lover's ear will hear the lowest sound,
> When the suspicious head of theft is stopp'd.
> Love's feeling is more soft and sensible

Than are the tender horns of cockled snails;
Love's tongue proves dainty Bacchus gross in taste.
For valor, is not Love a Hercules,
Still climbing trees in the Hesperides?
Subtle as Sphinx; as sweet and musical
As bright Apollo's lute, strung with his hair.
And when Love speaks, the voice of all the gods
Make heaven drowsy with the harmony.
Never dared poet touch a pen to write
Until his ink were temp'red with Love's sighs;
O, then his lines would ravish savage ears,
And plant in tyrants mild humility.
From women's eyes this doctrine I derive.
They sparkle still the right Promethean fire;
They are the books, the arts, the academes,
That show, contain, and nourish, all the world,
Else none at all in aught proves excellent.
Then fools you were these women to forswear;
Or, keeping what is sworn, you will prove fools.
. . . .
Let us once lose our oaths to find ourselves,
Or else we lose ourselves to find our oaths.
(*Love's Labors Lost*, IV.3.315–359)

Shakespeare, through Berowne, links love to the awakened heart *which everywhere perceives particularity*. To love is to perceive with more sensitivity—"it gives to every power a double power"; to sense more finely—"Subtle as Sphinx"—the physiognomy of the world: "Love's feeling...more soft and sensible/ Than...the tender horns of cockled snails." Love awakens the anaesthetized soul and its benumbed senses. The world is truly taken in, taken to heart, perceived as pure image in its precise particularity—in what William James called its "eachness."

Resounding this idea of eachness, James Hillman suggests that "only in this eachness does soul exist and cosmos show" where soul "is precisely the eachness of everywhere at any instant in any thing in its display as a phenomenon."[9]

173

It is this loving recognition of soul in the unique face of each instant that characterizes the poetics of love. But that is not all. In mythology, Love (Eros) is a God.

2. *Theophanies of Eros (Adagio sostenuto)*

Archetypal psychology finds its basis for the poetics of love here in Love's divinity: Eros, the "Mighty Daimon" of Socrates; the "Lord of Terrible Aspect" in Dante; the wounding, and wounded, youthful God in Apuleius; the chaos-born *Phanes* or *Protogonos* of the Orphics; the crimson-robed archangel of Sohrawardi. By allowing Eros a multiplicity of faces, we allow a variety of erotic metaphors. Archetypal psychology thus honors an ancient tradition which sees Eros as a nonhuman force of devastating power, polymorphous and Protean in its shape-shifting complexity.

An ancient Greek papyrus containing a prayer to Eros calls him "the source of all living,...unnameable and immeasurable," whose "golden wings...cover the whole world."[10] It speaks of him as "joining everything together" and breathing "life-giving thought into the soul." He is called "dark, mysterious one, who conceals discreet and crafty thought and inspires dark and ominous passion." Continuing, the papyrus describes Eros as "the hidden one who lives in stealth in every soul." It tells how Eros "kindles the invisible fire in all that is animate" by his touch. "Since time began," it says, this "first-born" one "tirelessly torments" with "desire through anguished rapture." And in spite of being called "lawless," "heartless" and "inexorable," he is also named "master of every movement of the spirit and of all things hidden...father of silence, through whom and to whom the light shines forth." He is both "tender infant" and "ancient of days." And he is the "archer," "the torch-bearer," who is also the "nocturnal visitor, joyful by night, maker of night," who also "hears and answers" from hidden "depths" of the sea.

Eros, the eldest, the first-born, the "golden-winged," as these Orphics knew him, emerged from "the wind-sown" egg of black-winged Night in the infinite bosom of Chaos.[11] His name was Phanes.

And this is how Eros still appears today: born of consciousness in chaos. His theophany as *Phanes* is as an apparition of original divinity. The Greek word *phaino* means to bring to light or to cause to appear. *Phaneros* means to show or display. *Phantasie* means the presentation to consciousness of perceptual images. *Theophany* means the apparition of the God and *angelophany* the apparition of the angel. Eros is not that which brings chaos; Eros is born of chaos. He is that inherent order in night and chaos, a theophany, an apparition before the eyes of the soul. The poet Rainer Maria Rilke describes the theophany of Eros in these terms:

> Lost, oh, suddenly, lost!
> Divinity in one swift embrace.
> Life turns round. Fate is born.
> And within a spring weeps.[12]

Psychology pays far too little attention to the theophanic nature of love. Caught by the developmental thinking of Great Mother psychologies, analysis looks at patients suffering under the influence of Eros as if it were something to grow out of or to be analyzed into personalistic familial projections.

Certainly it appears that some people are untouched by Eros. Whole schools of psychology as well! Eros as enemy? Yet, as James Hillman has asked, "can anyone live with authenticity unless he believes and trusts in the basic meaningfulness and rightness of the movements of his love?"[13]

But even here, however unwelcome and unannounced, the *puer* spirit of Eros can strike—right into the hearts of those respected paragons of anaesthetized senectitude of whatever age. Let's face it. We are not the masters of love. It masters us.

3. Ego Dominus Tuus (Molto moderato e cantabile)

Before going any further, we should recall two things. First, we should remember that in some Greek traditions, Eros was a daimon rather than a God—though this distinction was not always kept and is impossible to keep in any absolute sense. The

175

locus classicus for the description of Eros as daimon, or angelos—that mediating, intermediate being—is the teaching Diotima gives Socrates and which he repeats to his friends in the
Symposium. She says:

> He is a mighty daimon, Socrates; and everything that is
> of daimonic nature is half-God, half-man. And what is
> the function of such a being? To interpret and convey
> messages to the Gods from men and to men from the
> Gods...The daimon, being of an intermediate nature,
> bridges the gap between them, and prevents heaven
> and earth from falling asunder...it is by means of dai-
> mons that all intercourse and communication between
> Gods and men takes place. A man who possesses skill in
> such matters is called a daimonic man...Daimons are
> many in number and of many kinds, and one of them is
> Eros.[14]

Following Diotima and Socrates, archetypal psychology sees
Eros as daimon or angel, agreeing with Henry Corbin that every theophany has the form of an angelophany and that *it is not
Love that the lover falls in love with, but the divinity made manifest
by Love.*

The second thing we should remember is that we cannot
hope to understand the apparition of Eros through common-
place, bad copies. As Edgar Wind writes:

> It seems to be a lesson of history that the commonplace
> may be understood as a reduction of the exceptional, but
> that the exceptional cannot be understood by amplifying
> the commonplace. Both logically and causally the excep-
> tional is crucial, because it introduces (however strange
> it may sound) the more comprehensive category.[15]

In discussing the meaning of the Italian term *Fedeli d'amore*
with which he chooses to translate the Persian and Arabic
equivalents, Henry Corbin points out that it does not apply

indiscriminately to the entire community of Sufis. He explains that in making this distinction, he is following the indications given by the great Persian mystic, Ruzbehan Baqli of Shiraz (d. 1209), in his beautiful treatise entitled *The Jasmine of the Fedeli d'amore*:

> Ruzbehan distinguishes between the pious ascetics, or Sufis, who never encountered the experience of human love, and the *Fedeli d'amore,* for whom the experience of a cult of love dedicated to a beautiful being is the necessary initiation to divine love, from which it is inseparable. Such an initiation does not indeed signify anything in the nature of a monastic conversion to divine love; it is a unique initiation which transfigures *eros* as such; that is, human love for a human creature.[16]

This religion of love, Corbin continues, inspired the poets of Iran with "the magnificent *ta'wil*," according to which "the Prophet of Islam in person proclaims Zarathustra to be the prophet of the Lord of Love, the altar of Fire becomes the symbol of the Living Flame in the temple of the heart."[17]

Less than a century after Ruzbehan's death, the 29-year-old Florentine, Dante Alighieri, wrote a small book called *La Vita Nuova.* In it he sets out to depict the initiatory events which led to his embarking on "the new life" of the title. The year was 1295. Five years had passed since the death of his beloved, a young Florentine girl by the name of Beatrice Portinari.

It was still two centuries before Marsilio Ficino would be writing *de Amore,* his commentary on Plato's *Symposium,* and three centuries before Shakespeare would pen those unsurpassed words of eloquence in defense of the *Fedeli d'amore* in *Love's Labors Lost*.

Six centuries later, Dante's story could still captivate the imagination of the son of an Italian expatriate in England, Dante Gabriel Rosetti, who published his own illustrated translation of his namesake's treatise, while trying devotedly to serve the philosophy of the *Fedeli* in his own life and art.

177

In his book Dante Alighieri was addressing the company of the *Fedeli d'amore,* recounting in poetry and prose the story of his great love. "In the book of my memory," he begins, "after the first pages, where nothing much can be read, there is a section headed *Incipit vita nova.*" At a May Feast in 1274 Dante, aged nine, first met his beloved:

> Nine times already since my birth had the heaven of the light returned in its revolution to the exact same point when first the glorious Lady of my mind was made manifest to my eyes; even she who was called Beatrice by many who did not know what it meant to call her this. She had already lived in the world for so long a time as it takes the heaven of the fixed stars to move one twelfth of a degree towards the Eastern quarter; so that she appeared to me not long after she had passed the beginning of her ninth year, and I saw her almost at the end of my ninth year. Her dress that day was of a most noble color, a delicate and goodly crimson (*nobilissimo colore, umile e onesto sanguigno*), girdled and adorned in such a manner as best suited her very tender age. At that very moment I say in all truth that the spirit of life (*lo spirito de la vita*) which dwells in the most secret chamber of the heart (*la secretissima camera de lo cuore*) began to tremble so violently that the least pulses of my body shook. Tremblingly, it said these words: *Ecce deus fortior me, qui veniens dominabitur mihi* (Behold a God more powerful than I who comes to rule over me).[18]

For Dante the first sight of Beatrice is cosmic *and* personal. All the heavens had conspired, it seems, to bring about this theophany in a consciousness deeply shaken by beauty. And not in a grown man, but in a nine-year-old boy.

From this moment on, "Love," Dante says, "ruled my soul." He tells how Love often commanded him to go where perhaps he might see this "very young female angel" (*angiola giovanissima*). "And so, in my boyhood, I often went in search of her;

178

and I found her so praiseworthy and noble that certainly those words of the poet Homer might have been said of her: 'She did not seem the daughter of a mortal man, but of a God.'"

There is a parallel to this experience in the biography of an earlier master in the company of the *Fedeli d'amore*: the great twelfth-century Andalusian Sufi, Ibn 'Arabi. In his fortieth year, in the year A.D. 1201, this itinerant philosopher arrived in Mecca and there met a Persian shayk from Isfahan. This shayk had a fourteen-year-old daughter named Nizam Ayn al-Shams (Harmony Eye of the Sun and of Beauty) who was *actually* beautiful *and* mystically gifted. In honor of his love for her Ibn 'Arabi composed a book of poems, the *Tarjuman al-ashwaq*. So erotic were these poems that the public authorities attempted to prosecute Ibn 'Arabi. The philosopher quelled this persecution by writing a brilliant commentary to the poems, revealing their metaphysical meaning.

In his prologue, "The Interpreter of Desires," Ibn 'Arabi tells how one night, while he was performing the ritual of circumambulation around the Ka'aba, an angelophany occurred. A profound stillness had entered him. He left the paved surface and the pressing crowds, and while he was walking through the sand some lines of poetry began forming in his head. He spoke them aloud. They contained a desperate cry for reassurance from the "supreme Contemplated Ones"—to know if they were safe and sound or if they had perished. "No sooner than I had recited these verses," he writes, than I felt on my shoulder the touch of a hand softer than silk. I turned around and found myself in the presence of a young girl, a princess from among the Greeks. Never had I seen a woman more beautiful of face, softer of speech, more tender of heart, more spiritual in her ideas, more subtle in her analogies."[19]

Reprimanding the doubting sage with "the stern authority of a divine initiatrix," the young girl "divulges the entire secret of the sophianic religion of love." Corbin, however, warns us at this point to be aware that "we can only go astray if we ask, as many have done in connection with the figure of Beatrice in Dante: is she a concrete, real figure or is she an allegory?"[20]

This is a friendly warning. Corbin desires that we accept the inherently *twin* nature of consciousness and *not* make it be one thing or another. The experience of Ibn 'Arabi, like that of Dante, emphasizes the inseparability of the celestial and the terrestrial, the archetypal and the personal. As Corbin writes,

> a divine archetypal Figure can be contemplated only in a concrete Figure—sensible or imaginal—which renders it outwardly or mentally visible. When Ibn 'Arabi explains an allusion to...Nizam as...an allusion to "a sublime and divine, essential and sacrosanct Wisdom," we perceive how a being apprehended directly by the Imagination is transfigured...From the very first the figure of the young girl was perceived by the Imagination...as an "apparitional Figure."[21]

The way that we approach such figures is crucial to our psychologies. If we adopt an attitude which names this experience "idealization"—as certain schools of analysis and humanistic psychology do, dismissing such experiences as "projection"—we will see them as basically false. And we will see the imagination as a falsifier of reality.

Rather, this imagination is, as Corbin and the Sufis see it, *creative.* "The Active Imagination is essentially the organ of theophanies, because it is the organ of Creation and because Creation is essentially theophany."[22] When this imagination is induced, says Corbin, it "will not produce some arbitrary, even lyrical, construction standing between us and 'reality,' but will, on the contrary, function directly as a faculty and organ of knowledge just as real as—if not more real than—the sense organs. However, it will perceive in the manner proper to it."[23]

Corbin adds that in this process of "dematerialization" in which sense data are transmuted, resolved into the purity of the subtle world and restored as symbols, it is "the Earth, and the things and beings of the Earth, raised to incandescence, [which] allow the apparition of their Angels to penetrate the visionary intuition."[24]

The active imagination guides, anticipates, molds sense perception; that is why it transmutes sensory data into symbols. The Burning Bush is only a brushwood fire if it is merely perceived by the sensory organs. In order that Abraham may perceive the Burning Bush and hear the Voice calling him "from the right side of the valley"—in short, in order that there may be a theophany—an organ of trans-sensory perception is needed.[25]

With this understanding of the theophanic imagination we can return to Dante. We read in *La Vita Nuova* that exactly nine years after his first meeting with "the very young woman angel," the poet met her again out in the street. They were both close to being eighteen. Beatrice was dressed in the whitest white, walking between two older, distinguished women. She turned her eyes to Dante and with "her ineffable courtesy" (*la sua ineffabile cortesia*) spoke a greeting. As these were the first words of hers ever to have "made a move to his ears," his trepidation was transformed to rapture. Drunk with joy, Dante withdrew from people's eyes and hid himself in his room, possessed by her image, whereupon he fell asleep. It was then that he had the "marvellous vision":

In my room I seemed to see a cloud the color of fire (*una nebula de colore di fuoco*) and in the cloud, a Lord of Terrible Aspect, filling me with fear and awe, yet appearing astonishingly joyous in himself. He said many things, of which I understood only a few; among them were the words: *Ego dominus tuus.* (I am your master). In his arms there seemed to be a naked person, asleep, lightly wrapped in a crimson cloth (*una drappo sanguigno*). Regarding her intently, I saw that it was she who had earlier that day bestowed her greeting on me. In one hand he seemed to be holding something burning, and he seemed to say, *Vide cor tuum* (Behold your heart). After a time, he seemed to wake the sleeping one, and he forced her to eat the glowing heart in his hand. She did so unwillingly. Within moments his happiness turned to bitter grief, and weeping, he gathered the figure in his arms and together they rose into the sky. [my translation]

Dante felt such anguish at this point that he woke; it was about ten o'clock at night. Immediately, he put himself into a contemplative reverie in order to imagine himself deeper into the image and then composed a sonnet, addressed to all *Fedeli d'amore, "A ciascun'alma presa e gentil core"*:

> To every soul that's seized by Love
> and every Noble heart to whom these words
> are dedicated in Love's name:
> Greetings! And may you post me back a poem.
>
> The hours of the night in which stars shine
> had already in their course traversed a third
> when suddenly Love stood before me.
> His essence, terrifying to remember; though
>
> in himself he seemed ecstatic, at least to me.
> In his hand he held my heart, and in his arms he held
> My Lady, lightly wrapped and sleeping.
>
> Then he woke her, oblivious of her fear,
> giving her my burning heart to eat:
> whereupon I saw him turn and leave me, weeping.[26]

What respect Dante has for his dream! Where psychoanalysis[27] with its monotonously Oedipal method would deny the divinity in the fiery cloud, that "Lord of Terrible Aspect," seeing instead a disguised father image, and Jungians would waver between equally conceptual alternatives—seeing the figure as Negative Self or Shadow spiriting away the anima— Dante sees the figure imaginally, and in a sure move of archetypal reversion (*epistrophé*), calls the Lord *Amor*, or Eros. He thus makes an instinctive move into the creative, theophanic imagination of which this dream is such a beautiful example, and he realizes that the words spoken by the dream figure clearly apply to him. And although in the dream Beatrice is transported to a heavenly realm, this image is more than Dante can take at the moment. He only knows that it spells anguish. As William Anderson writes of the *Fedeli d'amore*, "One of the most important characteristics shared by the poets of the *dolce stil nuovo* is the attention they paid to their visions and dreams."[28]

The most important of the many replies Dante received from the poets to whom he had sent copies of this sonnet was that of Guido Cavalcanti, ten years Dante's senior and the most accomplished poet of his time. Cavalcanti recognized the genius in Dante and the young poet's natural inclination towards the *Fedeli d'amore*, and he drew Dante quickly into the select circle of the *dolce stil nuovo*. These men, all aspiring to enter the company of the *Fedeli d'amore*, shared certain social, aesthetic and metaphysical ideals which young Dante found congenial. The central idea of the group was that nobility was a matter of individual merit, not of heredity. This was the *gentil core*, the "noble neart," so often alluded to in their poetry.[29] The noble heart is the source of the only nobility recognized by the *Fedeli d'amore*:—the nobility of the imagination.[30]

For seven years following the "chance" encounter with Beatrice and her greeting of "ineffable courtesy," Dante lived in a state of perpetual communion with the creative imagination, punctuated only by sharp lightning flashes of terror. During all this time he made no open declaration of his true feeling for Beatrice, though he could often not hide his emotions on seeing her in public. To mislead the curious, Dante went to such lengths as to write love poems to a completely different woman, who became a screen for his true love.

There is no apparent reason for this secrecy. Dante himself gives none. And his best friends guessed his love, as did the women around Beatrice. It was a secret and not a secret.

Dante scholars after Luigi Valli have seen the secrecy as a sign that Dante belonged to a secret society of Sufis like the earlier troubadours and that he even spoke a secret language in his poetry.[31]

Archetypal psychology, however, understands the secrecy in another way, seeing it more as an inherent dimension of Eros consciousness, the diaphanous character of consciousness hermeticized by Eros. If theophany is a mirroring presence of the "alone to the Alone" (Corbin), then the theophany mediated by Eros is an intimacy which by its very nature cannot be shared, except with the Beloved. Lovers speak "the language of the birds." "Secrecy" is a secretion of theophanic Eros, what the Sufis term "inner taste."[32] The lover withdraws into the temple of the heart there to contemplate the image of the Beloved. Corbin tells us that the theophanic conception "is that of an Apparition which is a shining of the Godhead through the mirror of humanity, after the manner of the light which becomes visible only as it takes form and shines through the figure of a stained glass window."[33] Divinity is in mankind as an image is in a mirror. In other words, "Love tends to transfigure the beloved earthly figure by setting it against a light which brings out all its superhuman virtualities to the point of investing it with the theophanic function of the Angel."[34] But it is the soul that apprehends theophany. It recognizes "that the Beloved is this physical Form...at once in its spiritual and its physical nature, it is drawn toward that Form."[35]

Dante refers to Beatrice as "Madonna Intelligenza." Ibn 'Arabi speaks of the girl Nizam as "Sophia aeterna." Sohrawardi, that Prince of the *Fedeli d'amore*, calls the figure a Hermes in ecstasy and "the Crimson-robed Archangel" Gabriel, denoting the Holy Spirit in each individual. In each case the individual's experience is an absolutely unique perception of divinity in a concrete, human form.

When Beatrice is spoken of as an archetype, from the perspective of analytical psychology, she seems to lose her reality and become a figment of the intellect. On the other hand, if we speak of her as a real person, we shall no longer be able to distinguish the difference in structure between Beatrice's relationship with her *Fedele* and the relationship that any other girl on the earth can have with her boyfriend.

184

Madonna Intelligenza is that active intelligence which, "by awakening an awareness of itself in a person, awakens an appreciation of the Person who has awakened it." Such a relationship implies that "My Lady" is experienced as a person *and* as an archetype—as a person-archetype.[36]

It is through this angel, the active intelligence or *Madonna Intelligenza*, that "the human individual is attached directly to the celestial pleroma without the mediation of any magistery or ecclesiastical reality," writes Corbin.[37]

Or as Charles Williams put it: "What he [Dante] sees is something real. It is not more 'real' than the actual Beatrice who no doubt had many serious faults, but it is as real. Both Beatrices are aspects of the one Beatrice. The revealed virtues are real; so is the celestial beauty."[38]

4. The Fires of Love and the Alchemy of Seduction
(Lento con fuoco)

Thus, the fact that Beatrice is *Madonna Intelligenza* for Dante does not mean that he does not see her as Beatrice Portinari, the physical daughter of a Florentine banker. This love certainly does not exclude the physical. Dante says that his body was so oppressed by love, as by a surfeit of sweetness, that it felt heavy and lifeless; her greeting overpassed and overflowed his capacity. Everywhere among the *Fedeli* we read of the physical pathos of love. Dante says that he grew so frail and weak that many of his friends expressed concern for his health (*La Vita Nuova*, IV). Ibn 'Arabi writes that the apparitions of his beloved left him in such a state that he could not take any food for days, so intoxicated was he with the form that never ceased to be the object of his gaze, standing or seated, in movement or rest.[39] Sappho, terse to the point of anguish, can only cry:

> Pain penetrates
> Me drop
> by drop[40]

In another place she writes that she cannot even speak. "Thin fire" races under her skin, her eyes do not see and her ears are drumming. Cold sweat and shaking make her feel almost dead (Frag. 31).

Anne Carson, discussing Eros among the Greek poets, writes that "the physiology that they posit for the erotic experience is one which assumes eros to be hostile in intention and detrimental in affect. Alongside melting, we might cite metaphors of piercing, crushing, bridling, roasting, stinging, biting, grating, cropping, poisoning, singeing and grinding to a powder, all of which are used of eros by the poets."[41]

This catalogue, as moral critique of Eros' "heartlessness," is damning. But as a psychopoetic expression of love's alchemical operations on the soul it is awesome. What emerges is that Eros transforms mainly through fire. To Dante he appears in a fiery cloud (*nebulo fuoco*). He holds Dante's burning heart in his hand. Eros is the torchbearer. Whether his heat is felt as the melting fires of passion or the scorching flames of hell-torments, he burns. Forms transform. Eros brings metamorphosis.

In the *Phaedrus* (251) Plato sees the tortures of theophanic love alchemically as the growth of the wings of the soul. The new initiate, having had "full sight of the celestial vision" in a godlike face or physical form, "first of all shivers and experiences something of the dread which the vision itself inspired." He gazes on the form of his beloved and worships it as if it were a God. This leads him to receive through his eyes the emanation of beauty by which, in Plato's words, "the soul's plumage is fostered and grows hot, and this heat is accompanied by a softening of the passages from which the feathers grow, passages which have long been parched and closed up." The effect of the beauty experienced by the lover is as nourishing moisture—"the stump of each feather under the whole surface of the soul swells and strives to grow from its root; for in its original state the soul was feathered all over. So now it is all in a state of ferment and throbbing. In fact," says Plato, the soul of a man who is beginning to grow his feathers "has the same sensation of pricking and irritation and itching as children feel in their gums" when they are teething.

"Imprisoned below the surface together with the flood of longing, each embryo feather throbs like a pulse and presses... so that the soul is driven mad by the pain and the pricks in every part and yet feels gladness because it preserves the memory of the beauty of its darling." Struggling helplessly, baffled by the strangeness of his state, the lover tastes a mixture of pleasure and pain. In his frenzy he can neither sleep at night nor stay still by day, driven by a longing (*pothos*) to go wherever he might catch sight of the beloved. Happily, this sight can assuage the pain because the closed passages of the feathers are unstopped and they can grow again. "And," Plato says, "there is nothing to equal the sweetness of the pleasure which he enjoys for the moment." He will never willingly emerge from this state; no one in his eyes can compare with the beloved. Friends and relatives are forgotten; he thinks nothing of losing his property; he scorns conventional behavior; he is ready to make himself a slave. He is ill and the beloved is the only physician who can cure his illness. Men call this illness "eros," but—Plato punningly says—the Gods all it *pteros*, from the wings that must grow (*pteron*, "wing"). Thus, Eros himself must grow wings, and not simply the lover. But on whomever these wings must grow, the process is not all bliss.

In fact this ornithological psycho-metamorphosis is awarded Best Place in Plato's categories of divine madness. For Plato, every human soul has the potential of enjoying the benefits of Love's divine blessings, though he adds that "not every soul...finds it easy to use its present experience as a means of recollecting the world of reality."[42]

This passionate embodiment of *epistrophé* is described by Plato as the recognition in the traits of the beloved of the features of that God or Goddess with whom the lover is archetypally linked. Here archetypal psychology acknowledges Plato as the father of its metaphorical method of reversion, giving, one could say, a classical aesthetic to the otherwise debased idea of "transference," which is the root meaning of the word "metaphor"—every lover discovers the particular features of his or her divinity in the features of the beloved. To be in Zeus's train is to be drawn irresistibly to persons of dignity and wide-ranging rulership; just as to be in the train of Mars means to fall in love with battle lust, warlike boldness and steely temper.

The divinity whom Dante and his companions celebrated in the shape of the women they loved was Lady Sapientia, Sophia, Madonna Intelligenza—an archetypal figure capable of mediating beauty of the greatest imaginable reality.

Marsilio Ficino, who revived the Florentine cult of Orphic and Platonic love in the Renaissance, two hundred years later, defined love as the desire for divine beauty, and he wrote of beauty (commen. *de Amore*, 95) that it is:

> a certain lively and spiritual grace infused by the shining ray of God, first in the Angel, and thence in the souls of men, the shapes of bodies, and sounds; a grace which through reason, sight, and hearing moves and delights our souls; in delighting, carries them away, and in carrying them away, inflames them with burning love.[43]

It is beauty then which seduces the soul into falling in love. "Beauty," which, as Corbin writes, "is the theophany par excellence."[44] Beauty (*kallos*) calls forth, or provokes, love in the soul, just as the Greek root, *kaleo*, "I provoke," suggests. Once one has dared to look into the face of beauty, one is "lost," as Rilke says: "utterly lost." But to the degree that we insist on loving only the concrete physicality of the beloved, so does Love often rob us of our illusion of possession. The alchemy of seduction leads us straight into the fiery furnace of soulmaking, and there we must enter again and again, until, like Rumi, we can say:

> There is no intuitive certainty until you burn: if you desire that certainty, sit down in the fire.[45]

Or again like Rumi:

188

The voice of the fire tells the *truth*, saying *I am not fire. I
am fountainhead.*
Come into me and don't mind the sparks.
If you are a friend of God, fire is your water.
You should wish to have a hundred thousand sets
of mothwings,
so you could burn them away, one set a night.[46]

We know from Dante's own words in *La Vita Nuova* that the
death of Beatrice before she was twenty-five precipitated him
into the most profound soul crisis and forced him to change
from being dependent on Beatrice's physical presence to the
discovery of love as praise and timeless memory. This is the inner meaning of the "New Life" of the title.

The test of a *Fedeli's* faithfulness as a follower of Love is
when he loses the beloved as a concrete, physical presence, either through death or separation. Then he must confront a
world in which the temptation to make the beloved's physical
presence the only criteria of worth is overwhelming. This is
when the lover discovers of what metal his love is made.

In the voice of Zuleika, speaking of her beloved, Rumi
shows how she "let everything be the name of Joseph, from cel-
ery seed/to aloes wood. She loved him so much, she concealed
his name/in many different phrases, the inner meanings
known only to her/...anything she praises, it's Joseph's touch
she means, /any complaint, it's his being away."[47]

What we are witness to, on reading these lines from the
Mathnawi, is the ultimate transfiguring power of Eros. For Rumi's Zuleika-consciousness, even the beloved's absence is an
intimate presence—which speaks to her in secret phrases in all
the things of her world. What Rumi is describing is the final
breakthrough, the *Fedeli's* hard-won, diamond realization that
the soul of the beloved is in *every*thing.

When the strings of thy robe are loosened by
the intoxication of love,
Behold heaven's triumph and Orion's bewilderment!

189

How the world, high and low, is troubled
By love, which is purified from high and low!
When the sun goes up, where stayeth the night?
When the joy of bounty came where lagged affliction?
I am silent. Speak thou, O soul of soul of soul,
From desire of whose face every atom grew articulate.[48]

How did Rumi arrive at being able to write of love in this way? What happened to him? The extraordinary story of Rumi's transfiguration follows.

5. The Lunatic, the Lover and the Poet
(Largo dolce e legato)

At the age of thirty-seven, Mevlana Jalal 'uddin Rumi was at the peak of his career as professor of Islamic theology in Konya (the ancient Greek city of Iconium in Asia Minor) where he had succeeded his father in the role of spiritual teacher. His discourses drew thousands of listeners, among them many kings and princes, as well as commoners. As a student he had been taught by the best minds of his time. As a boy he had received the blessings of the great Sufi master, Farid al-Din 'Attar of Nishapur, who told the boy's father: "The day will come when this child will kindle the fire of divine enthusiasm throughout the world." For over ten years he had put all his energy into perfecting his profound and scholarly sermons. As a good Muslim he scorned music, and as a philosopher he probably considered poetry a lesser vehicle for the Truth. He was married; he had several children; and he was a deeply respected leader of the community. Then one day in November, 1244, as he was leaving the college where he had been teaching, something happened.

Sitting majestically on his horse, conversing with his students, who scrambled to walk beside him and to hold the stirrups of his mount, Rumi was suddenly aware of a weird figure that emerged from the Inn of the Sugar Merchants and moved through the throng towards him. It was a man of about sixty, a dervish, wearing an old, patched cloak of coarse, black felt. Leaping through the crowd, he grasped the bridle of the horse and shouted a question at the rider. Rumi answered. The man shouted another question (the books disagree as to what the questions were). Rumi answered again. This time the dervish fell to his knees in the dust. Rumi dismounted and knelt in the dust himself, touching the stranger's head and embracing him as if he were his long-lost, best friend. The crowd stopped. The students began murmuring. After a time, Rumi and the stranger stood up. Rumi gave the horse into the charge of one of his students and sent the crowd away. The two men left town and were not seen again for three months. The students discovered that they had gone to a hermitage in the country where they had remained hermetically cloistered. Who was this stranger?

No one knew much about him, except that he came from Tabriz and that he was a wanderer. His name was Shams, which means "The Sun." Rumi seemed spellbound. His students were outraged. It was as if a demon or djinn had appeared and taken possession of their master. He no longer appeared at his classes. After a time he even stopped wearing the professor's gown and took to wearing an old dervish cloak, like Shams. Worse, he seemed to dote on everything the old dervish said. Once when Rumi was giving a discourse to a few close students, Shams appeared, took his books and threw them into a nearby pool, saying "You must live by what you know." When Shams told Rumi not to speak, Rumi remained silent for days. The final proof that Rumi had gone mad was that, under Shams' influence, he had taken to listening to ecstatic music, composing poems and dancing. Rumi was drunk with the experience of divinity, but not in the abstract: Shams' presence was theophanic.

> Cross and Christians, from end to end,
> I surveyed; He was not on the cross.
> I went to the idol-temple, to the ancient pagoda;
> No trace was visible there.
> I went to the mountains of Herat and Kandahar;

191

I looked; He was not in that hill-and-dale.
With set purpose I fared to the summit of Mt. Qaf;
In that place was only the (Simurgh's) habitation
I bent the reins of search to the Ka'aba;
He was not in that resort of old and young.
I questioned Ibn Sina of his state;
He was not in Ibn Sina's range.
I fared towards the scene of *"two bow-lengths"* distance;
He was not in that exalted court.
I gazed into my own heart;
There I saw Him; He was nowhere else,
Save pure-souled Shamsi Tabriz
None ever was drunken and intoxicated
    and distraught.[49]

So writes Rumi in one of the *ghazals* he composed during this time. The meeting with Shams had, in fact, transformed Rumi into a great poet. In the years between 1245 and 1261, he composed some fifty thousand verses, comprising 3,500 ghazals and 2,000 quatrains. These were put together and called, by Rumi, the *Divan,* or Book, of *Shams-i-Tabriz.* And until recently, the only translations available in English were a selection from 1898 of forty-eight ghazals by Reynold Nicholson, a professor of Arabic at Cambridge.

The populace of Konya was shocked and indignant at Rumi's behavior and his association with Shams. Though Rumi told his closest friends that Shams was a great alchemist and a wide-ranging scholar of the sciences who had renounced all that to devote himself to the contemplation of love's mysteries, the people generally held that Shams was a magician who had bedevilled Rumi's mind. Rumi ignored public opinion:

If thou art Love's lover and seekest love,
Take a keen poniard and cut the throat of bashfulness.
Know that reputation is a great hindrance in the path;
This saying is disinterested: receive it with pure mind.[50]

Insofar as one is afraid to be who one is, reputation is a hindrance in the path. Being who he was, with Shams, was a joy for Rumi. It was hard going with the rest of the community. But Rumi had seen something, and he wasn't going to let go of it that easily.

What is to be done, O Moslems? for I
    do not recognize myself.
I am neither Christian, nor Jew, nor Gabr, nor Moslem.
I am not of the East, nor of the West, nor of the land,
    nor of the sea;
I am not of Nature's mint, nor of the circling heavens.
I am not of the earth, nor of water, nor of air, nor of fire;
I am not of the empyrean, nor of the dust,
    nor of existence, nor of entity.
I am not of India, nor of China, nor of Bulgaria,
    nor of Saqsin;
I am not of the kingdom of Iraqain, nor of the country
    of Khorasan.
I am not of this world, nor of the next, nor of Paradise,
    nor of Hell;
I am not of Adam, nor of Eve, nor of Eden and Rizwan.
My place is the Placeless, my trace is the Traceless;
'Tis neither body nor soul, for I belong to the soul
    of the Beloved.
I have put duality away, I have seen that the two worlds
    are one;
One I seek, One I know, One I see, One I call.
He is the first, He is the last, He is the outward,
    He is the inward;
I know none other except "Ya Hu" and "Ya man Hu."
I am intoxicated with love's cup, the two worlds
    have passed out of my ken;
I have no business save carouse and revelry.
If once in my life I spent a moment without thee,
From that time and from that hour I repent of my life.

If once in this world I win a moment with thee,
I will trample on both worlds, I will dance
   in triumph forever.
O Shamsi Tabriz, I am so drunken in this world,
That except of drunkenness and revelry I have
   no tale to tell.[51]

Rumi's son wrote about his father that "his Khidr was Shamsi Tabriz."[52] One's Khidr is, for the Sufis, the angel of one's being, the person-archetype who initiates into archetypal awareness. By instilling "an aptitude for theophanic vision,"[53] Khidr frees the Sufi from literal religion *and* literal psychology. This happens because Khidr requires that we be what he himself is. By leading the Sufi towards that which is truly individual in himself, Khidr reveals the active intelligence. His individuation is my individuation. It was as if Shams constantly held up the mirror of the invisible to show Rumi his secret face.

This initiatory angelophany is strikingly similar to that of the appearance of the Greek princess to Ibn 'Arabi in Mecca.[54] Rumi seemed blind to all else but Shams. In love, "Nowhere...- are we more blind," writes James Hillman:

> Love blinds in order to extinguish the wrong and daily vision so that another eye may be opened that perceives from soul to soul. The habitual perspective cannot see through the dense skin of appearances; how you look, what you wear, how you are. The blind eye of love sees through into the invisible, making the opaque mistake of my loving transparent.[55]

While Rumi says:

> I tasted everything,
> I found nothing better than you.
> When I dove into the sea,
> I found no pearl like you.
> I opened all the casks,

> I tasted from a thousand jars,
> Yet none but that rebellious wine of yours
> Touched my lips and inspired my heart.[56]

Soon the hatred for Shams among Rumi's closest circle grew so intense that Shams decided to leave. One day he was gone. After a long while a letter arrived from Damascus. Rumi wrote back with a ghazal of fifteen verses. It was at this time that he may have also written this ghazal, one of his finest:

> Happy the moment when we are seated in the palace,
>   thou and I,
> With two forms and with two figures but with one soul,
>   thou and I.
> The colors of the grove and the voice of the birds
>   will bestow immortality
> At the time when we come into the garden, thou and I.
> The stars of heaven will come to gaze upon us:
> We shall show them the moon itself, thou and I.
> Thou and I, individuals no more, shall be mingled
>   in ecstasy,
> Joyful, and secure from foolish babble, thou and I.
> All the bright-plumed birds of heaven will devour
>   their hearts with envy
> In the place where we shall laugh in such a fashion,
>   thou and I.
> This is the greatest wonder, that thou and I, sitting here
>   in the same nook,
> Are at this moment both in 'Iraq and Khorasan,
>   thou and I.[57]

Finally, a year and a half later, Rumi's devoted son, Sultan Veled, travelled to Damascus to find Shams and to ask him to return. Shams agreed. The dervish entered the town on horseback. Sultan Veled had walked beside his stirrup all the way from Damascus. Rumi was reunited with his Shams, and now they were closer than ever.

But Rumi's students grew jealous and angry again. A group of them, including Rumi's other son, 'Ala-ud-din Muhammed, plotted to get rid of Shams. In Jami's version,[58] one night in May, 1247, Shams and Rumi were sitting together in that sacred space of theirs when someone outside said that they wanted to see Shams immediately. As he rose, Shams said to Rumi: "I am called...to my death." Seven conspirators were waiting in the garden, and they all fell on Shams with knives. The dervish, Jami says, gave such a cry that the assassins were all struck dumb, and when they had recovered their senses, Shams was gone and only a few drops of blood remained. His body was never found.

This sudden, Dionysian disappearance bewildered Rumi. He could not be convinced that Shams was really dead. At first he refused to see anyone. Confining himself to his house, he fasted and meditated. But the longing for Shams was wild within him. It is said that Rumi went himself to Damascus, knocking on every door, asking if anyone had seen Shams.

> How long will I search for you from house to house and from door to door? How long will you evade me from corner to corner and from alley to alley?[59]

Many of the odes in the *Divan* are written in this tearing grief which Rumi felt on losing Shams. He began to dance in the streets, calling for his beloved, an imaginal volcano, a whirl-wind of intensity. Two years passed. By now he was regarded as quite mad. One day his spinning steps brought him into the street of the goldsmiths, some yards from the booth of a crafts-man called Zarkob. The rhythmic blows of Zarkob's hammer beating out a sheet of silver, caught Rumi's attention. He whirled closer, slower, stopped, listening.

Zarkob kept on pounding. Rumi stayed, listening. Zarkob looked up. Mevlana had returned. He had seen, in this man who was so unlike Shams, a divinity which immediately made his grieving transparent. It was like that moment when miner-als deep in the earth, under intense heat and pressure, change into crystal, into sapphires or rubies.

196

Sohrawardi wrote that "many years are necessary for one primal stone to be turned by the sun into a ruby in Badakshan or a carnelian in Yemen."

Through the disciplined, emancipated rhythms of the gold-smith's loving hammer, Rumi's spinning dance steadied, concentrated and deepened into soul. As his pupils began returning, Rumi taught them also how to spin, how to churn the milk of their experience into the clarified butter of compassion. The Mevlevi Order of the Whirling Dervishes began in Rumi's dance of praise for Shams, the angel of his being. Over the years that followed, Rumi evolved a way of creating poetry, spun like fine gold out of the turning point of the still world. The master unfolded his arms, like a fledgling bird, tilted back his head and whirled. As he whirled, he spoke, and during the next twelve years his third close friend, Husam-ud-din, transcribed the fifty-one thousand verses that made up the *Mathnawi*, long regarded by many as the Persian Koran. Rumi, according to Husam,

> never took a pen in his hand while composing the *Math-nawi*. He would recite wherever he was, in the *medrese* [the dervish college], at the Ilgin hot springs, in the Konya baths, in the vineyards. When he started, I would write, and I often found it hard to keep up. Sometimes he would recite night and day for several months. Once for a period of two years he spoke no poetry. As each volume was completed, I would read it back to him so that he could revise it.[60]

There is nothing like the *Mathnawi* in English or, in fact, in any language. As Rumi's inspired present-day translator Coleman Barks writes,

> To use Rumi's metaphor, the *Mathnawi* is an ocean, with myriad elements swimming and adrift and growing in it: folklore, the Qur'an, stories of saints and teachers, myth, the sayings of Muhammad, jokes from the street,

197

actual interruptions, whispered asides to Husam. There is an enormous generosity and humor at play here, and at work. Fresh, wild moments within a profound peace. Drunken, lyric dissolvings within a starry clarity. Spontaneous pleasure within discipline.[61]

Coda

Rumi lived until 1273 when he died at the age of sixty-six. Before he died he said:

> Do not search for me in the grave.
> Look for me in the hearts of learned men.

And he asked that these brief lines be his epitaph:

> *Not more than three words*
> *My whole life condensed in these three words.*
> *I was raw, now I am cooked and burnt.*

The *Mathnawi* is a treasury of gems shaped in the white heat of Rumi's creative imagination. It is an inexhaustible inheritance bequeathed the community—in the way that Dante's *Commedia*, Goethe's opus, Ibn 'Arabi's texts and Shakespeare's plays are. And each of these men in their lives was defeated by the angel of love, conquered by the adoration for another human individual. Each of these men was a true *Fedeli d'amore*, who followed Love faithfully wherever it led. As Ibn 'Arabi says:

> O marvel! a garden among the flames...
> My heart has become capable of all forms.
> It is a meadow for gazelles and a monastery
>   for Christian monks,
> A temple for idols and the pilgrim's Ka'aba,
> The Tables of the Law and the book of the Koran.
> I profess the religion of Love, and whatever direction
> Its steed may take, Love is my religion and my faith.[62]

198

Or as Rumi says:

> It is heartache that lays the lover's passion bare:
> No sickness with heart sickness may compare.
> Love is a malady apart, the sign
> And astrolabe of mysteries divine.
> Whether of heavenly mold or earthly cast,
> Love still leads us yonder at the last.[63]

It is this "yonder" that archetypal psychology calls the realm of the archetypal. Our longing for it, as Hillman has pointed out, is itself archetypal, it is an archetypal longing. In one sense, it is also "impossible"—impossible love as the love of the impossible. Our *pothos*, nostalgia, then ultimately "refers to our angelic nature, and our longings and seaborne wanderings are the effects in our personal lives of the transpersonal images that urge us, carry us, and force us to imitate mythical destinies."[64]

The task facing any psychotherapist or analyst wishing to practice and yet remain true to this archetypal longing is one of constant vigilance with respect to the subtleties of interplay between the world of the angel and what appears as simply psychopathology. The two are like two lovers each reflecting the face of the other. Even angels weep…at the beauty of God.

This must be the end of this sonata for four hands which has meant to give some standing, for psychology, to the figure of Eros—though neither as fickle libido, nor as pornographic reduction, nor even as professorial pleasure principle, but as daimon, spirit that always creates impossible longings and leads through all the circles of hell and purgatory to the white rose of the soul's cosmos. *L'amor che move il sole e l'altre stelle,* "love that moves the sun and all the other stars."[65]

6

PERSEPHONE

Midwife
and Muse of
Metempsychosis

An Undertaking in Psychopoetics

In 1898 on his last stay in Tahiti, spitting blood, tortured by a bad leg and suffering from double conjunctivitis, raging eczema and badly-treated syphilis; hounded by local authorities of church and state; abandoned by his wife, heartbroken over the death of his beloved daughter and submerged in debt with no income from paintings being sold by his wife in Europe, Paul Gauguin painted his last testament, the masterpiece he entitled *Where Do We Come From? What Are We? Where Are We Going?*

Three cries, three screams in crucifixion flung in the face of that eternal sphinx and enchantress, the World Soul. Another unfolding of that most radical of Western koans: *Know Thyself.* For always, when we ask who or what we are, we are asking where we come from and where we are going. And the first question is always—Where do we come from?

Like the perplexed mother who silences her curious child with the baffling surrealism of "It was the stork who brought you," Christianity, following Judaism, has answered the greater

This chapter developed from a lecture given at Dartington Hall, Devon, December 6, 1985.

200

question of origins for us, for centuries, by intoning, *basso pro-fundo*, that we have come from Adam, who was made from dust and the breath of God. Empirically-minded evolutionists, irritated by the lack of verifiability in this answer, dropped the breath of God and left us as Accidental Transforms of Struggling Mud. Most other cultures have far more imaginative myths of creation. Few of them share our dead-end, this-life-only view.

Nihilism, which regards death as total extinction, is, in fact, deeply embedded in the thought forms of our culture. It is usually disguised as a kind of rational materialism.

But our nihilism extends much further than the question of life after death. Its paralyzing gaze virtually arrests the spontaneous life of the imagination with regard to the really profound questions. What I am interested in here is the lifting of this repression so that imagination can inhabit more of its rightful country. It is a question not just of the possibility of other lifetimes than this one, but also of the "far" *memories* of those "other" lifetimes. C.G. Jung wrote that

> rebirth is an affirmation that must be counted among the primordial affirmations of mankind...In view of the fact that all affirmations relating to the sphere of the supra-sensual are, in the last analysis, invariably determined by archetypes, it is not surprising that a concurrence of affirmations concerning rebirth can be found among the most widely differing peoples. (*CW* 9i.206)

Most little children, if not mocked and made to feel stupid about it, will talk of other lives. When my daughter Natasha was three-and-a-half, she suddenly interrupted my bedtime reading to say, "I was a tiger once!" I stopped reading.

Me: Oh, really? Was that before you were Natasha?
Natasha: Yes—(pause)—I was many animals—
Me: And...after you were a tiger?
Natasha: Then I was a brown person. Like Heidi (her
African playmate).

201

Me: Then you were born as Natasha...?
Natasha: No. Then I was a white person, then a brown person. I was a white person, then I was Natasha.

This was delivered with the utmost assurance. And notice the precision of the sequence: "No. Then I was a white person, then a brown person. I was a white person, *then* I was Natasha."

Joan Grant, that extraordinary English sibyl who coined the term "far memory" for her ability to recall "other lives," remembered having "known" at the age of about a year old that she had died "on some earlier occasion." She had been listening to her mother tell her half sister about the fire alarm which had been installed beside her parents' bed. I quote from her book, *Many Lifetimes*:

> She explained how it worked, and then added it must never be used unless the fire was too serious to be coped with by the fire extinguishers: but it could summon fire engines which would arrive within minutes.
>
> Even while I was listening to their conversation I made up my mind to summon fire engines at the earliest opportunity. I would have to be alone in my parents' bedroom; be able to climb on the bed without assistance; discover how to break the glass cover and then pull the brass knob. I understood perfectly well that this would be considered exceedingly naughty. At best I should be scolded, and at worst have my knickers removed and be put on a high marble-topped chest of drawers, a form of punishment known as "Putting-a-hot-baby-on-cold-marble," which I found intensely humiliating. It also scared me, because I was fearful of pitching off it onto my head. I knew I had died from falling from a height on some earlier occasion.[1]

The archetypal rememberer of past lives is, of course, the Buddha, whose name comes from the Sanskrit for "awake" and means "one who came awake, or woke up." In one of the oldest

202

parts of the *Pali Canon*, the *Sutta Nipata*, the Buddha is shown telling his disciples about *his* "far memory":

> I, brethren, when I so desire it, can call to mind my various states of birth: for instance, one birth, two births, five, ten…a hundred thousand births: the various destructions of aeons, the various renewals of aeons…thus: I lived there, was named thus, was of such a clan, of such a caste, was thus supported, had such and such pleasant and painful experiences, had such a length of days, disappeared thence and arose elsewhere: there too I lived, was named thus, was of such a clan, of such a caste (and so on)—thus can I call to mind in all their specific details, in all their characteristics, in many various ways, my previous states of existence. (*Sutta Nipata*, ii.2-3)

Finding accounts of remembered past lives presents no difficulties, whether it be the visions of Edgar Casey, the sensationalism of Bridey Murphy or a bestseller account by Shirley Maclaine. I am not interested in whether the stories of past lives can be proven true, verified with empirical evidence, or documented and legally established. What does interest me is the meaning these "far memories" have for the soul. For whatever else they may be, these "memories" are not separated from the ground of our being, the psyche. If they are not literally true, they are imaginally true. Accepting these memories as imaginally true, we are making the same kind of move Freud made when he accepted the psychological reality of the "screen memory"—the "memory" of something which never happened.

Commenting on Freud's crucial discovery that the productions of the psyche presented themselves in his cases as reproductions of history, James Hillman asks, "Why does the psyche need to present experience dressed in costumes of the past, as if it were history? Why does the psyche historicize? What does historicizing do for the soul?"[2]

Hillman's answer bears upon the question of the validity of past life memories, even though his focus is on this life.

This "falsification" is nothing other than the historicizing activity of the psyche itself. The psyche itself makes
"history" that is altogether fictional. We are not merely
making history, but making it up as we go along. Henry
Corbin always insisted history is in the soul (not we are
in history). History making is a musing, poetic process...proceeding as an autonomous, archetypal activity, presenting us with tales as if they were facts. And we
cannot transcend history, not because we cannot get out
of time or escape the past, but because we are always in
the soul and subject to its musings.[3]

There is, of course, a very old and deep connection between
memory and the imagination. Inspired by Francis Yates and
the classical tradition of the *Ars Memoria* of which she was such
a great exponent, Hillman writes:

To be correct, this remembering-what-never-happened
must rightly be called imagining, and this sort of memory is imagination. *Memoria* was the old term for both. It
referred to an activity and a place that today we call var-
iously memory, imagination and the unconscious. *Memoria* was described as a great hall, a storehouse, a
theatre packed with images. And the only difference
between remembering and imagining was the memory
images were those to which a sense of time had been
added, *that curious conviction that they had once happened.*
[emphasis mine][4]

This move, if it could be effected within the realm of contemporary discussions on reincarnation, would free the whole
subject from the imprisoning literalism which now surrounds
it. Who wants to read another *Readers' Digest* report on "My
Life as a Priest of Atlantis"? Hillman continues:

Cut free from having-to-have-happened, from the need
to be historical, memories become pre-historical images,

that is, archetypal. The events called forth from the store-house of memoria are mythical in the Platonist sense of never having happened, yet which always are. They are eternally present not forgotten; not past; they are present now, just as Freud discovered them at work in the present psychopathology of everyday life.[5]

The way into these memorial halls is personal; we each have our own doorways which make us believe that *memoria* itself is personal, our very own.

To remove the idea of metempsychosis, or soul-migration, from the hackneyed literalisms of cheap fiction and the sensa-tionalism of New Age mysticism it is necessary to make an ar-chetypal excursion to the great halls of *Memoria,* the underworld theatre of ancestral images, and to seek out its ruler, the awesome Queen of the Dead, Persephone. I have named her "the midwife and muse of metempsychosis" be-cause in her maturity she is the divinity of the Round of Birth and Death, or Cyclical *Nekyia*—the periodic descent into the realm of the intangible dead and the return to the upper world of incarnate existence. By invoking her, we shall evoke a greater depth of imagining of the mysteries of incarnation, dis-incarnation and reincarnation.

Five Images

The first of five images of Persephone that I wish to invoke into the five archways of this evening's Memory Theatre is that of "the daughter of Demeter" from the *Homeric Hymn to Demeter*: the *Kore,* or maiden, with the "slender ankles," picking flowers in a lush meadow in the company of the "deep-breasted daughters of Oceanus." Young Persephone has already discov-ered roses and crocuses, violets, irises and hyacinths, and she is probably carrying a basket of them when she sees a wonder-fully bright narcissus with one hundred heads. The flower is so delightful that she stretches out both hands to pick it. But just then the earth "wide with paths," gapes and out comes "He

205

Who Accepts So Many...that son of Chronos with many names." Springing upon her with his immortal horses, the God catches hold of her, protesting, and takes her away, "weeping, /in his chariot of gold."[6]

The God that abducts and ravishes young Persephone, the one "Who Accepts So Many," whose many names include Aidoneus, Pluto, Hades, Brother of Zeus, and Ruler of the Underworld, was, for the ancient Greeks, The King of the Dead. And we learn from the poet that he carries out the abduction with Zeus's connivance, aided by the old Earth Mother, Gaia, who grew the incredible flower as a snare.

For archetypal psychology this account reads like a piece of mythological relativism; that is to say, each of the Gods seems to embody a specific cosmic perspective which can inform our style of thinking, doing and being. Each God presents a characteristic perspective on dying. From the perspective of Gaia, death is perfectly natural, and she doesn't think it evil to trick Persephone by growing the flower that tempts her to her doom, because all things die and are born again in the endless revolutions of great Nature.

Pluto, or Hades, however, is a killer, a divine death figure that would separate consciousness from its attachments.[7] Hermes, whom we will meet later in the story, is that consciousness which keeps the experience of life and death inseparable. As the God of thresholds Hermes is open to both life and death equally and sees no opposition between them. Hermes' perspective is masterfully put by the poet Rainer Maria Rilke in a letter (not long before his own death) to Withhold von Hulewicz:

Death is the *side of life* which is turned away from us, and upon which we shed no light: we must try to attain the greatest awareness of our existence, which is at home in both unlimited spheres, inexhaustibly nourished by both...The true shape of life extends through both spheres, the great circulation of the blood pulses through both: there is neither a here nor a hereafter, but

206

a vast one-ness in which those beings who surpass us, the angels, have their abode. [my translation][8]

But let us return to our image of *Kore*-Persephone, "gathering flowers, herself a fairer flower" (Milton). *Kore* not only meant "maiden" for the Greeks. In late antiquity the word *Kore* was explained as the feminine form of *Kouros*, which means "sprout." When Persephone reaches out to pick the many-headed narcissus, *then* the earth opens up and Pluto rushes out to pluck her away to the underworld. Pluto plucks her up like she plucks the flower.

Persephone-tugging-at-the-flower seems to be mirrored in the bursting-forth-out-of-the-ground of Pluto. Persephone tugs, but what comes up out of the ground is not the flower but Pluto driving a gold chariot with immortal horses. Perhaps the roots of this flower are deeper than just surface phenomena. If the roots of the flower descend into the underworld, the realm of the dead, then we might say that Persephone is unconsciously pulling on the bell rope of the House of Hades, calling forth her ravisher by this insistent tugging at the wondrously shining flower of many-headedness.

For the innocent psyche of slender-ankled Persephone, still tied to the upper world of human relationships and the tight coherence of life, the underworld first appears as a flower of many-headedness, a blossoming of multiplicities. What attracts her away from the sleep of the "single vision" of her mother's maternal materialism is a wondrously shining image of plurality.

As Hillman points out in his *The Dream and the Underworld*, the underworld spirits are plural. The Romans could only speak of the dead in the plural, as *di manes*. Even individual dead persons were spoken of in this way. And "the ancient Egyptian was thought to live after death in a multiplicity of forms, each of these forms was the full man himself." It is clear that the underworld is "an innumerable community of figures."[9] And could not this endless variety of figures reflect the endlessness of the soul, its innumerable incarnations, the ancestral dead?

207

Persephone knows-and-doesn't-know what lies ahead of her (or for that matter, behind her). She is just out gathering rosebuds with her girlfriends; she does not reflect on what she is doing. She is unsuspecting, completely absorbed in her world of flowers-to-be-picked. But this is also an example of the musing mind. We do not understand much about the nature of musing, but it is clear that it is not simply an even, unperturbed lapping of events at the lake's edge. There are sudden wellings up, epiphanies of images, incursions of things undreamt of, sources of hidden insight and exhilarating inspiration. In fact, the Great Goddess, *Mnemosyne*, mother of the Muses, has been compared to a spring, and her daughters seen as figures analogous to the spring Goddess. Carl Kerényi says of her:

> She is memory as the cosmic ground of self-recalling which, like an eternal spring, never ceases flowing. She even grants, again precisely through the Muses, pleasant, healing lapses of memory (*Theogony*, 55); in these one does not forget oneself, but only what is meant to be forgotten.[10]

Could we not see the appearance of the tricksterish, hundred-headed flower as a memory image? An image from the halls of *Memoria*, not something forgotten, not something past, but something present now, eternally present—a hundred-headed image with its roots deep in the underworld. Then Persephone-gathering-flowers would be the musing of virginal awareness responding with pure delight and fresh appreciation to the springing up of archetypal images, recognizing them as stories that concern the soul, memories of "past lives."

The muses, those daughters of *Mnemosyne*, or "The Great Memory" as W.B. Yeats used to call it, are usually considered to be nine in number, and Persephone, as far as I know, has never been counted as one of them—although Hillman has suggested that the tenth, invisible daughter must be Psyche.[11] I like this idea, but I would qualify it, for I feel that the tenth muse should be Persephone-as-Psyche.

Why Persephone-as-Psyche? First, because psyche, as Pindar says,[12] is that which "alone comes from the Gods," survives death. Psyche "sleeps while the limbs are active, but, to those that sleep, in many a dream it shows decision of things delightful and grievous creeping on." Second, because for the Greeks the psyche after death was an inhabitant of the underworld, an *eidolon*, or image in Hades, the realm of invisibles. Third, because another meaning of the word psyche, for the Greeks, besides the usual one of "soul," was "butterfly." Fourth, because psyche has from the very earliest times been personified as a *Kore*, or maiden, of great beauty. Fifth, because psyche "seems to have served for the early Greeks many of the purposes which the concept of the unconscious serves for us."[13]

Linking these five meanings of Psyche to Persephone, we can see that first she survives death and is like a dream of "things delightful and grievous creeping on" with regard to her mother-consciousness, Demeter. Second, she *does* become an inhabitant of the underworld, one of the invisible *eidola*. Third, Persephone, like the butterfly, dies to one form and reappears in another, having undergone a profound transformation. Fourth, Persephone is a maiden of extraordinary beauty. Even Aphrodite (in the story *Eros and Psyche*) recognizes that Persephone has a beauty she does not possess. Fifth, Persephone is an apt personification of consciousness beneath ego, especially in her hidden life-in-death as Queen of the Underworld and co-ruler of Hades.

Perhaps I am like Persephone-gathering-flowers when I muse over the possibility of having lived many lives. Or when I fall into those cracks in time, those lapses in concentration on upperworld matters, those holes that lead into the abysmal depths. Hillman writes:

The Persephone experience occurs to us each in sudden depressions...drawn downward out of life by a force we cannot see, against which we would flee, distractedly thrashing about for naturalistic explanations and comforts for what is happening so darkly. We feel invaded from below, assaulted, and we think of death.[14]

Pablo Neruda's great poem, *Solo la Muerte* (Only Death) resonates here. The poem begins:

> There are cemeteries that are lonely,
> graves full of bones that do not make a sound,
> the heart moving through a tunnel,
> in it darkness, darkness, darkness,
> like a shipwreck we die going into ourselves,
> as though we are drowning inside our hearts,
> as though we lived falling out of the skin into the soul.[15]

Although being raped into the underworld is not the only mode of experiencing this descent, it would seem that the awareness of *the objective reality* of the psyche, as Jung called it, is not usually something that happens to us easily. Like baby Joan, suddenly frightened of falling off the cold marble chest of drawers, there is usually some kind of shock, something that jolts us out of our psychic anaesthesia, a violation of the comfortable estrangement of the ego.

The reason for this usual lack of sensibility on the part of upperworld consciousness can only be one thing: the fear of death. And this is certainly why Socrates in his discussion of the transmigration of souls in the *Phaedo* links the recollection of past lives with the proper pursuit of philosophy, which he defines as "really having practiced how to face death easily."[16] The *Phaedo* is Plato's account of how Socrates died after having been condemned to death by the state of Athens. To pick up at the relevant point in this story, Socrates' friend Crito is telling him that the man who will be administering the drink of poison hemlock has been asking him for a long time to tell Socrates to talk as little as possible because talking makes one heated and this will affect the action of the poison, and then it may be necessary to take a second dose or even a third. Socrates listens and says that that is the man's own affair; he can make preparations for administering it twice or three times if necessary. Crito replies that he was pretty sure that Socrates would say this but that he had to ask, because the man had been bothering him for a long time. Then, Socrates says:

> Never mind him. Now for you, my jury. I want to explain to you how it seems to me natural that a man who has really devoted his life to philosophy should be cheerful in the face of death, and confident of finding the greatest blessing in the next world when his life is finished. I will try to make clear to you, Simmias and Cebes, how this can be so.

Ordinary people seem not to realize that those who really apply themselves in the right way to philosophy are directly and of their own accord preparing themselves for dying and death. If this is true, and they have actually been looking forward to death all their lives, it would of course be absurd to be troubled when the thing comes for which they have so long been preparing and looking forward.[17]

So for Socrates the true philosopher is not frightened of death because he has practiced facing death and has looked forward to it all his life. This is a strange idea for most of us, brought up to shun and fear death. But to be "half in love with easeful Death" as Keats was, is to add the dimension of depth to one's experience of the world.

How do I practice facing death and developing, if not a love of it, at least a less terrified view of it? According to Socrates, by not being beguiled by the view that nothing is real except "those physical things which can be touched and seen and eaten and drunk and used for sexual enjoyment" while being "accustomed to hate and fear and avoid what is invisible and hidden from our eyes, but intelligible and comprehensible by philosophy." In other words, I practice facing death by loosening my attachments to the literal, material world and by developing a love for the realm of invisibles, Hades, or the underworld.

For 1,500 years, including several centuries of the Christian era, the yearly September Mysteries at Eleusis provided just such an opportunity for the Greek populace. Just how profound this experience could be can be seen in the testimonials of Greek citizens, like Sophocles, who spoke of the importance of this experience for the end of life, whose whole character is made dependent on one's having participated or not in the Mysteries: "Thrice blessed are those among men who, after beholding these rites, go down to Hades. Only for them is there life; all the rest will suffer an evil lot."[18]

The Mysteries of Eleusis were also known as the Mysteries of the Two Goddesses, as Eleusis was the place where Persephone was finally reunited with her mother after her sojourn in the underworld. But we are jumping ahead of our story.

Staying with Socrates' suggestion that the philosopher practice facing death by seeing through material attachments to that which is invisible, I am reminded of the Buddhist teachings on attachments. All throughout North India and Nepal, scattered everywhere among the foothills of the Himalayas, are the teaching centers, monasteries, hermitages and caves where now live so many of the Tibetan lamas who escaped the genocidal fury of the Chinese some thirty years ago. What they teach to whoever approaches them to learn their wonderfully subtle forms of meditation is that one must begin one's career in meditation by contemplating at least once a day the subject of impermanence and death. This, they reckon, is absolutely essential for the development of a more metaphorical perspective. And they quote the Buddha's last words: "Oh, Brothers, I remind you: All composite things are subject to decay. Dwell in mindfulness." Or they quote the words of the tantric sage Naropa, who said: "All that is born must die; all that is joined must be parted." The Buddha himself, as the young, cosseted prince Siddhartha, was in fact propelled into his quest for enlightenment by the experience of seeing a dead man during one of his pleasure excursions from the palace.

The descent into the underworld is a letting go of upperworld concerns. Nowhere is this more clear than in one of the world's oldest surviving myths, the Sumerian story of Queen Inanna's descent to the Underworld, a story that dates from the third millenium b.c. Inanna, an early precursor of Persephone, actually chooses to make her descent, but she doesn't realize that her sister, Ereshkigal, the dread Queen of the Underworld, will demand that she totally divest herself of all her upper-world identity. At each of the seven gates leading into the underworld, Neti, the gatekeeper, refuses to let her pass until she has stripped off one of her precious attributes and relinquished it. She loses her crown, her necklace of lapis, her beads, her breastplate, her bracelet, her scepter, and finally, her royal robe. Only then, naked and defenseless, can she enter the presence of the Queen of the Dead.

The second image that I wish to invoke is that of Persephone in the underworld, ravished by Pluto. *The Homeric Hymn to Demeter* gives us no description of Persephone in Hades. We are merely told that she is carried off, resisting, weeping and screaming in a shrill voice for her "powerful father," Zeus. The poem then leaves Persephone and concentrates on Demeter's search for her in the upperworld. We follow the grieving mother as she scours the earth for her daughter, not eating or bathing for nine days, finally, accompanied by Hecate, arriving in the presence of Helios, the Sun God, to ask if he has seen where her daughter has gone. Just like a person that has died, Persephone disappears from the poem. She has become a shade, a denizen of the underworld, an *eidolon*, a pure, psychic image invisible to the physical eye. So to see her we must look with an underworld vision, an imaginal eye.

As Carl Kerényi has shown us in his evocative essay on the *Kore*, the two Goddesses "are to be thought of as a double figure, one half of which is the ideal complement of the other."[19] Thus, while Persephone experiences the abduction as a ravishing into the depths of the underworld and as an initiation into the realm of the Invisible, her mother experiences the same event as a grievous, painful loss of anima or soul. Kerényi writes that

to enter into the figure of Demeter means to be pursued, to be robbed, raped, to fail to understand, to rage and

213

grieve, but then to get everything back and be born again. And what does all this mean, save to realize the universal principle of life, the fate of everything mortal? What then, is left over for the figure of Persephone? Beyond question, that which constitutes the structure of the living creature apart from this endlessly repeated drama of coming-to-be and passing-away, namely the uniqueness of the individual and its enthralment to non-being. Uniqueness and nonbeing understood not philosophically but envisaged corporally in figures, or rather as these are envisaged in the formless, unsubstantial realm of Hades. There Persephone reigns, the eternally unique one who is no more.[20]

In fact, Persephone's break with the mother is the necessary outcome of her entry into the underworld. It is almost as if the myth says that as long as I am tied to the literal mother, I will not be able to see beyond the surface view of this-life-only. In the depths of the underworld, however, are the shades of all my mothers from all my lives. As Hillman comments:

Rape moves the Persephone soul from the being of Demeter's daughter to the being of Hades' wife, from the natural being of generation, what is given to a daughter by mothering life, to the psychic being of marriage with what is alien, different; and is not given. The experience of the underworld is overwhelming and must be made. This style of the underworld experience is overwhelming, it comes as violation, dragging one out of life and into the Kingdom that the Orphic Hymn to Pluto describes as "void of day." So, it often says on Greek epitaphs that entering Hades is "leaving the sweet sunlight."[21]

The new perspective which the Persephone soul gains in the underworld is, however, more attuned to the nightworld and the image of dreams. If we follow the dream over to its side of

214

the bridge into *its* own country, the nightworld, "our consciousness will be vesperal, a consciousness going into night, its terror and its balm, or a consciousness of Persephone, the excitement of pursuing images into their depths and mating there with the intelligence of Hades...Dreams are children of Night, and we have to look at their brightest dayworld image also through our selfsame smoky glasses...Instead of turning to the dream for a new start and for foresight to warn of pitfalls and repressions, there will be a going downward, first with feelings of hopelessness, then, as the mind's eye dilates in the dark, with increasing surprise and joy."[22]

I suggest that it is *this* kind of consciousness which we need to develop in order to approach the images of our "past lives" as they come towards us out of the smoky haze of the halls of *Memoria*. If we cannot do this and take them literally, we will find, like Odysseus, that any attempt to grasp the figures only ends in an empty embrace. The images, or *eidola*, of Great Memory are quintessentially insubstantial, like the persons we meet in our dreams. And, as was mentioned earlier they differ from images of the imagination only in that they are tinged with a sense of time, "that curious conviction that they had once happened."

What can we establish? Perhaps that the main obstacle to an open-minded encounter with the images of "far memory" is the fear of death; that the practice of facing death leads to being able to face death more easily; that as one loses one's horror of dying, one is more able to contemplate the images of the underworld with a kind of affection. Further, that the way to losing one's fear of death is a descent into darkness and depth and a giving up of the "sweet sunlight" of dayworld and upperworld views.

What do I see when the mind's eye dilates in the dark of the underworld? We have noted that the underworld was "an innumerable community of figures" and that, for the Romans at least, even individual dead persons were spoken of in the plural. The Greeks considered the realm of Hades as being amorphous. Hades was the place where the psyche went

215

when it departed from a person at death. *Hades* was their name for the underworld, the realm of the dead, but the word also meant "invisible." When Odysseus descends to the underworld, the *eidola charonton,* or the images of the departed, flock around him. He sees, among them, his mother and tries three times to embrace her, but each time his arms pass through empty space. The *eidola,* as Kerényi suggests, "have nothing of the 'living corpse' about them, which figures in the ghost stories of so many people. The soul of Patroclus still has the lovely eyes of the hero, though in the corpse these have long since decayed. The *eidola* in the realm of the dead represent, as it were, the minimum conceivable amount of form; they are the image with which the deceased individual, through his uniqueness, has enriched the world."[23] Granted, we don't hear of Odysseus, on his visit to the underworld, encountering or recognizing *eidola* of himself, that is, images of his past selves in previous existences, but he was really bent on only one thing and that was to seek counsel from the image of the dead Tiresias.

"According to the Pythagoreans," Kerényi remarks, "the image of the unique mixture of elements that produced the individual passes to the moon, never to be replaced. Every individual being is accordingly preserved not only in the past of a world temporally conceived (consisting of what has been and is), but in a definite portion of the spatial universe as well." He goes on to say that "Another such place is the House of Hades."[24]

Let us imagine the House of Hades as a storage place for the psyches, or images, of departed individuals. The House of Hades as the Halls of Memoria, Great Memory. And let us imagine Memoria as an archetypal place, *the* place of archetypes as well as the storehouse of individual incarnations. "As above, so below": the Gods are also in the underworld. Isn't everything there a reflection of what is above? Hades is *Zeus chthonios,* the sky God's double, rather than his brother, and each of the Gods has an underworld counterpart. There was Demeter *Erinys* or *Erebus.* The Romans had special temples for *Iuno Inferna,* Hera of the Underworld. Even golden Aphrodite appears there as Aphrodite *Epitymbidia* or *Tmyborchos*, Goddess of the tombs and the dead.

There is a thought in Plato, in the *Phaedrus*, that some souls, between incarnations, follow in the train of one of the Gods, and that it is the vague, half-conscious reminiscence of this sublime experience that draws them in their next incarnation on earth to look for "traces" in themselves "by which they can detect the nature of the God to whom they belong."[25] I suggest that this idea could be very fruitful for archetypal psychology in looking at the "soul history" of "remembered incarnations."

But now let us look at how an adept in the practice of far memory describes her method. I quote from Joan Grant:

> The technique of this type of far memory, as opposed to the isolated incident which is a spontaneous recall or recovered with the aid of hypnosis, entails learning how to shift the level of the majority of one's attention from the current personality to the earlier one while still retaining sufficient normal-waking-consciousness to dictate a running commentary of the earlier personality's thoughts, emotions, sensations. During the early stages I would often think I had been dictating clearly, only to discover at the end of a session that I had not spoken a word. On other occasions I would think I had been speaking so slowly that at least a minute had elapsed between each phrase: and then find that I had been talking so fast that Leslie [her husband], who could do Speedwriting but no shorthand, had been able to get down only a bare outline of what I had said.[26]

Joan Grant wrote this at the age of sixty after thirty years of perfecting her individual method. She writes that she was twenty-nine before she managed to evolve the technique of "being able to relive an earlier incarnation in detail and as a deliberate exercise." Until then, her conviction that she had had many lifetimes before she was born of English parents in April, 1907, rested on fragments of episodes from seven previous lives, four male and three female. As a child she found it difficult to understand that everyone did not have even a small degree of far memory. Until she was eleven, she presumed that a strange taboo was the reason for people's reticence about their "long history," as she calls it.

She makes a striking observation about the nonlinearity of far memory with regard to time:

> So far as I have been able to discover, it is no more difficult to recall an episode which took place several millennia ago than to recall one from the current or the preceding century. Here the analogy between a series of personalities and the segments of an orange is again apposite, Time being the center at which the segments join and from which they are equidistant. The concept of successive personalities being threaded by Time like beads on a string is intellectually expedient but misleading.[27]

Compare this perspective with James Hillman's comments on time in the underworld.

> When we consider the House of Hades, we must remember that the myths—and Freud too—tell us that there is no time in the underworld. There is no decay, no progress, no change of any sort. Because time has nothing to do with the underworld, we may not conceive the underworld as "after" life, except as the afterthoughts within life. The House of Hades is a psychological realm now, not an eschatological realm later. It is not a far-off place of judgement over our actions but provides that place of judging now, and within, the inhibiting reflection interior to our actions.
>
> This simultaneity of the underworld with the daily world is imaged by Hades coinciding indistinguishably with Zeus, or identical with Zeus *chthonios*. The brotherhood of Zeus and Hades says that upper and lower

218

worlds are the same; only the perspectives differ. There is only one and the same universe, coexistent and synchronous, but one brother's view sees it from above and through the light, the other from below and into its darkness.[28]

The linear approach to recalling past lives is given in the ancient, classical Buddhist text, the *Vishuddhi Marga,* or The Path of Purity, by the sage, Buddhaghosha. This method simply concentrates on meditating deeply on events which have just occurred and then recalling them in reverse succession. The practitioner, after he has returned from collecting alms and is absorbed in after-breakfast meditation, is instructed to

consider the event which last took place, namely, his sitting down; next the spreading of the mat; the entering of the room; the putting away of bowls and robe; his eating; his leaving the village; his going the rounds of the village for alms; his entering the village...Thus must he consider all that he did for a whole day and night, going backwards over it in reverse order.[29]

Once a full day's memory has been achieved without any gaps or obscure episodes, the practitioner pushes his memory to the day before, and the day before that, ten days before, a month, a year, ten years and so on. When memory is continuous as far back as conception, the supreme challenge is to harness sufficient intensity of concentration to reach even further to a name and form at the moment of death in the previous life. Buddhaghosha writes that "this point of time is like thick darkness and difficult to be made out by the mind of any person still deluded."[30]

A less systematic, completely nonlinear, but more dramatic method of "tapping far memory" is the use of symbols. In an early essay on magic, the Irish poet W.B.Yeats gives a personal account of such a dramatic event. He prefaces the account with a statement of three doctrines which he believes have been

handed down from ancient times and which are "the foundations of nearly all magical practices."

> 1. That the borders of our mind are ever shifting, and
> that many minds can flow into one another, as it were,
> and create or reveal a single mind, a single energy.
> 2. That the borders of our memories are as shifting, and
> that our memories are a part of one great memory, the
> memory of Nature herself.
> 3. That this great mind and great memory can be evoked
> by symbols.[31]

Yeats was invited by an acquaintance to a place in the country
outside London to witness a magical event. His acquaintance
longed to believe in magic but was full of skepticism. Yeats describes how they were received by "the evoker of spirits and
his beautiful wife" and brought into a "long room with a raised
place on the floor at one end, a kind of dais." Yeats sat with his
acquaintance in the middle of the room and the conjurer on the
dais, and his wife between them and him. The "evoker of spirits," as Yeats calls him, "held a wooden mace in his hand, and
turning to a tablet of many-colored squares, that stood near
him on a chair, he repeated a form of words." Yeats says that
"almost at once" his "imagination began to move of itself" and
bring before him "vivid images that, though never too vivid to
be imagination," as he had always understood it, "had a motion of their own," a life he "could not change or shape." What
develops is an extraordinary story; Yeats is able to see unfolded before his mind's dilated eye a critical past "incarnation" of his acquaintance—who sees nothing. Yeats thinks he
was forbidden to see. He writes, "His imagination had no will
of its own." Yeats tells how the seeress would often describe
precisely what he was seeing but that sometimes he "saw what
she described" before he heard her description. They watch a
man in black who—the seeress says—was perhaps a Fleming
of the sixteenth century. Yeats sees him pass along narrow
streets till he goes through a "door with some rusty ironwork

above it." Wishing to find out how far they had one vision in common, Yeats kept silent when he saw a dead body lying on a table by the door.

> The seeress described him going down a long hall and up into what she called a pulpit, and beginning to speak. She said, "He is a clergyman, I can hear his words. They sound like low Dutch." Then after a little silence, "No, I am wrong. I can see the listeners; he is a doctor lecturing among his pupils." I said, "Do you see anything near the door?" and she said, "Yes, I see a subject for dissection." Then we saw him go out again into the narrow streets, I following the story of the seeress, sometimes merely following her words, but sometimes seeing for myself.[32]

They follow the man into an underground laboratory, a cellar full of retorts and strange vessels. They see him go to a vessel that stands over a slow fire and take out "a thing wrapped in numberless cloths, which he partly unwrapped, showing at length what looked like the image of a man made by somebody who could not model." Weeks pass, the man is still busy in his cellar, but then he is seen lying sick in a room upstairs with a man in a conical cap standing beside him. They could also see the image in the cellar moving "feebly about the floor." Yeats also saw "images of the image passing from where it crawled to the man in his bed." The seeress tells him that these are "images of his terror." The man in the conical cap makes the sick man get out of bed and walk in much fear down to the cellar where he makes "some symbol over the image" which then falls back "as if asleep." Next, he puts a knife in the other's hand and says, "I have taken from it the magical life, but you must take from it the life you gave." They then see the sick man stoop and sever the head of the image from its body, and then fall as if he had given himself a mortal wound, "for he had filled it with his own life." They see the sick man again upstairs, lying there a long time, watched over by the man in the conical cap. They see that he would never quite recover and that the story would get abroad in the town and shatter his good name. They see that his pupils would leave him and men avoid him. He was an accursed magician.

As the story ended, Yeats looked at his acquaintance. He was white and awestruck. He said: "All my life I have seen myself in dreams making a man by some means like that. When I was a child I was always thinking out contrivances for galvanizing a corpse into life." Then he added, "Perhaps my bad health in this life comes from that experiment." I think you will agree that this exploration into a "past incarnation"—whether its origin lies in "far memory" or in the *Mundus Imaginalis*—was highly relevant to the destiny of this acquaintance of Yeats. (Was it not Alistair Crowley?)

The thought that bad health in this life could be the result of some action in a previous life is strange to us. Yet in the East, in the teachings of Hinduism and Buddhism, this kind of understanding, of karma, is the norm. In Sanskrit *karma* simply means "action." We will return to this theme.

I would like to turn now to the third image of Persephone—Persephone, Queen of the Underworld. We do not have many depictions from classical times of Persephone as queen, though there is one very lovely clay figure from Locri in Italy.[33] It dates from the mid fifth century b.c. and shows the Goddess sitting in a solid throne with decorated wings. Her hair is parted in the middle and held at the back. She has an expression of peaceful strength; and, what is a complete surprise, there is an exquisite dove standing in her lap! If we had any doubts as to Persephone's affinity with Aphrodite, the dove, which is sacred to Aphrodite, should reassure us. The figurine thus speaks of a beauty, a loveliness and a gentleness which is not usually associated with the Queen of the Dead. The commanding presence of the image is also not that of the shrieking maiden, being dragged off in wild disarray. She is absolutely at rest and in her right place—as well-seated as the great Egyptian Goddess Isis on her throne. Plutarch, in fact, in his brilliant essay on Isis and Osiris, does actually refer to the belief that identifies Osiris/Serapis with Pluto and Isis with Persephone.

It is Isis, of course, who frees Lucius in the end from his metamorphosis into an ass in the famous second century tale by Apuleius. Isis, who is also—in Lucius' prayer—the "dread Persephone to whom the owl cries at night, whose triple face awes the wild rages of the shades, who holds fast the gates of hell, who wanders through many sacred groves and is propitiated with many different rites—whose misty radiance nurses the happy seeds under the soil." It is she who reminds Lucius that when he reaches the destined end of his life and descends to the underworld, he will see her as queen of the profound Stygian realm, shining in the darkness of Acheron with a kindly and tender light.

In the underworld Persephone reigns as queen over *the uniqueness of what is individual.* It is she who watches over the specific uniqueness of soul within the multiplicity of psyches in the House of Hades. It is she who gives value to that which is individual.

I was very impressed with the particularity with which Joan Grant described her images of far memory, both concerning herself and other people. In her work as a consultant-on-past-lives for the psychiatrist Denys Kelsey, she began to see how specific "past life" experiences, when cut off from the rest of the personality, created troublesome symptoms in the individual's current life. She called these phenomena "ghosts," and it is very interesting to compare her definition of a ghost with C.G. Jung's definition of a "complex." First Joan Grant:

> A ghost is a dissociated fragment of a personality which has become split off from the rest, and it remains self-imprisoned in a timeless present, whilst the integrated components continue the normal process of evolution...symptoms are, in effect, the ghost's appeal to be accepted once more into the "family" of the personality, and the release of the ghost can result in the instant disappearance of a previously intractable symptom.[34]

Now, Jung:

> Complexes are psychic fragments which have split off
> owing to traumatic influences or certain incompatible
> tendencies...The tendency to split means that parts of
> the psyche detach themselves from consciousness to
> such an extent that they not only appear foreign but lead
> an autonomous life of their own...In a word, complexes
> behave like independent beings...Today we can take it
> as moderately certain that complexes are in fact splinter
> psyches...I am inclined therefore to think that autono-
> mous complexes are among the normal phenomena of
> life and that they make up the structure of the uncon-
> scious psyche. (CW 8.253, 204, 218)

My fourth image is Persephone eating the pomegranate. In
the myth we are told that when Hermes arrives in Hades to es-
cort Persephone back to the light of day, Pluto cunningly offers
her a pomegranate—"a sweet one"—as a precaution so that
she will not stay all the time in the upper world."[35]

Here Pluto is behaving strangely like Satan in the Garden of
Eden. The pomegranate is the Apple of Hades, and in eating it,
Persephone, like Eve in the garden, is assimilating a knowledge of good and evil. For once we contemplate the question of
rebirth in depth we must inevitably confront the reality that
every action has consequences, what the West now so glibly refers to as "the oriental idea of the law of karma." The archetypal image of karma is that of the seed. And the most
impressive characteristic of the pomegranate is that it is
packed with seeds. An old Buddhist proverb reads:

> Out of pungent seeds pungent fruits are born;
> Out of sweet seeds sweet fruits.
> By this example the wise should know
> The bitter result of evil deeds and
> The sweet result of good ones.[36]

In his later years C.G.Jung was very preoccupied with the question of rebirth. In his autobiography he writes that "the idea of rebirth is inseparable from that of karma."[37]

The rather peculiar quandary which Jung fell into as regards the origins of one's karma seems typically perverse seen from the perspective of Buddhist thought. He speculates:

> The crucial question is whether a man's karma is personal or not. If it is, then the pre-ordained destiny with which a man enters life represents an achievement of previous lives, and a personal continuity therefore exists. If, however, this is not so, and an impersonal karma is seized upon in the act of birth, then that karma is incarnated again without there being any personal continuity.[38]

This question vividly reflects the personalism of Western psychologies, for in the end, even an impersonal karma would still be experienced as something happening *to me*. Jung does not seem to know that the concept of *karma*, as developed over centuries by Indian sages, can *only* be personal. One experiences the fruit of one's *own* actions. As it says in the *Abhidharma samuccaya*: "What is ascription of Karma? It is the experience of the fruition of the Karma one has done oneself. Being dissimilar to others it is called one's own."[39]

The whole point about the image of the seed is that it contains its own latent future. Buddhist sutras talk of the seed as being created by one of three kinds of action: physical, verbal, mental. The seed falls to the "ground" where, given the right conditions of "moisture" and "sunlight," it will "sprout." A text reads:

> The deeds committed by Devadatta do not mature in the ground nor in the water, nor anywhere else, but solely in the psychosomatic constituents and the operational fields of him who owns them. Where else can they mature?[40]

According to the *Karma Satatka sutra*,

> The deeds of beings
> are not exhausted even in hundreds of aeons;
> ...when the proper time arrives, they will mature into
> their fruits.[41]

The Buddhist texts also state that the sun and moon may collapse but that the workings of karma are infallible, and in this system, it is one's karma which determines where one is born, in what kind of world, in what kind of conditions, in what species and in what kind of body. This outcome is considered to be the maturating and ripening of the seeds of karma. I am not going into details here. The point is that karma in these systems is considered to be very specific. It is said that one cannot expect to taste the lovely fruit of the mango tree if one has not planted that particular seed. If one has planted the seed of a lime tree, one will taste the bitter fruit of the lime. A lime seed will not produce a mango tree. Thus the practitioner is encouraged to develop an increasingly differentiated awareness and reflectiveness as to the consequences of his or her actions.

Pausanius (Book II.17.4), that great traveller of ancient Greece who left us such wonderful descriptions of the sacred sites, remarks that he may not tell why the Goddess bears a pomegranate in one place: it is an *aporrhetoteros logos,* a story told under strict injunction of silence, in other words, a secret. However, he does (IX.25.1) stress its relation to bloody death and explains this by referring to the dark red color of the opened fruit. Kerényi, in his book on Eleusis, writes that

> the bloodlike color and abundance of seeds may have
> played a part in the origins of the Persephone myth; yet
> it is doubtful whether we shall ever be able to trace the
> myth back to its remote beginning, particularly as it was
> a tragic myth and a secret legend underlying Mystery
> ceremonies.[42]

The Mysteries at Eleusis, which revolved entirely about the figure of Persephone, were extremely secret. No one was allowed to speak of the essential part of the Mysteries under pain of death. We also know that there were prohibitions against eating pomegranates at certain feasts at Eleusis. Was this a reminder of the sacred secrets of the Mysteries?

This secrecy appears to be in complete contradiction to the Buddhist tradition—which aims at making the teaching on karma available to all beings out of compassion for the sufferings they undergo due to their ignorance of the laws of karma.

There are, however, secret teachings and esoteric "mystery" initiations in the Buddhist tradition, namely those within the Vajrayana or Tantric schools, but these are seen as more condensed forms of teachings which are otherwise freely available to all.

If we were to look for an outer, *exoteric,* form of the Eleusian mysteries, we would have to turn back to the myth itself, the story. And here, we do find a great deal to make us ponder. We can see that it is a profound story, one that ceaselessly produces insights in whoever takes the trouble to meditate upon it. It is no wonder that this myth informed the heart of the sacred Mysteries of Eleusis which was by far the most important mystery religion of ancient Greece for over 1500 years.

And although Socrates pretends to transcend the Mysteries, his vocabulary in many of the dialogues of Plato is marked by allusions, associations and references to Eleusis and what happened there. Could it be then that when he is giving his farewell speech to his friends in the prison that he is also transmitting the essence of his knowledge of the Mysteries? He has clearly told them that although the body perishes, "the psyche, the invisible part...goes away to a place that is, like itself, glorious, pure, and invisible—the true Hades or unseen world—into the presence of the good and wise God."[43] He then takes the cup, prays to the Gods that his removal from this world to the other may be prosperous, drains it to the bottom, and in the storm of weeping from his friends that follows, tells them to calm down and to be brave. As the poison begins to take effect, he lies down and when his disciples pinch his toes, he says he cannot feel them. The coldness spreads upwards, and he seems to have died. They cover his face with a sheet. But suddenly, he uncovers his face and speaks his last words: "Crito, we ought to offer a cock to Aesclepius. See to it, and don't forget."[44]

Crito says he shall, and he asks if there is anything else, but Socrates makes no reply. He is dead. And he has died with a joke on his lips. Any Greek of Socrates' circle would know that people offered a sacrificial cock to Aesclepius before asking for a healing dream with the hope of waking up cured when they went to sleep in the *abaton*, or dream room, in the temple of Aesclepius. Socrates is telling his friends in the most humorous and gentle way that he sees death as a sleep and a dream and that he is not afraid of going to the unseen world to meet the good and wise God, Hades.

I would like to recall that other meaning of the Greek word *psyche*—butterfly. Is it not an extraordinary image for death-in-life and life-in-death? The caterpillar sleeps and wakes up a butterfly!

And is it not also remarkable that one of the central events of the Mysteries that we do know about was that at a certain point on the last night the hierophant—"the one who showed what was sacred"—simply held up a freshly harvested ear of wheat for all to see? *There* was the seed which had returned after its death in the ground, now reborn as a new life.

Some traditions speak of a movement of consciousness right from the least animate level up to the human. Joan Grant had the following vision:

> A man starts with only enough energy to organize a single molecule. As this energy increases, and his consciousness begins to expand, he requires more complex forms through which to express them. After growing too adult to be contained by the mineral phase of existence, he enters the vegetable kingdom and then graduates, by a series of incarnations as various species of animal, to his first incarnation as a member of the race of homo-sapiens.[45]

228

The Buddhists teach that mind can incarnate in six basic and different *lokas,* or existential worlds—those of the blissful Gods, the jealous Gods, the human, the animal, the hungry ghosts and the hell beings. The Sufi teachings see the whole world as vehicle for soul. Again we turn to Jalal 'uddin Rumi:

> From the moment you came into the world of being,
> A ladder was placed before you that you might escape.
> First you were mineral, later you turned to plant
> Then you became animal: how should this be
>   a secret to you?
> Afterwards you were made man, with knowledge,
>   reason, faith;
> Behold the body, which is a portion of the dust-pit,
>   how perfect it has grown!
> When you have travelled on from man, you will
>   with certainty become an angel;
> After that you are done with this earth: your station
>   is in heaven.
> Pass again even from angelhood: enter that ocean,
> That your drop may become a sea which is a hundred
>   seas of Oman.
> Leave this "Son," say ever "One" with all your soul;
> If your body has aged, what matter, when the soul
>   is young?[46]

We have arrived at the last image of Persephone—Persephone returned to the earth and reunited with her mother in Eleusis—"the place of happy arrival." At this point the *Homeric Hymn* says that "right away she [Demeter] brought in a harvest...And the whole earth/was heaped with leaves and flowers."[47]

It is like the arrival of spring—or as so many artists and poets have described it—like the birth of Venus/Aphrodite—who when she emerges out of the sea walks on the land, leaving flowers and grasses springing up in her footsteps as she walks.

Of course, there is the realization that Persephone must spend one-third of the year below with Hades because of having eaten the pomegranate, but that is only right. After all, do we not spend one-third of our lives asleep, approximately eight hours out of every twenty-four? So Psyche maintains her connection with Hades, the underworld, the realm of images and ghosts and of the "ancestral" dead—through dream. Dream—which is going on all the time even though we in our waking consciousness are unaware of it. And for those of us who dare to enlarge our conception of life to include "many lifetimes" there is a great deal to explore and to remember as well as to imagine.

I began with a reference to Gauguin's question "Where Do We Come From?" And I have not answered it. But I hope that I have opened a door in the usual and narrow, conventional parameters. My biological family of origin is obviously only a step on the way towards an answer. Pushing the answer back to another family in another century, in another country, is not much better, though it does allow more room for imagination. But perhaps all this can be seen as prelude to entry into an imagination of our archetypal origins. This is a move away from the whole fixation on literal, biological sources, a move that befits archetypal psychology. In the cosmos seen Platonically, we have arrived here after a sojourn among the Gods, and our origins are in the stars.

From the perspective of archetypal psychology, the emphasis is not on the ego at all; it is more a question of accepting that we are a plurality, a multiplicity, that, if anything, the psyche is polycentric. In an imaginal sense, the whole conception of reincarnation with all its many levels, worlds, beings and possibilities is one of poetics, because only poetry can do justice to the great beauty and mystery of our "origins."

The French philosopher Henry Corbin said it so well—at the end of a paper on Jung's *Answer to Job*:

> What we are concerned with is a world where socialization and specialization would not wrench from the soul its individuality nor its spontaneous perception of the life of things and of the religious beauty of living beings; a world where love would precede all knowledge and

where the sense of death would only be a nostalgic yearning for the resurrection.[48]

Psychology is painfully lacking in any sense of the poetry of life and death, of origins and endings. With its single-minded, problem-solving compulsion, it has only scorn for the imagination. But, 'where there is no imagination of death, there is a death of the imagination.'

At the very end of his life, wrestling with the inevitable exhaustion of consumption, D.H. Lawrence crafted the remarkable poem called "The Ship of Death." In it he stresses, like Socrates, the absolute necessity of the *practice* of death, working *in life* toward a soul image that will carry one into the unknown realm of death and what follows, with full acceptance.

> Oh build your ship of death, oh build it in time
> and build it lovingly, and put it between the hands
>   of your soul.
> Once outside the gate of this walled silvery life of days,
> once outside, upon the grey marsh beaches, where
>   lost souls moan
> in millions, unable to depart,
> having no boat to launch upon the shaken, soundless,
> deepest and longest of seas,
> once outside the gate,
> what will you do if you have no ship of soul?
>
> Oh lovely last, last lapse of death, into pure oblivion
> at the end of the longest journey.
> peace, complete peace—!
> But can it be that also it is procreation?
> Oh build your ship of death
> oh build it!
> Oh, nothing matters but the longest journey.[49]

231

7

WHO IS BEHIND ARCHETYPAL PSYCHOLOGY?

An Imaginal Inquiry

When you see a severed head
rolling down the path toward our field,
ask of it, ask of it—the secrets of the heart:
for of it you will learn our hidden mystery.
— JALAL 'UDDIN RUMI

With its metaphorical method of mythic reversion, archetypal psychology implicitly lays claim to being a psychology of psychologies, if not *the* psychology of psychologies. Is archetypal psychology, however, out of bounds for its own method? If as archetypal psychology asserts, fantasy is always going on, then what is the archetypal fantasy within archetypal psychology itself? Through *epistrophé* any phenomenon can be led back or "reverted" to its archetypal source.[1] Suppose we try to lead archetypal psychology back to an archetypal source?

In thus asking who is behind archetypal psychology, we are not asking for the name of a literal person. If we were, we would begin with the obvious: James Hillman, who named archetypal psychology in 1970.[2] We would also point to the two immediate fathers of archetypal psychology: Carl Gustav Jung and Henry Corbin.[3] We might also list various contemporary authors, cited by Hillman as contributing to the broadly Neoplatonic tradition within which he situates his work: "Vico and the Renaissance (Ficino), through Proclus and Plotinus, to Plato."[4]

Originally published in *Spring* 1988.

232

In this transhistorical lineage Socrates must be regarded as the imaginal ancestor of Plato, Plotinus and Proclus, Ficino and Vico. But to what or to whom can we "return" Socrates? Where revert this intellectual colossus who declared that he knew nothing apart from the nature of love, who with invincible rhetoric out-argued the best minds of his time while simultaneously celebrating the blessings of divine madness? What can we make (archetypally) of such an apparently composite, multiplistic, subversive, underworld-friendly, querulous, entertaining, brilliant, lunatic, grim and jovial sage? I think there is a clue in Alcibiades' speech in the *Symposium*:

> I propose to praise Socrates, gentlemen, by using similes. He will perhaps think that I mean to make fun of him but my object in employing them is truth, not ridicule. I declare that he bears a strong resemblance to those figures of Silenus in statuaries' shops, represented holding pipes or flutes: they are hollow inside, and when they are taken apart, you see that they contain little figures of the Gods.[5]

Silenus is a close companion of Dionysos. Socrates was said to resemble him. (Silenus was often represented as an old, bald, dissolute man, with a flattened nose, riding on an ass.) Alcibiades, however, saw another kind of resemblance: a pipe-playing Silenus who contained images of Gods within his own emptiness. Imagining many Gods, Socrates was, first of all, pluralistic in his psychology. The particular archetypal person whom Alcibiades sees is Silenus. Another lover may have seen Socrates as Apollo, lofty mind of clear reason. A third might have seen Hermes beckoning toward the underworld. Plato himself gives a variety (*Phaedrus*, 252d–253c).

Yet is it Socrates that we are after? Even if archteypal psychology is at times Socratic, the imaginal person moving through its lineaments is far more of a poet and musician. Only in his last days on earth did Socrates turn his hand to poetry. As he told Cebes (*Phaedo*, 59e):

> In the course of my life I have often had the same dream, appearing in different forms at different times, but always saying the same thing: "Socrates, practice and cultivate the arts!"

In prison, awaiting execution, Socrates begins composing poetry, explaining to the amazed Cebes that he does this in the attempt to discover the meaning of his recurring dream. He says that it had never occurred to him before this to doubt his interpretation of the words as referring to the practice of philosophy. But now he questions that.

It is clear that Socrates was more afraid of ignoring this oneiric voice than of drinking the hemlock! He tells Cebes that ever since the trial, while the festival to Apollo was delaying his execution, he felt that the dream was actually urging him to practice "the more popular form of art," and quite possibly, to acknowledge his gratitude to the God.

> I thought it would be safer not to take my departure before I had cleared my conscience by writing poetry and so obeying the dream. I began with some verses in honor of the God whose festival it was. (*Phaedo*, 61a)

Socrates is clearly aware of the importance of the *daimonic*; he knows, in Friedländer's words, that without the realm of the daimonic "heaven and earth break asunder."[6] Yet there is a subtle aura of embarrassment and ambiguity in the philosopher's expression of "the many Gods within." For this reason (and because of his neglect of the arts), we must look deeper for the archetypal figure moving within archetypal psychology.

Like Socrates, archetypal psychology does have (and advocates) a pluralistic, polycentric psyche.

> Following the traditional descriptions of the *anima mundi*, Jung wrote of the *lumen naturae* as a multiplicity of partial consciousnesses, like stars or sparks of luminous fishes' eyes...By providing a divine background of personages and powers for each complex, polytheistic psychology would find a place for each spark.[7]

234

To archetypal psychology, "the primary rhetoric…is myth."[8] But with the proviso that "even if the recollection of mythology is perhaps the single most characteristic move shared by all 'archetypalists,' the myths themselves are understood as metaphors—never as transcendental metaphysics whose categories are divine figures…The study of mythology allows events to be recognized against their mythical background."[9] And more precisely:

> Psychology needs to specify and differentiate each event, which it can do against the variegated background of archetypal configurations, or what polytheism called Gods, in order to make multiplicity both authentic and precise. Thus the question it asks of an event is not *why* or *how,* but rather *what* specifically is being presented and ultimately *who,* which divine figure, is speaking in this style of consciousness, this form of presentation.[10]

Thus we do not here ask for the *why* or *how,* or even the *where,* of archetypal psychology, but for the *what* and the *who,* trying to stay true to its method and its nature.[11] So far, with respect to our question of *who,* we have noted that archetypal psychology should view events in terms of their mythical background (*epistrophé*), should be polytheistically oriented, and should give each God its due. Beyond these points, we must stress the importance for archetypal psychology of soul/anima, the underworld and the imagination.[12] In his 1972 Terry Lectures at Yale, Hillman said:

> Here I am working toward a psychology of soul that is based in a psychology of image. Here I am suggesting both *a poetic basis of mind* and a psychology that starts neither in the physiology of the brain, the structure of language, the organization of society, nor the analysis of behavior, but in the processes of imagination. [emphasis mine][13]

Central to all these traits is, of course, the concrete concern for soul, a concern that lives beyond the walls of the consulting room, and, along with this, the idea that "the soul is born in beauty and feeds on beauty, requires beauty for its life."[14] In his Eranos lecture from 1979, "The Thought of the Heart," Hillman makes it quite clear that psyche is *the life of our aesthetic responses*—"that sense of taste in relation with things." And referring to the Apuleian tale of *Eros and Psyche*, Hillman says of Psyche that "we know her first by her primary characteristic given with her nature: Psyche is beautiful."[15]

If the soul requires beauty for its life, a psychology in service of soul is also a psychology in the school of beauty. Consequently, archetypal psychology, apart from its character as a polytheistic psychology and a theophanic psychology, is also an *aesthetic psychology*. And the mythic person within it must be an artist, even a poet. Now if we ask ourselves, what mythic figure is not only an artist, but an artist whose art is dedicated to the Gods, polytheistically, in their particularity, an artist who embodies the imagination and who is associated with the anima and the underworld and who sings of the beauty of Psyche, we must conclude that the mythic person for whom we have been searching is Orpheus.

Elizabeth Sewell's *The Orphic Voice* suggests that Orpheus's unusual relation to myth promises to give him special significance: "*In this particular story mythology is considering in the person of the poet, the power and the fate of poetry or thinking or myth. In the Orpheus story, myth is looking at itself. This is the reflection of myth in its own mirror.*" [emphasis mine][16]

In Sewell's words, the constant reappearance of the Orpheus myth, in ever new metamorphoses, forms a tradition of inquiry into the question *What power and place has poetry in the living universe?* [17] The Orpheus myth itself provides "a method by which to pursue the inquiry" that Orpheus mythologizes.[18] Indeed, Orpheus personifies the myth-making nature of the psyche—he is myth looking at itself.

Following Sewell, though with a twist, I see the tradition as actually *having obscured* three Orphic images: first, Orpheus among the animals; then, Orpheus in the underworld; last, the head of Orpheus, singing.

236

1. *Orpheus among the Animals*

As one great Orphic voice, Rainer Maria Rilke, says:

> Animals of silence came out of the clear, untroubled
> forest, leaving their nests and dens,
> and it seemed that why they were so quiet
> was not from fear or craftiness,
>
> it was listening. Now, howling, roaring, growling
> mattered little in their hearts. And where before
> there hardly was a hut to hold this listening—
>
> a lean-to of dimmest longing
> with shaky door-jambs at the entrance—
> you built temples in their hearing for them.[19]

Orpheus's relaxed, unafraid stance among the animals, whether facing the king of beasts or a snake in the grass, and *their* calm alertness, ears cocked, listening intently, display a deep communion in soul. Listening, they enter his mythic music, become pure image, pasture in his imaginal meadows, share the same sun, the same night, the miracle of vegetation.

Orpheus opens an imaginative perspective on the animal, saying that when you remain quiet and play, images, as animals, will come out of hiding and come close. This is certainly true about animals in dreams, and it seems equally true of animals in myth. There is a love that images show us in dreams and myth. The archetypal psychologist is an imaginal animal lover. He sees that the animals of poetry are images; the images, animals. If the animals don't come, the poet "stalks" them.[20]

Animals and Darkness: The images in the mirror of the myth of Orpheus grow clearer if we follow Sewell's move and imagine the scene in darkness!

> It will help the figure to help us—by waking a jaded imagination and incidentally by producing a much closer image of our own state in this inquiry—if we shift

the happening from day into night. Imagine, then...the singer in almost complete darkness in which his reordering of creation has just begun, but as if it were a dream he is having, or that of the beast whose masks, fierce or gently, appear suddenly like emblems or heraldic devices out of the darkness only to puzzle the mind catching at beauty and significance...Nothing is seen except in glimpses, a phantasmagoria out of which nevertheless a world of new order is shaping.[21]

Sewell actually demonstrates Orphic *epistrophé* when she speaks of darkness as *a method for thinking about myth*.[22] The use of light, she claims, is connected with the perspective of treating myth as *cipher*, a code which can be *de*-ciphered.

The Orphic *method of darkness* necessarily invokes something fundamentally other than the literal single-vision of day-world consciousness. The method of darkness sees metaphor as condensed myth, myth as metaphor. Lorca says, "the metaphor links two antagonistic worlds by means of an equestrian leap of the imagination."[23]

Lorca is an Orphic voice and a daimonic man. In Gongora, he found an Orphic predecessor, a mentor, though in speaking about him Lorca was also describing the archetypal poet. He wanted everyone to know that the jewel of metaphor, like the alchemists' *lapis*, was lying right under our very noses in the language everyone used. "Language is founded on images," he writes. "A poetic image is always a transference of meaning."[24]

According to Lorca, Gongora's originality lies in his method of stalking the image. From Lorca's description of stalking we see that the literal world is a reflection of the archetypal. About Gongora Lorca writes that he was

a man with an amazing feeling for myth. He studied the archetypal images of classical culture and shunning the mountains and their luminous visions, seated himself on the shores of the sea where the wind

> *curtained him round with turquoise*
> *on the blue couch of the sea*

and there he bridled and curbed his imagination, with-drawing like a sculptor before commencing work...His imaginative strategy is perfect. There are times when each image is an accomplished myth.[25]

The Orphic method, then, is fundamentally Teiresian and Homeric, as well as polytheistic; it is the vision of the blind poet who looks into the faces of animal masks emblazoned on the night of Imagination and reads them, not as ciphers to be decoded and fixed into meanings, but as living *glyphs* of divinity.

> Orpheus and myth are the methods for our natural history, and they warrant a figure of darkness for they are in themselves riddles, dark sayings, hieroglyphics, in that field where minds and language engender their productions of thought.[26]

Hillman connects the glyph and the dark vision with the animal:

> Within the ark it was dark, or course, for the ark was covered with pitch, inside and out (Genesis 6:14). By what light, then, did the creatures see? What is the vision of these seeds in the ark, the essential vision? Jewish legend says that God sent Archangel Raphael to Noah with a book of wisdom in which were written a'l the secrets and mysteries. By means of this book, Noah knew how to fulfill his task and gather the animals. With him into the ark he took this book and it was made of sapphires, and by means of its light all the creatures in the ark could see.
>
> The incorruptible substance of the *caelum* is the light by which the corruptible animals see. The natural animals have an imaginal vision; the physical world perceives by a metaphysical light. To restore to our human

eye that sapphire light we must be pressed in among the animals against the pitch wall. The way to the imaginal lies in the animal.[27]

The way to the imaginal lies in the animal. And a book of sapphires by means of whose light we can see in the dark. A light which is no light, but a kind of seeing, a kind of vision brought by the animal of the image, a vision which stems from living with darkness, rather than against it.

It is significant that Kerényi, in sounding the etymology of Orpheus, departs from the usual (medieval) tradition which derives Orpheus from *oraiphone*, "best voice," and instead links the name with *orphne*, "darkness": "Orpheus was connected with darkness, both in his journey to the underworld and also later, when he communicated his initiations at night, as was proper."[28]

The Tortoise and the Lyre: To Orpheus among the animals belongs the lyre, the instrument upon which Orpheus plays the music specific to each God. The lyre symbolizes with him. Or it is a kind of Jacob's ladder upon which he ascends and descends in communion with the celestial worlds.

Nichomachus (*Excerpta ex Nicho*, 1) relates that Hermes, after having constructed the seven-stringed lyre, taught Orpheus how to play it. The same source says that when Orpheus was killed by the Thracian maenads, his lyre fell into the river Hebron and was taken out to sea and carried by the waves to Lesbos; there it was taken to Terpander, who became the unrivaled lyrist of his day. Another version is given by Eratosthenes: the Muses gathered the remains of Orpheus and buried them in Leibethra (where the nightingales ever since have sung sweeter than anywhere else).[29] Having no one to whom to give the lyre, they asked Zeus to set it among the stars as a memorial to him and to themselves. Today we still know this constellation as Lyra (with its chief star, Vega, the brightest star in the northern sky after Arcturus). It is a small but conspicuous constellation of the summer sky just outside the mainstream of the Milky Way. The old name for this constellation among the Greeks was Chelys, "shell of the tortoise," one of the oldest names for the lyre.

Reverting the lyre to a constellation in the heavens is another way of indicating its archetypal nature.

According to Nichomachus, there were seven strings on the original lyre. He tells how the names of the musical notes were derived from the seven planets and their positions in relation to the earth. Originally, these names were given to the strings of the lyre according to their position in relation to the performer. The lyre is an instrumental image of archetypal differentiation. The ensemble of strings provides an endless range of possible tonal sequences. With the discovery of the octave, not only did a metaphor for metaphor appear, but the idea of a scale was born. As Plato says in the *Republic* (3.617b), referring to the seven classical octachords called *harmonias,* "from all eight [strings] one *harmonia* is formed." These octave-species are what we call the Greek *modes*: the Lydian, the Phrygian, the Dorian, the Hypolydian, the Mixolydian, the Ionian and the Aeolian. The Greeks were quick to see that each of the different octave-species had its specific ethos or moral character: that of the Dorian was "dignified and distinguished," for example, whereas the ethos of the Hypodorian was "haughty, pompous and somewhat conceited." They called the Phrygian "inspired, enthusiastic, emotional and violently exciting" and the Hypolydian, "voluptuous, intoxicating and bacchic."[30] The octave-species or harmonias are thus modes and moods, and Orpheus is the knower of these modes. This is not a secular, mundane activity or an academic pastime. It was understood to be the activity of the *theologos,* the one who spoke with and about the Gods. Thus the lyre is in effect a metaphor for the differentiating, individuating activity of archetypal psychology in its imagination of particular Gods within the body styles, moods, and rhetorics of specific events.

Before Hermes handed on the lyre—either directly to Orpheus or, as in some versions, to Apollo, who then gave it to Orpheus—he commemorated the Gods in song. The *Homeric Hymn to Hermes* tells us how he first sang for Mnemosyne,

Great Memory, Mother of the Muses (and thus mother to Calliope, the mother of Orpheus). After that, Hermes sang all the immortal Gods, according to their ages and the manner in which they had been born. *Hermes initiates the practice of theology and connects it with song and the lyre.* And Orpheus becomes not only the first mortal poet and musician but the first theologian after Hermes, the first human to sing the Gods and to know their different stories, features, characters, moods and styles of theophany.

All this is made possible because of the lyre. And what made the lyre possible? A tortoise. In the *Homeric Hymn to Hermes* we learn that soon after his birth in a cave on Mt. Cyllene, Hermes gets out of his cradle to steal the golden oxen of Apollo. However, just outside the entrance to the cave he sees a tortoise eating grass. He speaks to it, calling it a "lucky omen," a "darling" and the "friend of the feast." He asks it where it got its beautiful shell, and he tells it that although it is "good medicine against black magic while alive," it will "make great music, dead." He raises the tortoise in both hands and carries "the treasure" back into his cave, whereupon he takes "a knife of grey iron" and stabs out its life and scoops out its marrow.

The hymn goes on to describe how Hermes quickly and deftly devises a way of stretching cowhide over the shell, fixing a bridge and two arms to it and tying seven chords of sheep gut to the crossbar. A new "animal" is born. Kerényi's comment is exquisite:

> The irony of his words springs from his divinity and is as merciless as Being itself. It is based on "seeing through." Seeing through is divine. Greek tragedy offers its spectators a divine standpoint in that it allows them to participate in such a penetrating vision. The spectator sees in the king the guilty fugitive while he is still ruling and governing. In the same way Hermes "sees through" the tortoise. There is no doubt what he sees there. He names the unsociable beast with an expression that

alludes to a divinely established description of the lyre, "friend of the feast." He sees already the glorious instrument while the poor tortoise is still alive."[31]

Music, poetry, theology—all founded on a murder. A merciless "seeing through" which is divine. Co-emergent with the creation of the lyre is the creation of metaphor: *poiesis—mythopoiesis*. This is precisely how the soul acts:

> Soul-as-metaphor also describes how the soul acts. It performs as does a metaphor, transposing meaning and releasing interior, buried significance...The perspective darkens with a deeper light. But this metaphorical perspective also kills: it brings about the death of naive realism, naturalism and literal understanding.[32]

The Hermetic murder of the tortoise is thus the death of the exclusively literal mode of seeing. This death is at the heart of the whole Platonic tradition of psychology. "Essential to the psychology of Platonists is the movement of seeing through the illusions of literal and personal reality in terms of archetypal verities."[33] Seeing through is thus prior, and basic, to the death of literalism. And this death liberates multiplicity from the confines of a monotheism of meaning.[34] The seeing through which is at the heart of the story of Hermes making the lyre is thus a true *archai*, a primary paradigm, an archetypal image for the Platonic mode of metaphorical thought, indissolubly connected with Orpheus and the Orphic tradition in its every sense.

The Lyre as Metaphor and Instrument of Polytheism: Everything about the lyre seems to lead away from the unity and monotony of monotheism into increasing complexity and differentiation. Apollo—whose name, Plutarch (*The E at Delphi*, 393c) having derived it from *a* and *poly*, means "not many"—cannot be held to be the ruling principle of the lyre nor of the Orpheus myth, though monotheistic movements tried for centuries to make Orpheus an Apollo figure. Early

Christianity tried to monotheize Orpheus, even spreading prosaic rumors of Orpheus recanting his polytheistic views and preaching the superiority of monotheism.[35] The medieval church followed suit, forcing Orpheus to perform as an early Christ figure.

It wasn't until the Renaissance of Ficino's Florence that Orpheus returned as pagan theologian of polytheism. The tradition of Orpheus as *theologos* and teacher of the *teletae*, or mysteries, is yet older. According to the words which Aristophanes puts into the mouth of Aeschylus in his play *The Frogs* (1030ff.), Orpheus was famous for two things: "From the very earliest times the really great poet gave us the Mysteries and taught people it was wrong to kill."

The idea that Orpheus was the founder of the Mysteries is well attested among the ancient Greeks. Clement of Alexandria describes Orpheus as "The Thracian who was at once hierophant and poet" (*Protrept,* 7.74.3). Pausanius (9.27.2) speaks of Orpheus as the author of hymns which were composed for use in Mysteries. It was an accepted notion that Orpheus was strongly connected with Eleusis, even regarded as the author of the mythos of the rape of Persephone and the search by her mother.[36] Finally, according to Ivan Linforth,

> when paganism was engaged in its death struggle with Christianity, the particular manifestation of the religious spirit which was inherent in the things that bore [Orpheus's] name seemed to the Neoplatonists at once so vital and so comprehensive that he was proclaimed by them as the founder of Greek polytheism itself.[37]

The Renaissance—Marsilio Ficino and Orpheus: If the Neoplatonists saw Orpheus as the founder of Greek polytheism, the Florentine Renaissance saw the great flowering of soul in its time as intimately related to the return of Orpheus: "This age, like a golden age, has brought back those liberal disciplines that were practically extinguished, grammar, oratory, painting, sculpture, architecture, music and the ancient singing of songs to the Orphic lyre."[38]

In his circle Marsilio Ficino was celebrated as an embodiment of Orpheus.[39] The poet Naldo Naldi even traces Orpheus's soul from Homer to Ficino, saying that after the death of Ennius the soul of Orpheus had to wait sixteen hundred years for its next incarnation. The famous bust of Ficino by Andrea Farucci in the Santa Maria dei Fiori in Florence echoes Naldi in depicting Ficino in the guise of a lyre player—his face radiant and his mouth opening to sing—holding, like a lyre, a volume of Plato in his hands. And the poet Poliziano says that Ficino's lyre, far more successful than the Thracian Orpheus (meaning Ovid's, no doubt), brought back Eurydice from the underworld—"the true Eurydice, that is, Platonic wisdom with its broad judgment."[40]

Orpheus's voice and lyre are not only metaphors to describe Ficino's teaching. Ficino played an Orphic lyre, ornamented with a picture of Orpheus charming the animals and the landscape with his music.[41] Corsi, in a biography published just seven years after Ficino's death, says that he expounded the hymns of Orpheus and sang them to the lyre "in the ancient style with remarkable sweetness."[42] Cosimo de Medici finishes a letter to Ficino, saying, "Come, and bring your Orphic lyre with you."[43]

In his pastoral poem *Altercazione*, Lorenzo de Medici, grandson of Cosimo and pupil of Marsilio, tells how he encounters Orpheus one day on a walk outside Florence. He has left the city and his official tasks to seek peace among the hills and fields and to muse on life lived close to Nature. He is interrupted by a cynical shepherd who argues that the country is just as corrupt as the city; there is just as much ambition and greed. But his angry rhetoric is silenced by the sounds of someone singing to the lyre:

> ...una nova voce a sé gli trasse
> da piu dolci armonia legati e presi
> Pensai che Orfeo al mondo ritornasse...[44]

(A new voice drew us to itself. [We were] captured and
bound by its sweeter harmony. I thought that Orpheus
had returned to the world.)

The singer was, of course, Marsilio Ficino.

Besides a common starting point in soul, similar styles of
fantasying and striking likenesses among their main themes,
Renaissance Neoplatonism and archetypal psychology also
share a common method.[45] Ficino, in the tradition of the Neoplatonists, held that the relationship between the images of the
sensible world and the ideas of the angelic world is one of identity at different levels of reality. Neoplatonic tradition spoke of
a "threefold being" in man: body, soul, spirit. For Ficino, to
communicate with the world of soul meant the use magic (Orphic song, poetry, painting, sculpture, ritual, dance, theater); to
communicate with the world of spirit meant the *comparative
method*, what Ficino called *Orphica comparatio*—"that is, we
pursue images or symbols of the phenomenal world to their
originals"[46]—an essential aspect of the method of *epistrophé*,
which is not to be taken as a literal tracing but as the recognition that there are Gods in all things.

It is one of those delightful examples of angelic intuition
that the very first Greek texts which the young Ficino—in the
first year of a lifelong commission from Cosimo de Medici—set
his hand to translating were the *Orphic Hymns* and the *Orphic
Argonautica*.[47]

2. Orpheus in the Underworld

> I will tell you the secret of secrets. Mirrors are the doors
> by which Death exits and enters. Don't tell anyone.
> What is more—look for a lifetime in mirrors and you
> will see Death at work, like bees in a hive of glass.
> —JEAN COCTEAU, *Orphée*

The second Orphic image I want to consider is a turning-in-
side-out of the first image, that of Orpheus among the animals:
there the musician as teacher-philosopher and *therapeutes* of the

Mysteries; here the poet, shaman-musician and daimon-denizen of the underworld. This latter image gives the former its depth and soulfulness. Orpheus's power to move even the stony heart of the world has its roots in the heart of the kingdom of darkling shades:

> Only the man who has also raised
> his lyre among the darkling shades
> may be allowed a sense
> of infinite praise.
>
> Only he who has eaten poppy
> with the dead and shared their poppy
> will never lose
> the softest tones.
>
> Even though the pool's mirror
> often trembles:
> know the image.
>
> Only in the kingdom of doubleness
> do voices sound
> undying and tender.[48]

The Orphic voice in Rilke unerringly connects the poet with the realm of essences, the kingdom of doubleness, *Mundus Imaginalis* (Corbin), and shows that entry into the Mysteries of this kingdom is possible only to one who can raise his lyre among the shades and eat poppy with the dead. The Orphic voice originates in an imaginal body, and the imaginal body lives among specters, ghosts, ancestral spirits, all the *eidola* of Hades. Orpheus is that which deepens imagination by imagining always greater depths to be ensouled.

Cocteau, speaking to a bemused Parisian audience about his first Orphic film, said: "Poets, in order to live must often die, and shed not only the red blood of their hearts, but the white blood of their souls, that flows and leaves traces which

247

can be followed."[49] Orpheus as *angelos chtonios,* the archetypal figure who draws us into the depths of any moment—is the "necessary angel" (Wallace Stevens)—because "to know the psyche at its basic depths, for a true psychology, one must go to the underworld."

The question arises: If Orpheus had an established position in the underworld in the eyes of his followers, then how did they understand his presence there?[50] In order to imagine an answer let us look at the Delphic painting by Polygnotos as Pausanius describes it. Orpheus is situated among many figures from Greek myth: dead heroes, shades, suffering souls and the classic scene of Odysseus with his men about to sacrifice the black ram to feed the shade of Teiresias. Pausanius writes (Bk. 10.3.2): "If you look lower down the picture, just beyond Patroclus, you see Orpheus sitting on a mound, holding a lyre in his left hand and touching a willow with his right; he is touching the branches and leaning up against the tree…Orpheus looks Greek, he is not wearing Thracian clothes or a Thracian hat. Promedon is leaning up against the other side of the willow tree. There are people who believe Polygnotos brought in Promedon's name as if he were making up a poem; but others have said he was a Greek who loved listening to all kinds of music, and Orpheus' singing most of all."[51]

This is an Orpheus who, it appears, is able to establish an aesthetic communication even with the shades of the underworld. It is as if Orpheus here is dreaming the underworld. He is not just any kind of dreamer, but precisely the dreamer of the underworld—Orpheus as *mythopoiesis,* myth looking at itself.

Orpheus dreaming the underworld. Not only that, but singing to the shades of his dreams. As dreamer of the underworld, Orpheus is as close as one could get to a personification of what Hillman has, for years, been calling (and calling for): an *imaginal* ego. This is an ego which has *learned how to dream,* an ego weakened in its heroic, upperworld attitudes:

> An imaginal ego is at home in the dark, moving among images as one of them. Often there are inklings of this ego

248

in those dreams where we are quite comfortable with absurdities and horrors that would shock the daylight out
of waking consciousness. The imaginal ego realizes that
the images are not his own and that even his ego-body
and ego-feeling and ego-action in a dream belong to the
dream image. So the first move in teaching ego how to
dream is to teach it about itself, that it too is an image.[52]

Orpheus singing the image that is a metaphor of himself. Or is
it a song about death, something darkly ironic, profoundly
nostalgic? Like the lines by Pablo Neruda:

There are cemeteries that are lonely,
graves full of bones that do not make a sound,
the heart moving through a tunnel,
in it darkness, darkness, darkness,
like a shipwreck we die going into ourselves,
as though we were drowning inside our hearts,
as though we lived falling out of the skin into the soul.[53]

Perhaps Orpheus is singing about Persephone. After all, as we
noted earlier, he was thought to be the one who first sang her
story, bringing the *teletae*, the Mysteries, and their mythos to
the people. Perhaps he is singing of how she was forced into
the depths of Hades, singing about what happened to her
there.

Until Persephone has been raped, until our natural consciousness has been pathologized, our souls project us as
literal realities. We believe that human life and soul are
naturally one. We have not awakened to death. So we
refuse the very first metaphor of human existence: that
we are not real.[54]

When Persephone finally reigns in the soul, we see life through
her darker eye. And this is the Orphic eye, the "method of
Darkness." The dark eye is also a pathologized eye which sees

249

life in kinship with death, in fact, in a marriage with death, a *Todeshochzeit*, as that thanatological physician Alfred Ziegler describes it.[55]

Loss, Pathologizing and Soulmaking: Can one imagine a more terrible image of loss than that of Orpheus, having moved Death itself to give him back his beloved, turning at the threshold of the upperworld to look at her and losing her forever? The Western imagination has been haunted by this image for at least two thousand years. It was bequeathed to us by the Roman writers Virgil and Ovid, in whose poems we find this explanation given for Orpheus's failure to bring Eurydice back. And it has merged imperceptibly with our notion of the poet as a genius of pathologizing. From Sappho to Dante to Shakespeare to Rilke, poetry finds its gold through the refining fires of loss. And loss does characterize underworld experience:

> A life that is lived in close connection with the psyche does indeed have an ongoing feeling of loss. It would be noble to believe this to be the enduring sacrifice that the soul required, but it does not feel noble. Instead we experience the humiliating inferiority of uncertainty and an impairment of potential…A sense of infirmity goes with soul.[56]

In keeping with the idea that he can be seen as the mythologizing tendency of the psyche, Orpheus, in a most startling manner, seems to embody all the essential characteristic inherent to the mode of metaphor itself: that sense of weakness, inferiority, mortification, masochism, darkness and failure.[57]

This weakness characterizing Orpheus is reflected in the repeated attacks on the poet throughout history. The heroic attitude toward Orpheus is exemplified in Plato's Phaedrus, who claims that the Gods did not grant Orpheus his wife when he made his descent to Hades because "he seemed to lack spirit, as is only natural in a musician; he hadn't the courage to die for love like Alcestis, but contrived to enter Hades alive" (*Symposium*, 179c).

Virgil's Orpheus has been described by one scholar as sentimentally indulgent and, though magnificent, fundamentally flawed. The same author describes Ovid's Orpheus as a "melodramatic, egoistic poet of overblown rhetoric."[58] There is a noticeable tendency in Western literature to emasculate Orpheus, to make him effeminate and pathetic.

Shakespeare, however, gives the most dignified image of the pathologizing Orpheus. Shakespeare's image moves the myth to a psychic location where the poet is himself the instrument of his art; his suffering becomes the basis for his poetry and song. Shakespeare gives the archetypal *pothos*,[59] or longing, of Orpheus a ground of *pathos*. He writes of Orpheus as one

> Whose golden touch could soften steel and stone
> Make tigers tame, and huge leviathans
> Forsake unsounded deeps to dance on sands.
>
> *Two Gentlemen of Verona*, 3.2.79–81

And Shakespeare introduces these lines with an unsurpassed image: "For Orpheus's lute was strung with poets' sinews."

For Shakespeare, says Sewell, Orpheus's instrument is the poet's body. In "that splendid metaphor he unites himself, as poet, immediately with the Orphic power and becomes the myth he is describing...The image holds also a muted anguish at the notion of being strung, fiber by fiber, on something. It almost suggests the rack in those tight, drawn sinews, with a further hint on intimate dissection, for sinews, used as lute strings, can only come from a body that has been unpicked. It is as if the finale of the Orpheus story were present also, poets sharing of necessity the dismemberment of their master."[60]

We need an Orpheus who is not just a poet of self-indulgent sentimentality, just as we need a poetry which can carry our suffering and give it voice, just as we need a language in psychology which will do justice to the depths of our pain, our loss and our failures. Archetypal psychology is the first psychology to address itself to language in this way. In its concern for a language of soul, archetypal psychology is truly Orphic; that is, it sees that poetic imagination is as vital for the language of psychology and psychopathology as it is to the language of poetry.

3. The Singing Head

> Mythology, like the severed head of Orpheus, goes on singing even in death and from afar.
> —ELIZABETH SEWELL

> Many there are who bear the wand but few there are who become Bakchoi.
> —SOCRATES, *Phaedo*

Since the first mention of the dismemberment of Orpheus (frag. *Bassarides,* Aeschylus), there has always been disagreement over the reasons for it. Two views that do not warrant much attention are (1) that Orpheus was hostile to Dionysos and was killed at the behest of Dionysos by the maenads and (2) that Orpheus was killed by women who were angry at him for his rejection of their sexual advances and his preference for young men. The first view is untenable when one understands the strongly Dionysian character of much of the Orpheus myth and cult. The second view is untenable because it is literalistic, personalistic and absurd—a late and obvious invention to make a "human" narrative out of a divine mystery. Personal reasons for the death of Orpheus are not the archetypal ones.

Phaedrus, in the *Symposium,* claims that the Gods caused Orpheus to be slain by women as punishment for cowardice; Isocrates (*Busiris,* 11.38) claims it was because Orpheus had told stories that discredited the Gods. Linforth argues that if the Greeks could give two totally different causes for Orpheus's death, then clearly "the legend itself, as it was generally known in the fourth century B.C., recognized no cause, or at least no cause which was essential to the legend."[61] In other words the death of Orpheus is a mystery.

There seems little doubt among the Greeks that Orpheus was the founder of the Dionysian Mysteries. Apollodorus (1.3.2) says that "Orpheus discovered the Mysteries of Dionysos"—that is to say, he found them elsewhere and introduced them into Greece. Proclus, Lactantius, Diodorus and Herodotus concur.[62] Guthrie writes that "to the question who was the God of the Orphic religion? there can be but one answer—Dionysos."[63]

In his dismemberment Orpheus becomes Dionysos—the Loosener (as Dionysos was known) being loosened from himself. He is Dionysos suffering a psychic death, a death into psyche. Orpheus is thus a true psychopomp, for *he* conducts *himself* to the underworld. The dismembered Orpheus is an image of initiation into the experience of the imaginal ego—psyche sparkles in every piece/place of our depths.

Following the great scholar Rohde, who called Dionysos "The Lord of Souls," archetypal psychology insists upon a reappraisal of this God.[64] If Dionysos is the Lord of Souls, then he is "the soul of nature, its psychic interiority. His 'dismemberment' is the fragments of consciousness strewn all through life."

The idea is an old one, found as far back as the Orphism of ancient Greece. Guthrie writes that "The belief ascribed to the *discipuli Orphei* is that the dismembered Bakchos was the soul of the world." Iamblichus also labels as Orphic the belief in the pluralization of the world soul.[65]

Viewing *anima mundi* as the scattered fragments of Dionysos gives to each thing a touch of ecstatic divinity; viewing *anima mundi* as the scattered fragments of Orpheus reveals these same things as poetry. "Psyche as the *anima mundi*, the Neoplatonic soul of the world, is already there with the world itself, *so that a second task of psychology"—beyond that of providing soul with an adequate account of itself—is "to hear psyche speaking through all the things of the world, thereby recovering the world as a place of soul."* [emphasis mine][66]

The alchemical perspective developed in Jung's later writings does not see only confusion, splitting, anarchy and schizophrenia in images of dismemberment. Jung also recognized that individuation itself entails the differentiation of unconscious unity. The body begins to become conscious of itself as a composite of differences, the parts as distinct from each

253

other, each with its own light. It seems that the Dionysian experience is crucial for understanding what Jung meant when he wrote of "the fundamental dissociability of the psyche and its multiple consciousness."[67]

The image of the dismembered Dionysos is a metaphor for the awareness of the parts of the body as distinct *and* for the world as ensouled in all its parts—as *anima mundi*. Both understandings are of great importance for archetypal psychology. The head itself—for archetypal psychology as well as for the *discipuli Orphei* of old—is an image of psyche. More—the singing head of Orpheus is like a poetic celebration of Pindar's *aionos eidolon* (psyche) which "alone comes from the Gods" and survives death, "sleeps while the limbs are active, but, to those that sleep, in many a dream shows decision of things delightful and grievous creeping on." For the Greeks the head was the beginning, the source of generation.[68] The seed of life was in the head. The head was packed with seed, like a pomegranate. It was the seat of the soul; it contained psyche, which alone survived death, appearing as an *eidolon*, or image, in Hades. What more wonderful source could there be for archetypal psychology to be "returned to"? Imagination as a singing head![69]

For the Greeks it was a universally accepted notion that the head of Orpheus continued to speak after his dismemberment. Linforth describes graphic representations on a red-figured hydria and a cylix, practically contemporary with Euripides' *Alcestis*, representations in which men or women gaze at a (speaking) head while a young man or a scribe writes down the words that proceed from its lips. "But Orpheus is dead. This we know from the picture on the other side of the cylix and from the picture on the hydria, in which the grief of the three figures is manifest. This means that the immortal voice of Orpheus continues to dictate poems even after his death. Thus we find an explanation of the continuous production of new Orphic poems throughout antiquity."[70] Here is the head of Orpheus as *inspirateur*. We need to revalue the head as the seat of genius (as the Romans knew it) and as the seat of the daimon (as the Greeks knew it).

Philostratus says that after the head of Orpheus was found on the shores of Lesbos, it was taken to a sanctuary of Dionysos, where it spoke/sang/told stories before Apollo came and silenced it. The act of placing the head in the sanctuary of Dionysos is a mythic image of reversion. Orpheus is returned to his archetypal source, the God Dionysos.

We all know how Apollo wants to silence the speech of the soul. It is not the head as oracle which threatens Apollo, as is commonly believed; what bothers Apollo is the spontaneous speech of the soul, its images and its polytheistic imagination. Apollonic iconophobia is inherent to the structure of Western consciousness.

Today, however, the head of Orpheus is singing again, and not only in archteypal psychology. Most relevant to this discussion and the future of Orphic consciousness in nonpsychological circles is an extraordinary novel, *The Medusa Frequency* (1987) by Russell Hoban. After Cocteau, Hoban is the first writer of our time to give the head of Orpheus a chance to speak. He treats the head of Orpheus as a daimon.

The protagonist of this novel, a self-deprecating balloon writer for Classic Comics by the name of Herman Orff, meets the head of Orpheus while walking along the muddy banks of the Thames near Putney Bridge. It is an "eyeless and bloated head, sodden, covered with green slime and heavy with barnacles."[71] The head asks Orff if he knows what it *is* to him, and Orff answers, "Probably not." The head then says, "I am the first of your line. I am the first singer, the one who invented the lyre, the one to whom Hermes brought Eurydice and perpetual guilt. I am your progenitor, I am the endlessly voyaging sorrow that is always with you, I am that astonishment from which you write in those brief moments when you can write."[72]

Orff takes the head home with him.

The head offers to tell its story. In this version "Orpheus" gives his parentage as Calliope–Hermes. 'He' also tells the story of how, as Orpheus, he made the first lyre by killing the tortoise. Later the head explains that being Orpheus was his

255

punishment for killing the tortoise.[73] This has the ring of true Orphic imagination. Hoban speaks with the Orphic voice.

Sewell says that "Orphic genius, each time it occurs, is more than just the appearance of one particular mind, active in thinking and writing. It constitutes itself a point of transformation or metamorphosis, a living instance of post-logic in the context of its own historical period. In this tradition, each such mind is itself an example of the process it seeks to discover and perfect."[74] As the mythologizing nature of the psyche, Orpheus continually discovers new reflections of myth.

At another point in the novel, the head asks: "Might it be that the whole universe has no purpose but to explain the killing of the tortoise?...Perhaps the universe is a continually fluctuating event that configures itself to whatever is perceived as center."[75] The head proposes a way of looking at myth which is based on the image, a way that is not linear or narrational but rather simultaneous:

> "My story is not a sequence of events like knots on a string," said the head; "I could have started with the loss of Eurydice and ended with the killing of the tortoise— all of it happens at once and it goes on happening; all of it is happening now and any part of it contains the whole of it, the pictures needn't be looked at in any particular order."[76]

The novel's protagonist deeply misses a woman he once loved, a woman who left him. The story is permeated with a longing for the beloved that is mixed with a sense of loss and a memory of life suffused with her presence. The head shares Herman's longing. This nostalgia seems to be at the heart of the Orpheus myth—it is because of it that the poet can create. Archetypal psychology says that this nostalgia is not a nostalgia for anything literally attainable; it is an archetypal nostalgia, a nostalgia for the archetype.[77] The head tells Orff: "In the stories they always say I turned around to look at her too soon but that isn't how it was: I turned *away* too soon, turned away before I'd ever

256

looked long enough, before I'd ever fully perceived her."[78] Orphic pathos is inherent to the awareness of the impermanence of life itself. The head tells how Eurydice told him as she left that now he would sing better than ever:

> Art is a celebration of loss, of beauty passing...not to be held. Now that I'm lost, you will perceive me fully and you will find me in your song; now that underworld is closed to you the memory of the good dark will be with you always in your song. Now you are empty like the tortoise-shell, like the world-child betrayed, and your song will be filled with what is lost to you.[79]

Prognosis and Shadow

A voice in the shadows speaks: *You have omitted one thing very urgent. The prognosis. The shadow. The fate of Orpheus is to: (a) found religion, (b) be torn apart, (c) have soul (Eurydice) perennially in the underworld, (d) become codified into spiritual discipline, (e) be considered only aesthetic. These sorts of possibilities could happen to archetypal psychology if it is only or truly Orphic. Actually, these sorts of attacks are now made on archetypal psychology by its detractors. Having read your chapter on Orpheus, and your book, we now know the reason why. Those detractors smell Orpheus in the woodpile.*

You've hit the point exactly. Archetypal psychology *is* harboring Orpheus, but the woodpile has become a library and the hounds of monotheism will run themselves ragged trying to corner him among its friendly forests of metaphor. Besides, archetypal psychology is not only Orphic, nor is it literally Orphic. Archetypal psychology is not a literal repeat of the Orpheus myth in any of its versions: it is not mimetic to Orpheus in the sense of enacting his story. It is Orphic in that its primary rhetoric is myth and its primary intention the recovery of soul in speech through image work *and* the recovery of soul in everyday life through a concern for soul in the things of the world. The danger (to take your points in reverse order) of its becoming "only aesthetic" would be realized if it were to fall into a onesidedly aesthetic mode, a monotheism of Aphrodite. The same is true with regard to the possibility of its being codified into a spiritual discipline: this could only happen if it fell into the hands of academic priests determined to organize it according to an Apollonic structure of consciousness—again another mode of monotheism.

Your point about Eurydice is more tricky—because it ignores the basic ambiguity of the underworld story. Keeping in mind that Eurydice does not even figure in the earliest appearances of Orpheus and that he, from very early on, seems to have an established position in the underworld *apart from* any link with her, let us ponder the ambiguity of her place in the myth. Robert Graves claims that Eruydice's death by snake bite and Orpheus's subsequent failure to bring her back figure only late in myth. He thought that these events were mistakenly deduced from pictures showing either Dionysos, whose priest Graves believed Orpheus to be, descending himself to Hades in search of his mother, or Orpheus being welcomed in Hades "where his music charmed...Hecate into giving special privileges to all shades initiated into the Orphic Mysteries."[80]

Ivan Linforth is adamant that the first passing reference to Orpheus's descent for his wife unmistakably implies a successful recovery. This reference is to be found in Euripides' *Alcestis* (lines 357–362) where Admetus, husband of the doomed Alcestis, says that he wishes he had the voice and melody of Orpheus so that he could charm Pluto and Persephone into giving him back his wife. The first century B.C. *Lament for Bion* and the Alexandrian version of the myth told by Hermesianax give similar accounts of the poet's successful journey. For both Virgil and Ovid, however, Orpheus fails to retrieve Eurydice.

When later Christian writers purged Orpheus of his pagan polytheism and identified him with Christ, they could not allow him to fail. So like Christ, Medieval Orpheus heroically vanquishes Hell and "saves" the lost soul.

With the coming of the Renaissance, Angelo Poliziano, one of the poets of Ficino's Florentine convivium, wrote a musical drama, *La Favola di Orfeo* (1477), returning the story to its Roman

258

version: Orpheus fails to bring Eurydice out of the underworld and is attacked and dismembered by maenads. A few years into the sixteenth century Monteverdi picked up the idea and created his *Orfeo* (considered to be the first opera), giving the story a happy end by allowing Apollo to intervene and take Orpheus up to join the immortals. (Opera has struggled ever since with the meaning of loss and the descent to the underworld.)

So it goes, into our century when Rilke's Orpheus loses Eurydice to the underworld and Cocteau's (1926 stageplay) Orpheus loses Eurydice but is reunited with her in "Heaven." Harrison Birtwhistle's 1987 opera *Orpheus* actually stages several contradictory endings simultaneously, with three actors playing Orpheus.

The ambiguity stressed by archetypal psychology as inherent to the metaphorical nature of psychic reality is thus basic to the myth of Orpheus. It is not that *either* Orpheus succeeds *or* he fails in bringing back Eurydice. It is that he is *both* successful *and* unsuccessful in bringing her back.

A monistic and literalist perspective would want it clearly one way or the other. And as we have seen, different Orphic voices present different outcomes. The myth upholds this ambiguity. What seems to be the myth's shattered mirror is actually a plurality of perspectives reflecting Orpheus from different angles. Looking at whether Orpheus is "successful" in returning Eurydice to the upperworld we see both responses to this question echoed by archetypal psychology. In either case Orpheus leads us to soul in the hidden depths. We have seen that Orpheus's essential activity of pathologizing always brings us closer to soul. Pathologizing, "the psyche's autonomous ability to create illness, morbidity, disorder, abnormality and suffering in any aspect of its behavior and to experience and imagine life through this deformed and afflicted perspective," is "a royal road of soulmaking" and "unerringly leads the soul into the deepest ontological reflections."[81] For archetypal psychology, soul is intimately associated with the underworld.

However, archetypal psychology is also passionately concerned with the return of soul to the world. In a 1981 talk with just this title and theme ("*Anima Mundi*: The Return of the Soul to the World") James Hillman makes the radical move of imagining the *anima mundi* as crucial for contemporary psychology, imagining it "as that particular soul spark, that seminal image, which offers itself through each thing in its visible form."[82] In this turn of archetypal psychology the emphasis is upon the world as a display of self-presenting forms. This is Eurydice returned to the world, not as a "personality," but as the soul of the world, glowing in each event as the physiognomy of the world itself. "Not only animals and plants ensouled as in the Romantic vision, but soul is given with each thing, God-given things of nature and man-made things of the street."[83] This move into a depth psychology of extraversion is an open celebration of Eurydice's return.

What about the fate of Orpheus, his being torn apart? To invoke dismemberment as the fate of Orpheus is to stop short, as we have seen: he goes on living in the things of the world, in tandem with Eurydice. And even the dismemberment doesn't extinguish his song. The tearing apart is not his final end. The severed head, like mythology, "goes on singing even in death and from afar." And the lyre? We have forgotten the lyre. But the myth says that it is taken up among the stars. Sewell writes:

> Figures of mind may be thought of as being the terminus of one end of the scale of nature. The stars, those infinitely remote elemental, fiery powers, are at the other. Between the two lies the whole range of form...So the Orpheus myth ends with two things: the affirmation of the unity of all the forms in nature, between the galaxies and the mythological lyre—the power of the human mind figuring in its own characteristic function of language—which joins them; and there is also the floating, singing head, which is poetry and thinking.[84]

Orpheus, like the indestructible life force which the Greeks called *zöe*, or Dionysos, can be torn apart, but he can never be

260

destroyed. Thus insofar as archetypal psychology is Orphic, it too can be torn apart but not destroyed—unless one gags the Orphic voice and silences the singing head.

Finally, the fate of archetypal psychology is not so much to found religion as it is to *ground* religion in the imaginal world (*Mundus Imaginalis*). "Literal religion approaches Gods with ritual, prayer, sacrifice, worship, creed...In archetypal psychology Gods are *imagined*. They are formulated ambiguously, as metaphors of experience and as numinous borderline persons. They are cosmic perspectives in which the soul participates."[85] To lose the metaphorical perspective of this and to go about instituting rituals and reviving a dead faith in the fashion of literalism would be to silence the head of Orpheus and to suffocate the poetic imagination.

Conclusion

> I am in search of a myth that can carry psychology,
> enabling psychology to carry soul.
> —JAMES HILLMAN

> Everything is metaphor and metaphor is the only
> activity.
> —RUSSELL HOBAN

Here we come to the end of this condensed account of the mythic animation of archetypal psychology by the archetypal figure of Orpheus/Dionysos—first poet, priest, theologian, shaman, musician, *therapeutes* of Western culture. It has been my thesis in this concluding chapter that a revisioning of psychology cannot take place without the simultaneous revivification of the myth of Orpheus. More precisely, a revisioning of psychology *is* a recollection of the myth. By revision I do not mean the unification or integration of fragmented schools, theories, and practices divided by disjunctive perspectives, perspectives at loggerheads with one another and fissured by internal schisms.[86] No, the revisioning of psychology recovers the Renaissance delight in polyphony, contradiction, ambiguity, the *gloria duplex*, the enigmatic, the paradoxical, the regard for the anima and the animal, the respect for the mysteries of theophany. The emergence of archetypal psychology echoes the Renaissance call by Marsilio Ficino to restore the polytheistic imagination to the psyche and the psyche to Orpheus. It also follows Ficino's move to reintroduce the Neoplatonic (Orphic) method of *epistrophé,* while placing soul central to any account of the world.

The Renaissance recovered Orpheus singing to the animals and hymning the Gods, celebrating their individuation. It also tried to come to grips with Orpheus in the underworld. A century after Ficino, Shakespeare gave us the profound image of the artist who is his own instrument. The voice of Orpheus continued to sing in the poetry of Keats and other Romantics engaged in soulmaking, and it has flowered most eloquently in our century's great Orphic poet Rainer Maria Rilke. The myth goes on metamorphosing.

Like Rilke, both Freud and Jung made descents to the underworld, and their psychologies are the fruit of that experience. But neither of them managed to release the voice of Orpheus from the spell of Apollo, though Jung did much to prepare the way for a true poetic eloquence. The singing head, the third image of Orpheus, has waited until the twilight of the millennium to come into its own. By insisting upon an aesthetic psychology in a voice of subtly variegated modulations, we are closer now to evoking all three images of Orpheus. By our returning psychology to the image, a way has been found out of the impasse of dogmatism. There can be no dogmatism of the image, for "the greatest enemy of dogma is the imagination's spontaneous freedom."[87] Like his contemporary Russell Hoban, James HIllman has addressed the rotting head of Orpheus, and it has begun to speak. A strange new language is being born, an angelology of the word, a theophany of the image. Now from all sides the world begins to speak, to murmur and to sing.

> Raise no monument. But let the roses
> blossom every summer for his sake.
> For this is Orpheus. His metamorphosis
> into this one and that one. We need not worry

about all those other names. Once and for all,
if there is singing, there is Orpheus. He comes and goes.
Is it not already much if he sometimes survives
the roses in the bowl by a day or two?

He has to vanish, so you will understand!
Even though himself he fears this disappearance!
The moment his words rise above what's here,

he's already on his way beyond your gaze.
The lyre's chords do not entangle his hands.
And he obeys, in the very act of overstepping.[88]

NOTES

CHAPTER 1

[1]Andrei Tarkofsky, *Sculpting in Time,* trans. by Kitty Hunter-Blair (London: Bodley Head, 1986), 89.

[2]*Andrei Rublev,* USSR. Prod. Co., Mosfilm Studio. Dir.: Andrei Tarkofsky; Script: Andrei Mikhalkov-Konchalovsky and Andrei Tarkofsky; Phot.: Vadim Yusov; Music: Vyacheslav Ovchinnikov; Cast: Anatoly Solonitsyn (Rublev), Ivan Lapikov, Nikolai Grinko, Nikolai Sergeyev, Irma Rausch, Nikolai Burlyayev (Morishka), Rolan Bykoz.The italicized passages in this chapter represent my own account of the film.

The locations of the film include Pskov, Novgorod, Vladimir, Lake Ladoga and the Andronikov Monastery in Moscow.

Although the film was made in 1966, it was not released until 1969 when it was shown in Cannes, where it won a prize. It was not shown in Russia until 1971.

Andrei Rublev (1360-1430) is regarded as the most distinguished of Russia's medieval icon painters. It is from the work of Rublev and his teacher Theophanes that the major school of late medieval Russian icon and mural painting, known as the Moscow School, developed. And, though Rublev did not sign his paintings, enough of them have been identified through written evidence to make it possible to recognize his very unique style. It shows a delicacy of line and a luminosity of color that was never quite equalled again in Russian art. He also humanized the figures of the icons and gave them a tenderness and expressiveness which was lacking before. Very little is known of the painter's life, except the places he lived in and painted in—Sagorsk, Vladimir, Andronikov—and the rough dates of his life.

Of all the icons known to be by Rublev, the one referred to in English as "The Old Testament Trinity" is one of the most famous, one of the great masterpieces of the craft. Tarkofsky dwells at some length on it at the end of the film in the color sequences of the remains of Rublev's work in Moscow's Tretyakov Gallery. I am told that in Russian the title is far more precise. It is: "Abraham's hospitality to the Angels." In it the three archangels—Raphael, Gabriel and Seraphiel—are seated at a table under the oak tree in Mamre where they appeared to Abraham one day as three travellers in the desert. The chalice of food he offered them is the only object on the table. Commenting on this, Henry Corbin said that of all the images in which this theme appears, Andrei Rublev's masterpiece occupies a place of honor (Corbin, *Creative Imagination,* p. 130; see note 9). The "feeding of the stranger" (*philoxenia*) is, in this case, a nourishing of the divine image. And this is precisely what Tarkofsky is doing in this film—feeding the imagination of divinity.

[3]Andrei Tarkofsky was born in 1932 in Russia, the son of the poet Arseni Tarkofsky. He studied at the Soviet Film School, G.I.K., under Michael Romm. His first three features after film school all won major prizes. After *Andrei Rublev*, other films of his that have attracted attention are *Solaris, Mirror, The Stalker, Nostalgia* and *Sacrifice*. He died in December, 1986.

[4]James Hillman, *Interviews* (New York: Harper & Row, 1983), 59.

[5]Jalal 'uddin Rumi, *Mathnawi*, Book III, lines 3700ff., ed. and trans. by Reynold Nicholson, E.J.W. Gibb Memorial Trust, 1930, distributed by Luzac & Co., London, reprinted 1982.

[6]James Hillman has written a beautiful paper on this subject. See James Hillman, "The Thought of the Heart" (Dallas: Spring, Eranos Lectures, No. 2, 1981).

[7]James Hillman, "Image Sense," *Spring* 1979, 142.

[8]Hillman, "Thought of the Heart," 31ff.

[9]Henry Corbin, *Creative Imagination in the Sufism of Ibn 'Arabi* (originally published in French, 1958), tr. by Ralph Manheim (Princeton, NJ: Princeton University Press, 1969/1981), 47.

[10]For more discussion on the iconoclasm in Christianity see James Hillman, *Healing Fiction* (New York: Station Hill Press, 1983), 70ff.

[11]Hillman, "Thought of the Heart," 14.

[12]Rainer Maria Rilke, *The Selected Poetry of Rainer Maria Rilke*, ed. and trans. by Stephen Mitchell (New York: Random House, 1982), 111.

[13]Hillman, "Thought of the Heart," 23-4.

[14]Rainer Maria Rilke, "The Panther," in *Rilke—Selected Poems*, with English translations by C.F. MacIntyre (Berkeley: University of California Press, 1958), 65.

[15]Hillman, "Image Sense," 142.In an exchange with James Hillman some years after this paper was first presented the question of the archetypal nature of the horse arose. As Hillman was emphasizing its "vitality" and "power" and seeing it as "extroverted libido," especially as used by so many warring armies, I pointed to the martial perspective of this fantasy, and claimed the horse rather for the imagination: "The image is always of a specific horse and that bespeaks the precise state of the imagination at that particular moment." Hillman then underlined the impressive differentiation of the horse's motoric system, which allowed it to flick off a fly from its skin with complete accuracy, suggesting, in compromise, that we might see the horse as "muscular imagination."

Another wildly imaginative Russian, Marc Chagall, gives us a fitting emblem for the end of this chapter: "At the sight of horses, who are always in a state of ecstasy, I think: are they not, perhaps, happier than us? You can kneel down peacefully before a horse and pray. It always lowers its eyes in a rush of modesty. I hear the echo of horses' hooves in the pit of my stomach...I would like to go up to that bareback rider who has just reappeared, smiling; her dress, a bouquet of flowers...I would run after her horse to ask her how to live, how to escape from myself, from the world, whom to run to, where to go" (from *Le Cirque* 1967 (New York: Pierre Matisse Gallery, 1981).

[16] R.M. Rilke, in a letter to Rudolf Bodlander, March 23, 1922. Quoted in *The Selected Poetry*, 339.

[17] W.B. Yeats, "Byzantium," *The Collected Poems of W.B. Yeats* (New York: Macmillan, 1983), 248.

CHAPTER 2

[1] The journals of Edvard Munch in the Munch Museet library, Oslo, as quoted in Ragna Stang, *Edvard Munch: The Man and the Artist* (Oslo: Aschehoug-Tanum,1977), note T2800.

[2] James Hillman, *Archetypal Psychology: A Brief Account* (Dallas: Spring, 1985), 16.

[3] Ibid.

[4] Ibid., 1.

[5] Carol Ravenal, "Three Faces of Mother: Madonna, Martyr, Medusa in the Art of Edvard Munch," *The Journal of Psychohistory*, vol. 13, no. 4, Spring 1986, 400.

[6] C.G. Jung, *Collected Works*, vol. 9, (London, Routledge & Kegan Paul, 1956) par. 159. Subsequent references to Jung's *Collected Works* will be cited in text as *CW* with volume and paragraph numbers following.

[7] James Hillman, *Loose Ends* (Dallas: Spring, 1975), 37.

[8] Gaston Bachelard, *Water and Dreams: An Essay on the Imagination of Matter* (Dallas: The Pegasus Foundation/The Dallas Institute of Humanities and Culture, 1942/1983), 16.

[9] Ibid.

[10] Wolfgang Giegerich, "The Rescued Child or the Misappropriation of Time—On the Search for Meaning," *Harvest—Journal for Jungian Studies* (London: The C.G. Jung Analytical Psychology Club, no. 32, 1986), 13.

[11] Hillman, *Loose Ends*, 16.

[12] Jalal 'uddin Rumi, *Open Secret: Versions of Rumi*, trans. by John Moyne and Coleman Barks (Putney, Vermont: Threshold Books, 1984), 7.

[13] Gaston Bachelard, *The Poetics of Reverie: Childhood, Language and the Cosmos* (Boston: Beacon Press, 1960/1969), 53.

[14] Ibid.

[15] Edvard Munch, note 29, Oslo Kommunes Kunstsamlinger.

[16] Edvard Munch, *Livsfrisens Tilblivelse* (Oslo: 1929).

[17] Edvard Munch, to Ingeborg Motzfeldt Lochen, January 3, 1937, as quoted in Ragna Stang, *Edvard Munch: The Man and the Artist* (London: Gordon Fraser,1979), 63, note 17.

[18] Hillman, *Archetypal Psychology*, 17.

[19] Hans Jaeger, *Dagen* (1886), as quoted in Stang, op. cit., 60, quotation 14.

[20] Munch, *Livsfrisens Tilblivelse*. But mostly likely written in 1890 in St. Cloud. See Reinhold Heller, *Munch—His Life and Work* (London: John Murray, 1984), 63.

[21] Ibid.

[22] Ingrid Langaard, *Edvard Munch, Modningsaar* (Oslo: Gyldendal Norsk Forlag, 1960), 32.

[23] Henry Corbin, *Creative Imagination in the Sufism of Ibn 'Arabi*, trans. by Ralph Manheim (Princeton, NJ: Princeton University Press, 1969/1981), 274.

[24] Ibid.

[25] Munch, *Livsfrisen Tilblivelse.*

[26] See Hillman, "Pothos," in *Loose Ends.*

[27] Munch, *Livsfrisens Tilblivelse.*

[28] Ibid.

[29] Ibid.

[30] Ibid.

[31] *Sappho, A New Translation*, trans. by Mary Barnard (Berkeley: University of California Press, 1958), 24.

[32] Bachelard, *Poetics of Reverie*, 82.

[33] Ibid.

[34] Edvard Munch, note 2771, Oslo Kommunes Kunstsamlinger.

[35] The 1886 original of *The Sick Child* may be viewed at the Munch Museete in Oslo. The fourth version, painted in 1907, is on permanent view in the Tate Gallery in London.

[36] Arne Eggum, *Edvard Munch: Malerier-Skisser og Studier* (Oslo: J.M. Stenersens Forlag, 1983), Foreword.

[37] Langaard, *Edvard Munch*, 28.

[38] Edvard Munch, note T2759, Oslo Kommunes Kunstsamlinger.

[39] Carl Kerényi, *The Heroes of the Greeks* (London: Thames & Hudson, 1974), 51.

[40] Niel Micklem, "The Intolerable Image: The Mythic Background of Psychosis," *Spring*, 1979, 1ff.

[41] Edvard Munch, as quoted in Langaard, 286, from *La Revue Blanche*, December 1, 1985, where it accompanied a lithograph of *The Scream*. Copies, many of them poorly drawn, of Munch's *Scream* appear in connection with everything from campaigns against abortion to pleas for aid to starving populations in Africa. As an icon of our time it is ubiquitous: a *Mona Lisa*—but shorn of her hair and tortured by military police in a soundproofed cell. Not long ago a photographer from London's *Evening Standard* spotted a teenager on Kensington High Street with Munch's *Scream* handpainted on the back of his leather jacket. The photographer asked him if he was a particular fan of Munch. He looked blank and then replied that he was a Dead Kennedy's fan and had copied the painting from their album sleeve.

[42] Ravenal, *Three Faces*, 384. This writer's whole approach to the artist, which on the surface seems to be an "understanding," is, in fact, loaded with derogatory and patronizing attitudes; for example, she sees Munch's art with Newtonian single vision as a "reflective and analytical tool" couched in "cogent and personal symbols," quite ignoring its archetypal nature.

The following passage, continuing on from the above, reveals her literalizing and personalistic stance: "These symbols *revealed his personal history* and the maelstrom beneath. While not ultimately curative, the canvas, *or two dimensional surface,* became a repository of his defenses against sex and aggression. There was sufficient renewal in work itself to generate the will and *capacity for continued productivity.* However, it was not ultimately reparative, *as a psychoanalysis might be,* for there was *no character change or increased ability to sustain a mature relationship with any other individual"* [emphasis mine] (p. 386).

[43] James Hillman, *Inter-Views* (New York: Harper & Row, 1983), 38. This is a central idea for Jung as well—cf. his often reiterated phrase, "esse in anima," or being-in-soul, which means that soul or psyche is not in us, but we are in it. Psyche is thus always greater than any description or explanation of it.

[44] Sigmund Freud, "Das Medusenhaupt" (1922), Ges.W.17, 47: trans. by J. Strachey, "The Medusa Head," Int. J. Psa., 1941, 22.

[45] Hillman, *Archetypal Psychology,* 39.

[46] Kerényi, *Heroes,* 50.

[47] Micklem, *Intolerable Image,* 13.

[48] Ibid., 16.

[49] Ibid.

[50] Ibid.

[51] Ibid.

[52] Richard Browton Onians, *The Origins of European Thought* (New York: Arno Press reprint, 1973), 95–122.

[53] R.D. Laing, *Ritualisation and Abnormal Behaviour,* in "The Philosophical Transactions of the Royal Society of London," B, vol. 251, 1966, 331-335.

[54] Micklem, *Intolerable Images,* 16.

[55] Mario Praz, *The Romantic Agony* (Oxford: Oxford University Press, 1953/1983), 25.

[56] Edvard Munch, *The Tree of Life,* Oslo Kommunes Kunstsamlinger.

[57] Sigbjorn Obstfelder, *Edvard Munch, et Forsok in Samtiden* 7 (1896), 21.

[58] Edvard Munch, note T2547, Oslo Kommunes Kunstsamlinger.

[59] Corbin, *Creative Imagination,* 275.

[60] Ibid., 338, note 48.

[61] Andrei Tarkofsky, *Sculpting in Time,* trans. by Kitty Hunter-Blair (London: Bodley Head, 1986), 109.

[62] Edvard Munch, *Edvard Munch's Brev,* in Arne Eggum, "The Theme of Death," exhibition catalogue, *Edvard Munch, Symbols and Images* (Washington, DC: National Gallery of Art, 1978).

[63] Tarkofsky, *Sculpting,* 108.

[64] Ibid., 109.

[65] Pola Gauguin, *Edvard Munch* (Oslo: Aschehoug, 1933).

[66] Eggum, *Edvard Munch,* 136.

[67]James Hillman, *The Myth of Analysis* (New York: Harper Colophon Books, Harper & Row, 1972/1978), 102.

[68]James Hillman, "The Thought of the Heart" (Dallas: Spring, Eranos Lectures, No. 2, 1981), 26.

[69]Tarkofsky, *Sculpting*, 42.

[70]Edvard Munch, note dated 22 April, 1899, Munch Museum Arkives, as quoted in Heller, *Munch*, 171.

[71]Edvard Munch, to K.E. Schreiner, note T2748b, Munch Museum Archives.

CHAPTER 3

[1]"The music starts, and from the opening in the courtyard of the horses comes the procession of the bullfighters; the *paseo* or parade. The… matadors walk abreast, their dress capes are furled and wrapped around their left arms, their right arms balance, they walk with a loose-hipped stride, their arms swinging, their chins up, their eyes on the president's box. In single file behind each matador comes his cuadrilla of banderilleros and his picadors in the order of their seniority. So they come across the sand in a column of three or four. As the matadors come in front of the president's box they bow low and remove their black hats…" —Ernest Hemingway, *Death in the Afternoon* (London: Jonathan Cape, 1932), 61–62.

[2]Published as part 3 of Hillman, *The Myth of Analysis* (New York: Harper Colophon Books, Harper & Row, 1972/1978).

[3]Hillman, *Myth of Analysis*, 266.

[4]James Hillman, "On the Necessity of Abnormal Psychology: Ananke and Athene," in *Facing the Gods* (Dallas: Spring, 1980), 33.

[5]Lorca maintained that the gypsy *siguiriya* was the genuine, perfect prototype of that group of Andalusian songs known by the name of *cante jondo*, "deep song."

[6]Federico García Lorca, *Obras Completas*, vol. 1 of 2 (Madrid: Aguilar, 1954/1980), 583. Subsequent references to the *Obras Completas* will be cited in text as *OC* with volume and page numbers following. Except where otherwise indicated, the translations are my own or my composites of several other translations.

[7]Hillman, *Myth of Analysis*.

[8]*Levantado* is the Spanish term for the first of the three phases of the bull in the fight. "He is called levantado, or lofty, when he first comes out, carries his head high, charges without fixing any object closely and, in general, tries confident in his power, to sweep the ring clear of his enemies. It is at this time that the bull is least dangerous to the bullfighter" (Hemingway, *Death in the Afternoon*, 141).

[9]This is Lorca's own geographical image, given in the beginning of his great talk on the *duende* in 1933.

[10]Edward Stanton, *The Tragic Myth—Lorca and Cante Jondo* (Lexington: University Press of Kentucky, 1978), 56.

[11]Ibid., 55.

[12]Ibid., 81.

[13]The *veronica* is the touchstone of all cape work. "It is where you can have the utmost in danger, beauty, and purity of line. It is in the veronica that the bull passes the man completely and, in bullfighting, the greatest merit is in those maneuvers where the bull passes the man in his charge" (*Death in the Afternoon,* 169). "...the whole hot bulk of the bull passing the man, who looks down calmly where the horns almost touch, and sometimes do touch, his thighs, while the bull's shoulders touch his chest, with no move of defense against the animal and no means of defense against the death that goes by in the horns except the slow movement of his arms and his judgement of distance..." (*Death in the Afternoon,* 168). "Those passes were designed to show the matador's skill and art with the cape, his domination of the bull and also to fix the bull in a certain spot before the entry of the horses. They are called veronicas after St. Veronica who wiped the face of Our Lord with a cloth and are so called because the saint is always represented holding the cloth by the two corners in the position the bullfighter holds the cape for the start of the veronica" (*Death in the Afternoon,* 67).

[14]The translation here is provided by Christopher Maurer in *Deep Song and Other Prose* (London: Marion Boyers, 1980). Here and following, passages provided by this source are cited as CM with page number following.

[15]James Hillman, "Bachelard's Lautremont, Or Psychoanalysis without a Patient," in Gaston Bachelard, *Lautremont,* trans. by Robert S. Dupree (Dallas: The Dallas Institute Publications, 1986), 106.

[16]Bachelard, *Lautremont.*

[17]Bachelard, *Lautremont,* 69, quoting Paul Eluard, *Donner à Voir.*

[18]Marcel Auclair, *Enfance et mort de Garcia Lorca* (Paris: Editions du Seuil, 1968), 72.

[19]Hillman, *Myth of Analysis,* 274.

[20]As told by Rafael Nadal to Ian Gibson, in "Federico García Lorca su maestro de musica y un articulo olvidado," in *Insula* (March, 1966), 14.

[21]"The *media-veronica* that stops the bull at the end of the passes is a *recorte*. A *recorte* is any pass with the cape that, by causing the bull to try to turn in less than his own length, stops him brusquely or checks his rush by cutting his course and doubling him on himself." (*Death in the Afternoon,* 67).

[22]James Hillman, *Archetypal Psychology—A Brief Account* (Dallas, Spring, 1983/1985), 29–30.

[23]There are three acts to the fighting of each bull and they are called in Spanish *Los tres tercios de la lidia,* or the three thirds of the combat. The First Act, in which the bull charges the picadors, is the *Suerte de Varas,* or the trial by lances. The dictionary lists several meanings for *suerte* (f.): chance, hazard, lots, fortune, luck, good luck, haphazard; state, condition, fate, doom, destiny, kind, sort; species, manner, mode, way, skilful maneuver, trick, feat, juggle, a piece of ground separated by landmarks. The translation of "trial" or "maneuver" is quite arbitrary.

[24]Hillman, *Archetypal Psychology,* 27.

[25] James Hillman, *Re-Visioning Psychology* (New York: Haper & Row, 1975), 12.

[26] The lecture on the Gypsy Ballads was a talk Lorca gave often during 1935 and 1936. His poems, the *Gypsy Ballads*, were published in 1928 and had become the most widely read modern poems in the country. The word *amargo* means "bitter."

[27] Salvador Dali, *The Secret Life of Salvador Dali*, trans. by Haakon M. Chevalier (New York: Dial Press, 1942), 84.

[28] Pablo Neruda, "They tried to Extinguish the Light of Spain," *Passions and Impressions*, trans. by Margaret Sayers Peden (New York: Farrar, Straus and Giroux, 1983), 95.

[29] James Hillman, *Healing Fiction* (Barrytown: Station Hill Press, 1983), 37.

[30] Carl Kerényi, *Dionysos—Archetypal Image of Indestructible Life* (London: Routledge & Kegan Paul, 1976), 52. The animal as God, the Gods as animals, is an idea held by many ancient peoples, as far back as the Egyptians. Our modern cosmologies have, however, lost the sense of the animal as divinity. But archetypal psychology has begun to retrieve this "animal eye." See James Hillman's essay, "Cosmology for Soul," in *Sphinx* 2(London: The London Convivium for Archetypal Studies, 1989).

[31] Tragedy, like the bullfight, ends in death. Both are ritualistic dramas moving us to pity and terror. Tragedy, however, has lifted ritual death out of the literal and into metaphor. Lorca's three great tragedies, *Blood Wedding, Yerma,* and *The House of Bernarda Alba,* have all the dramatic tension of fate and chance, ambiguously mixed, found in the "liturgy of the bulls." Here, Dionysos, as Lord of Metaphor, is the teacher.

[32] *Suerte* (see note 23) contains all the ambiguity of the Dionysian, implying both chance and fatedness. In the second phase of the bullfight, the "trial" is that of the banderillas. "These are pairs of sticks about a yard long, seventy centimeters to be exact, with a harpoon-shaped steel point four centimeters long at one end. They are supposed to be placed, two at a time, in the humped muscle at the top of the bull's neck as he charges at the man who holds them. They are designed to complete the work of slowing up the bull and regulating the carriage of his head which has been begun by the picadors; so that his attack will be slower, but surer and better directed. Four pairs of banderillas are usually put in…The entire act of the banderillas should not take more than five minutes" (*Death in the Afternoon,* 95-96).

[33] Hillman, *Myth of Analysis,* 281.

[34] Ibid., 258–259.

[35] Ibid., 274.

[36] Ibid., 273.

[37] The second phase of the bull's condition in the fight (see note 8). "When the bull is *parado,* he is slowed and at bay. At this time he no longer charges freely and wildly in the general direction of any movement or disturbance; he is disillusioned about his power to destroy or drive out of the ring anything that seems to challenge him, and his initial ardor calmed, he recognizes his enemy, or sees the lure that his enemy presents him instead of his body, and charges that with full aim and intention to

kill and destroy. But now he is aiming carefully and charging from a quick start. The bull has no desire to play, only to kill" (*Death in the Afternoon*, 141).

[38]The translation here is provided by Felicia Hardeson Londre in *Federico García Lorca* (New York: Federick Ungar, 1984), 163.

[39]In the bullfight the first act is "the trial," the second act is "the sentencing" and the third "the execution." This last act begins after the salutation of the president of the corrida and the dedication of the death of the bull. These events are followed by the work of the matador with the muleta. "Muleta means literally crutch, but in bullfighting it refers to the scarlet-serge-draped stick with which the matador is supposed to master the bull's head and keep it lowered while he kills the animal by a sword thrust high up between his shoulder blades," (*Death in the Afternoon*, 96).

[40]Hillman, *Myth of Analysis*, 293.

[41]Ibid., 294.

[42]Ibid., 295.

[43]*Death in the Afternoon*, 90. Hemingway also makes the point that the greater an artist a bullfighter is, the less likely he is to be a "great killer." These are usually two separate functions of the bullfighter. The aesthetic sense can only be a handicap to a great killer. "To most of the bullfighters who are artists...the necessity to kill seems almost regrettable. They are not matadors but toreros, highly developed, sensitive manipulators of cape and muleta. They do not like to kill, they are afraid to kill, and ninety times out of a hundred they kill badly," (*Death in the Afternoon*, 171).

[44]Raphael Lopez-Pedraza, "Reflexiones Sobre El Duende," in *Ansiedad Cultural* (Caracas, 1987), 70.

[45]As recounted by Rafael Nadal in his commentary on Lorca's "Sun and Shadow," trans. by Kathleen Raine and R.M. Nadal (London: Enitharmon Press, 1972), 3.

[46]"*Aplomado* is the third and last general stage the bull goes through. When he is *aplomado*, he has been made heavy, he is like lead; he has usually lost his wind, and while his strength is still intact, his speed is gone. He no longer carries his head high; he will charge if provoked; but whoever cites him must be closer and closer. For in this state the bull does not want to charge unless he is sure of his objective, since he has obviously been beaten, to himself as well as the spectator, in everything he has attempted up to that time; but he is still supremely dangerous," (*Death in the Afternoon*, 142).

[47]Federico's brother, Francisco, writes that for him "Federico's theatre begins with my first childhood memories. The first toy that Federico bought with his own money, by breaking open his savings bank, was a miniature theatre. He bought it in Granada, in a toy store called The North Star, which was on the Street of the Catholic Kings. No plays came with this little theatre. So they had to be made up. This must have been his first attempt at drama...He liked to play at the theatre and at marionettes, to dress up the maids and make them go out into the street—grotesquely dressed sometimes, or dressed as ladies—wearing my mother's or my Aunt Isabel's street clothes."—Francisco García Lorca in the introduction

to *Three Tragedies* (London: Penguin Books in association with Martin Secker and Warburg, 1987), 9. From these and other accounts it is apparent that Lorca was very early attuned to the Orphic mode of "seeing through" the literal to the archetypal or mythic in the events around him. For the development of the connections between Orpheus, poetry and archetypal psychology see chapter 7 of this book, "Who Is Behind Archetypal Psychology?"

[48]Neruda, "They Tried," 62.

[49]Quoted by Ian Gibson, *The Assassination of Federico García Lorca* (London: Penguin Books, 1983), 34.

[50]Ibid.

[51]Ibid.

[52]Ibid., 58.

[53]Quoted in "Conversation With Bagaria," in Maurer, *Deep Song,* 128.

[54]Pablo Neruda, *Memoirs,* trans. by Hardie St. Martin (London: Souvenir Press [E & A] Ltd., 1977), 123–124.

[55]In connection with this image which Lorca related to Neruda we might place Jung's remark: "Perhaps—who knows?—these eternal images are what men mean by fate," (CW 7.183).

[56]Auclair, *Enfance et mort,* 28–29.

[57]Federico García Lorca, "Lament For Ignacio Sanchez Mejias," 2. The Spilled Blood, trans. by Stephen Spender and J.L. Gili, in *The Selected Poems of Federico García Lorca,* edited by Francisco García Lorca and Donald M. Allen (Norfolk, CT: New Directions, 1955), 145.

[58]Federico García Lorca, *Sonnets of Dark Love,* trans. by Eva Loewe and Noel Cobb, in *Sphinx* 1 (London: The London Convivium for Archetypal Studies, 1988; also reprinted in revised, authorized version, pamphlet and cloth edition, The Green Horse Press, P.O. Box 417, London NW3 6YE, England).

[59]Lopez-Pedraza, "Reflexiones."

[60]Ibid.

[61]Neruda, *Passions and Impressions,* 96.

[62]Lorca, "Lament," 4. Absent Soul.

CHAPTER 4

PART I

[1]James Hillman, *Archetypal Psychology—A Brief Account* (Dallas: Spring,1985), 45.

[2]James Hillman, *The Myth of Analysis* (New York: Harper & Row), 39.

[3]Robert Bly, *News of the Universe* (San Francisco: Sierra Club, 1980), 3.

[4]Ibid., 4.

[5]Wallace Stevens, *Opus Posthumous* (London: Faber & Faber, 1990), 183.

[6]Hegel observed that the free activity of spirit was more important to the Romantics than the harmonious balance of objective classical form. The

274

lack of objective form, is however, only a stage. The Romantic impulse, by breaking old forms, is also bringing unknown, emerging forms to birth. It was Coleridge, I believe, who said that there is a difference between "form proceeding" (emerging) and "shape superimposed."

[7]James Hillman, "Pothos: The Nostalgia of The Puer Eternus," in *Loose Ends* (Dallas: Spring,1975), 53.

[8]Bly, *News*, 70.

[9]This longing of the soul is not historically bound, nor is it bound to any particular place or race or culture. It is transhistorical. Among the many Sufi mystics who speak of it, the great poet-mystic Jalal 'uddin Rumi articulates it thus:

> I am not of the kingdom of Iraqain, nor of the country of Khorasan.
> I am not of this world, nor of the next, nor of Paradise, nor of Hell;
> I am not of Adam, nor of Eve, nor of Eden and Rizwan.
> My place is the Placeless, my trace is the Traceless.

Rumi continues, leaving us in no doubt as to the erotic character of this spiritual longing:

> 'Tis neither body nor soul, for I belong to the soul of the Beloved.

—Rumi, *Divan Shamsi-Tabriz*, translated and selected by Reynold Nicholson (Cambridge: Cambridge University Press, 1898/1977), 125.

[10]Hillman, "Pothos," 54.

[11]Ibid., 60.

[12]Ibid., 60–61.

[13]Ibid., 60.

[14]Hillman, *Archetypal Psychology*, 21.

[15]Quoted in Aneile Jaffe, *Word and Image* (Princeton: Princeton university Press,1979), 213.

[16]James Hillman, "An Inquiry into Image," in *Spring* 1977, (Dallas: Spring), 62-68.

[17]Hillman, *Archetypal Psychology*, 13.

[18]Gaston Bachelard, *The Right to Dream* (Dallas: Institute of Humanities and Culture, 1970/1988), 165.

[19]Ginette Paris, *Pagan Grace* (Dallas: Spring, 1990), 52–53.

[20]Marcel Brion, *Robert Schumann and the Romantic Age* (London: Collins, 1956), 133.

[21]Jean Paul, as quoted in G. Abraham, *Schumann: A Symposium* (London: Oxford University Press, 1952), 39.

PART II

[1]Julius Alf and Joseph Kruse (Eds.), *Robert Schumann—Universalgeist der Romantik* (Dusseldorf: Droste Verlag,1981).

[2]Marcel Brion, *Robert Schumann and the Romantic Age* (London: Collins, 1956), 25.

[3] As quoted in R.H. Schauffler, *Florestan* (New York: Holt, 1945), 475.

[4] Eric Sams, "Schumann and the Tonal Analogue," in *Robert Schumann: The Man and His Music,* edited by Alan Walker (London: Barrie & Jenkins, 1972), 390.

[5] William James, *A Pluralistic Universe—The 1908 Hibbert Lectures in Oxford* (Cambridge, Massachusetts: Harvard University Press, 1977), 71.

[6] As quoted in Ronald Taylor, *Robert Schumann—His Life and Work* (London: Panther/Granada, 1985), 47.

[7] Letter to F. Wieck, Heidelberg, November 6, 1829, in *The Letters of Robert Schumann,* edited by Karl Storck and translated by Hannah Bryant (London: John Murray, 1907), 44.

[8] Robert Schumann on Hector Berlioz' "Symfonie Fantastique," in *Neue Musicalistische Zeitschrift,* 1835, in Henry Pleasants, *The Musical World of Robert Schumann* (London: Victor Gollancz, 1965), 84.

[9] Ibid., 85.

[10] Samuel Taylor Colerdige, *Biographia Literaria* (London: J.M. Dent & Sons, 1980), 139.

[11] Published by Breitkopf & Hartel in 1850.

[12] In Thomas Alan, *The Aesthetics of Robert Schumann* (London: Peter Owen,1969), 25.

[13] R.D.Laing, *The Voice of Experience* (London: Allen Lane, 1982), 9–10.

[14] Thomas Moore, *The Planets Within* (Great Barrington: Lindisfarne Press, 1990), 88.

[15] Laing, *Voice,* 10–11.

[16] Sams, "Schumann," 392.

[17] Ibid., 393.

[18] Ibid.

[19] Taylor, *Robert Schumann,* 73.

[20] Sams, "Schumann," 395.

[21] Ibid.

[22] Leslie Gerber in sleeve notes to Murray Perahia's rendition of *Papillons,* on CBS label no. 76635.

[23] Letter to Henrietta Voigt, summer, 1834, in Storck, *Letters.*

[24] Taylor, *Robert Schumann,* 73.

[25] Sams, "Schumann," 396.

[26] Ibid.

[27] Ibid.

[28] Recalling the archetypal idea of the essential doubleness of consciousness, it is easy to see the initiatory potential of Jean Paul's novel for this consciousness. It is also possible to see Schumann's *Papillons* as a musical transcription of that initiatory power. Referring to how Schumann's music mirrors "the mysterious culmination of that disconcerting, yet marvellous book," Brion says: "I use the word mysterious here in its classical sense, ritualistic and liturgical. The mystery of the ancients brought initiation...In this sense—though I am afraid few listeners ever grasp it—*Pap-*

illons has this initiating quality," (Brion, *Robert Schumann*, 134).

[29]Sams, "Schumann," 398.

[30]Brion, *Robert Schumann*, 274.

[31]Ibid., 128.

[32]Robert Schumann, *Tagebucher:* 1827–1838, Band I (Leipsig: VEB Deutscher Verlag Fur Musik), 339.

[33]Ibid.

[34]Henry Corbin, *Avicenna and the Visionary Recital,* trans. by W.R. Trask (New York: Bollingen, 1960).

[35]Peter Ostwald, *Schumann, Music and Madness* (London: Victor Gollancz, 1981), 85.

[36]Ibid., 74.

[37]Joan Chisell, *Clara Schumann* (London: Hamish Hamilton, 1983), 36.

[38]Laing, *Voice,* 28.

[39]"Objective scientific psychiatrists believe what they call disease theory is the best strategy to adopt to bring undesired experience and conduct under control as quickly, painlessly and cheaply as possible" (Laing, *Voice,* 9).

[40]James Hillman, *Re-Visioning Psychology* (New York: Haper & Row, 1975), 13.

[41]In Gaston Bachelard, *Lautremont,* trans. by Robert S. Dupree (Dallas: The Dallas Institute Publications, 1986), 69, quoting Paul Eluard, *Donner àVoir.*

[42]Hillman, *Re-Visioning,* 12.

[43]Ibid., 31–32.

[44]Ibid., 12.

[45]Ibid., 34.

[46]*Allgemeine Musicalische Zeitung,* Leipzig, December 7, 1831.

[47]Eric Sams, "Schumann's Hand Injury," in *Musical Times* (London: December, 1971), 1156–1159.

[48]Taylor, *Robert Shcumann,* 96.

[49]Letter to Franz Otto, August 9, 1833, in Storck, *Letters,* 89.

[50]E.T.A. Hoffman, *The Serapion Brethren,* trans. by Ewing, 51–53. From here it is but a step to John Keats: "I am certain of nothing but of the holiness of the Heart's affections and the truth of Imagination" (Letter to Benjamin Bailey, November 22, 1817).

[51]Brion, *Robert Schumann,* 153.

[52]The first twenty-four measures of *Preambule* are what remain of Schumann's variations.

[53]In Schubert it is in bars 9-10 of D.365 and in Schumann in bars 10-11. Cf. Sams, "Schumann," 397. Sams gives many more examples of the distinctive style of Schumann's method.

[54]Moore, *Planets,* 91.

[55]Ibid., 186.

[56] Marsilio Ficino, *Opera Omnia*, 2 vols. (Basel: 1576; reprint edition, Torino: Bottega d'Erasmo, 1959), 542.

[57] Ibid., 819. Ficino advocates a combination of the spirits of the Sun and of Mars in any human endeavor requiring intensity.

[58] Moore, *Planets*, 173.

[59] Hillman, *Re-Visioning*, 37.

CHAPTER 5

[1] In his commentary on Plato's *Symposium*, Marsilio Ficino says: "O, the incomparable beneficence of love! For other gods finally reveal themselves with difficulty, and then, for only a brief time, after long searching. Love runs to meet us even before we start looking"—Marsilio Ficino, *On Love*, trans. by Sears Jayne (Dallas: Spring, 1985).

[2] James Hillman, *Re-Visioning Psychology* (New York: Harper & Row, 1975), xi.

[3] James Hillman, *Silver and the White Earth*, part 1, *Spring* 1980, 46. Hillman adds that this task may not be left only to the poets any more than the tasks of lunacy may be left only to the insane.

[4] Sappho, Fragment 40, my translation.

[5] Marsilio Ficino in *de Amore* claims that it was Orpheus who first used the expression "bitter-sweet" about Eros.

[6] The Sufi method of "ta'wil" is, according to Henry Corbin, "without question, a matter of harmonic perception, of hearing an identical sound (the same verse, the same *hadith*, even an entire text) on several levels simultaneously." See Henry Corbin, *Spiritual Earth, Celestial Body—From Mazdean Iran to Shi'ite Iran*, trans. by Nancy Pearson (Princeton, NJ: Princeton University Press, 1977), 54.

[7] Marsilio Ficino called the *nete* "summer" and the *hypate* "winter."

[8] Jalal 'uddin Rumi, in Coleman Barks and John Moyne, *Open Secret* (Putney, VT: Threshold Books, 1984), 45.

[9] James Hillman, *Cosmology for Soul—From Universe to Cosmos, Sphinx 2* (London: The London Convivium for Archetypal Studies, 1989).

[10] "Prayer to Eros," K. Preisendanz, *Papyri Graecae Magicae*, 2 vols. (Stuttgart and Leipzig, 1973), vol.1, 129. Quoted in Marie-Louise von Franz, *Projection and Re-collection in Jungian Psychology* (London: Open Court, 1980), 133–4.

[11] This description is given in Aristophanes' play *The Birds*, 693ff. W.K.C. Guthrie —in his *Orpheus and Greek Religion* (London: Methuen, 1935/52), 95–96—says about the question of the Orphic source of Aristophanes' words that "it becomes increasingly difficult to withhold belief, and I for one am ready to give up the struggle and affirm that in describing Eros as he did, Aristophanes must have been playing with the phrases of a poem in the Orphic tradition."

[12] Rainer Maria Rilke, *Eros*, trans. by Eva Loewe and Noel Cobb, ©1989 in *The Changing Faces of Love—Twenty Poems of Rainer Maria Rilke* (London:

Embers Press and the Green Horse Press, forthcoming).

[13]James Hillman, *The Myth of Analysis* (New York: Harper & Row, 1972), 82.

[14]Plato, *Symposium,* 203b.

[15]Edgar Wind, *Pagan Mysteries in the Renaissance* (London: Faber & Faber, 1958/1968), 238.

[16]Henry Corbin, *The Creative Imagination in the Work of Ibn 'Arabi* (Princeton, NJ: Princeton University Press, 1969), 100–101.

[17]Ibid.

[18]My translation throughout, based on translation by Dante Gabriel Rosetti.

[19]Quoted in Corbin, *The Creative Imagination in the Work of Ibn 'Arabi,* 140.

[20]Ibid., 139.

[21]Ibid.

[22]Ibid., 190.

[23]Corbin, *Spiritual Earth,* 11. And to crown the argument: "Reality is itself a theophanic apparition" (Corbin, *Creative Imagination,* 190).

[24]For a poetics of Love to become a psychopoetics of Love (soulmaking), we must give first place to the Imagination as the soul's organ of perception. This is the true Imagination, the *Imaginatio vera* of Paracelsus, also known as the *astrum in homine,* or "the star in man."

[25]Corbin, *Creative Imagination,* 190.

[26]Dante, *La Vita Nuova,* III, my translation.

[27]Sigmund Freud, in claiming to "trace back" the concept of taboo "to its sources," for example, reveals the incapacity of psychoanalysis to accept the gods as archetypal places. His "tracing back" is *not* the Neoplatonic mode of *epistrophé* or the *ta'wil* of the Sufis. His "humanistic" method leads back, but only to itself, the human ego. He says: "Neither fear nor demons can be regarded by psychology as "earliest" things, impervious to any attempts at discovering their antecedents. It would be another matter if demons really existed. But we know that, like gods, *they are creations of the human mind,*" [emphasis mine]—Freud, *Totem and Taboo,* 24.

[28]William Anderson, *Dante, the Maker* (London: Hutchinson, 1983), 114.

[29]The "core" here is the heart of beauty, the heart awakened to the world, the recipient of images—the "secret chamber in which the vital spirit lives"—not only the heart of the lion, Courage, nor quite the confessional heart of Augustine, and certainly not Harvey's heart—that mechanical, muscular pump. See James Hillman, *The Thought of the Heart* (Dallas: Spring, 1981).

[30]In our own time the poet Wallace Stevens writes "The imagination gives to everything it touches a peculiarity, and it seems to me that the peculiarity of the imagination is nobility, of which there are many degrees."—Stevens, *The Necessary Angel—Essays on Reality and the Imagination* (London: Faber & Faber, 1960/1984), 33.

[31]Erich Auerbach, for example, says of Cavalcanti and his circle that "these men opposed nobility of heart to nobility of birth, and though actively

engaged in political affairs, give the impression of a secret society of initiates...love mysticism and philosophical and political elements form a unity that is often hard to account for. They appear to have striven more clearly and consciously than the poets of any other country to create a sublime style in their native language. They addressed the elite of the cor gentile and it was their endeavour to create a conscious elite."—Auerbach, *Literary Language and its Public in Later Latin Antiquity and the Middle Ages,* trans. by R. Mannheim (London), 296.

[32]Corbin, *Creative Imagination,* 229. See also page 121 for Corbin's discussion of the secrecy of divine suzerainty.

[33]Ibid., 275.

[34]Ibid., 154.

[35]Ibid., 151.

[36]Ibid., 60.

[37]Ibid., 11.

[38]Charles Williams, *The Figure of Beatrice* (New York: Octagon Books, 1978), 27.

[39]Corbin, *Creative Imagination,* 382, n. 13.

[40]*Sappho: A New Translation,* by Mary Bernard (Berkeley: University of California Press, 1958), frag. 61.

[41]Anne Carson, *Eros—The Bittersweet* (Princeton, NJ: Princeton University Press, 1986), 40–41.

[42]All quotations from Plato's *Phaedrus* are taken from the translation by Walter Hamilton (London: Penguin, 1983).

[43]Marsilio Ficino, *On Love,* trans. by Sears Jayne (Dallas: Spring, 1985), Speech V, chapter 6, 95.

[44]Corbin, *Creative Imagination,* 263.

[45]Jalal 'uddin Rumi, *Mathnawi* V, 858, trans. by Reynold Nicholson (Cambridge: E.J.W. Gibb Memorial Trust, 1930).

[46]Rumi, *Mathnawi* V, 420ff., in Barks and Moyne, *Open Secret,* 76–77. Novalis, in 1797, wrote: "Whoever flees pain will no longer love. To love is to feel the opening forever, to hold the wound always open," (Journals).

[47]Rumi, *Mathnawi* VI, 4020ff., in *Open Secret,* 82.

[48]Rumi, *Divan Shams-i-Tabriz,* trans. and ed. by R. Nicholson (Cambridge: Cambridge University Press, 1898/1952), 7.

[49]Ibid., 71.

[50]Ibid., 3.

[51]Ibid., 125127.

[52]Afzal Iqbal, *The Life and Work of Jalaluddin Rumi* (London: Octagon Press, 1983), 113.

[53]Corbin, *Creative Imagination,* 61.

[54]Rumi may even have heard of Ibn 'Arabi's encounter, as the Andalusian sage had arrived in Konya twenty years before Rumi's family came to settle there and had married the widow of a friend, adopting his new stepson, Sadr al-Din al-Qunawi, and training him in Sufi ways of

thought. This boy later became one of Rumi's closest friends, a fellow mystic and enthusiast of the work of Sohrawardi. Of these two greatest of Sufi masters, Rumi and Ibn 'Arabi, Corbin writes: "Both are inspired by the same theophanic sentiment, the same nostalgia for beauty, and the same revelation of love. Both tend toward the same absorption of the visible and invisible, the physical and the spiritual, into a *unio mystica* in which the Beloved becomes a mirror reflecting the secret face of the mystic lover, while the lover, purified of the opacity of the ego, becomes in turn a mirror of the attributes and actions of the Beloved."—*Creative Imagination*, 70.

[55] James Hillman, *The Myth of Analysis*, 91.

[56] Rumi, *Divan*, quoted in A. Reza, *Rumi, the Persian, the Sufi* (London: Routledge and Kegan Paul, 1974), 76.

[57] Rumi, *Divan*, Nicholson, 153.

[58] Ibid., xxiv. Jami, Persian poet and one of the great mystics of Islam (d. A.D.1495).

[59] Iqbal, *Life and Work*, 126.

[60] Rumi, *This Longing—Poetry, Teaching Stories, and Selected Letters*, versions by Coleman Barks and John Moyne (Putney, VT: Threshold Books, 1988), x.

[61] Ibid., ix.

[62] As Quoted in Corbin, *Creative Imagination*, 135.

[63] Rumi, *Mathnawi* I, Nicholson, 109.

[64] James Hillman, "Pothos," in *Loose Ends* (Dallas: Spring, 1975), 61.

[65] The last line of Dante's *Divina Commedia*.

CHAPTER 6

[1] Joan Grant, *Many Lifetimes* (London: Victor Gollancz, 1974), 176ff.

[2] James Hillman, *Healing Fiction* (Barrytown, NY: Station Hill, 1983), 43.

[3] Ibid.

[4] Ibid., 41.

[5] Ibid.

[6] Jules Cashford (Tr.), *The Homeric Hymns*, unpublished.

[7] James Hillman, *The Dream and The Underworld* (New York: Harper & Row, 1979), 166.

[8] R.M. Rilke, letter to Witold von Hulewicz, November 13, 1925.

[9] Hillman, *Dream*, 41.

[10] Carl Kerényi, *Hermes—Guide of Souls* (Zurich: Spring, 1976), 31.

[11] Hillman, *Dream*, 42.

[12] Pindar: *Frag.* 131 (96).

[13] Richard Broxton Onians, *The Origins of European Thought* (New York: Arno Press, reprint, 1973), 103 n.4.

[14] Hillman, *Dream*, 49.

[15] Pablo Neruda, *Twenty Poems,* trans. by James Wright and Robert Bly, (Minnesota: The Sixties Press, 1967), 21.

[16] Plato, *Phaedo* 80B, trans. by Hugh Tredennick, in *Plato—The Last Days of Socrates* (London: Penguin, 1980), 133.

[17] Ibid., 107 (64).

[18] Sophocles, quoted in Carl Kerényi, *Eleusis—Archetypal Image of Mother and Daughter,* trans. by Ralph Manheim (New York: Schocken Books, 1977), 14.

[19] Carl Kerényi, *Kore,* in C.G. Jung and C. Kerényi, *Essays on a Science of Mythology: The Myth of the Divine Child and the Mysteries of Eleusis,* trans. by R.F.C. Hull, Bollingen Series XXII (Princeton, NJ: Princeton University Press, 1949/1973), 109.

[20] Ibid., 123.

[21] Hillman, *Dream,* 48.

[22] Ibid., 191.

[23] Kerényi, *Kore,* 124.

[24] Ibid., 125.

[25] Plato, *Phaedrus* (125).

[26] Grant, *Many Lifetimes,* 5.

[27] Ibid., 4.

[28] Hillman, *Dream,* 29–30.

[29] Buddhaghosha, *Vishuddi Marga,* as quoted in J. Fisher, *The Case for Reincarnation* (London: Granada Publishing, 1985), 142ff.

[30] Ibid.

[31] W.B. Yeats, *Selected Criticism and Prose* (London: Pan Books, 1980), 80.

[32] Ibid., 82.

[33] The clay figurine from Locri is in the National Museum at Reggio Calabria.

[34] Grant, *Many Lifetimes,* 239–240.

[35] Cashford (Tr.), *Homeric Hymns.*

[36] Sgam.po.pa, *Jewel Ornament of Liberation,* trans. by Herbert Guenther (London: Rider & Company, 1959).

[37] C.G. Jung, *Memories, Dreams, Reflections,* trans. by Richard and Clara Winston (London: Fontana, 1963/1983), 349.

[38] Ibid.

[39] Sgam.po.pa, *Jewel Ornament,* 81.

[40] Ibid.

[41] Ibid.

[42] Kerényi, *Eleusis,* 137.

[43] Plato, *Phaedrus,* (80B).

[44] Ibid. (118).

[45] Grant, *Many Lifetimes,* 2.

[46] Jalal 'uddin Rumi, *Divan Shamsi Tabriz,* ed. and trans. by Reynold Nicholson (Cambridge: Cambridge University Press, 1898/1977), 47.

[47] J. Cashford, op.cit..

[48] Henry Corbin, *The Eternal Sophia* (1953), trans. by Molly Tuby, in *Harvest—Journal for Jungian Studies,* number 31 (London: C.G. Jung Analytical Psychology Club), 22.

[49] D.H. Lawrence, "The Ship of Death," in D.H. Lawrence, *The Complete Poems,* collected and edited by Vivian de Sola Pinto and Warren Roberts (London: Penguin, 1984), 962–964.

CHAPTER 7

[1] James Hillman, *Archetypal Psychology: A Brief Account* (Dallas: Spring, 1985) 24–25.

[2] James Hillman, "Why 'Archetypal Psychology'?" in *Spring* 1970, 212–219.

[3] Hillman, *Archetypal Psychology,* 2–3.

[4] Ibid., 4.

[5] Plato, *Symposium,* 215.

[6] Paul Friedländer, *Plato* (Princeton, NJ: Princeton University Press, 1969), 1:43.

[7] James Hillman, "Psychology: Monotheistic or Polytheistic?" in David Miller, *The New Polytheism* (Dallas: Spring, 1981), 114.

[8] Hillman, *Archetypal Psychology,* 19.

[9] Ibid., 19–20.

[10] Ibid., 34.

[11] Asking "where?" is more of a political or sociological question, as in Andrew Samuels' and Peter Bishop's attempt to "place" archetypal psychology. See Andrew Samuels, *Jung and the Post-Jungians* (London: Routledge & Kegan Paul, 1985) and Peter Bishop, "Post-Jungianism and the Place of Archetypal Psychology," *Spring* 1987, 143–151. Before archetypal psychology can be "placed," however, it needs to be seen from within its own perspective. The first placing must be archetypal.

[12] For anima, see James Hillman, *Re-Visioning Psychology* (New York: Harper & Row, 1975), *The Myth of Analysis* (New York: Harper & Row, 1972), and especially *Anima: An Anatomy of a Personified Notion* (Dallas: Spring, 1985). For underworld, see James Hillman, *The Dream and the Underworld* (New York: Harper & Row, 1979). For imagination, see James Hillman, *Re-Visioning Psychology* and *Healing Fiction* (Barrytown, NY: Station Hill, 1983).

[13] Hillman, *Re-Visioning,* xi.

[14] James Hillman, "The Thought of the Heart" (Dallas: Spring, Eranos Lectures, No. 2, 1981).

[15] Ibid.

[16] Elizabeth Sewell, *The Orphic Voice* (London: Routledge & Kegan Paul, 1955), 4.

[17] Ibid. Sewell also says that "the Orpheus line of descent among the poets establishes its own subsidiary line of spiritual heredity, whereby later Or-

phic voices recognize and acknowledge their ancestors," (*Orphic Voice,* 61).

[18] Ibid., 4.

[19] Rainer Maria Rilke, *Die Sonette an Orpheus,* 1.1, in R.M. Rilke, *Gesammelte Gedichte* (Frankfurt am Main: Insel Verlag, 1962), 487. Translation by Eva Loewe and Noel Cobb ©1988.

[20] Federico García Lorca, "La Imagen Poetica de Don Luis Gongora," in *Obras Completas* (Madrid: Aguilar, 1954/1980), 1.1043–44.

[21] Sewell, *Orphic Voice,* 56.

[22] Ibid., 82ff.

[23] Lorca, *Obras Completas,* I.1038.

[24] Ibid., I. 1032.

[25] Ibid., I. 1038. My translation.

[26] Sewell, *Orphic Voice,* 56.

[27] Hillman, "The Animal Kingdom in the Human Dream," in *Eranos Jahrbuch 51,* 1982, 326–327.

[28] Carl Kerényi, *The Heroes of the Greeks* (London: Thames and Hudson, 1959), 273.

[29] O. Kern, Ed., *Orphicorum Fragmenta* (Berlin: 1922/1963), text 113.

[30] Solon Michaelides, *The Music of Ancient Greece: An Encyclopedia* (London: Faber & Faber, 1978), 110ff.

[31] Carl Kerényi, *Hermes: Guide of Souls,* trans by Murray Stein (Dallas: Spring, 1976), 26.

[32] Hillman, *Archetypal Psychology,* 21. "Seeing through" is one of the main modes of archetypal psychology. It is a "process of deliteralizing and a search for the imaginal in the heart of things by means of ideas," (*Re-Visioning,* 136).

[33] James Hillman, "Plotino, Ficino and Vico," in *Loose Ends* (Dallas: Spring, 1975), 149.

[34] Hillman, *Re-Visioning,* 149. Further, "literalism prevents mystery by narrowing the multiple ambiguity of meanings into one definition. Literalism is the natural concomitant of monotheistic consciousness." But see the whole section entitled "Psychologizing or Seeing Through," 115–164.

[35] For an excellent discussion of this, see J.B. Friedman's account of the "Testament of Orpheus" in his *Orpheus in the Middle Ages* (Cambridge, MA: Harvard University Press, 1970), 124.

[36] Proclus represented Orpheus as highly honored at Eleusis (*In Plat. Rempublicam* 2.312) and Theodoretus states explicitly that Orpheus instituted the Eleusinian Mysteries: "The rites [*teletae*] of the Dionysia, the Pan-athenaea, the Thesmopyhoria and the Eleusinia were introduced into Athens by Orpheus. He also went to Egypt and transformed the rites [*orgia*] of Isis and Osiris into the rites of Deo and Dionysos" (*Graecarum affectionum curati.*o 1.21).

[37] Ivan Linforth, *The Arts of Orpheus* (New York: Arno Press reprint, 1941/1973), 306; cf. 141.

[38] John Warden, Ed., *Orpheus: the Metamorphoses of a Myth* (Toronto: Uni-

versity of Toronto Press, 1982), 88.

[39]Thinking no doubt of the music and magic of his teacher Marsilio Ficino, Pico della Mirandola wrote: "Nothing is more effective in natural magic than the Hymns of Orpheus, if the proper music, mental concentration and other circumstances which the wise are aware of be applied," (*Orphicae Conclusiones* 2, *Opera Omnia* 106).

[40]Warden (Ed.), *Orpheus*, 102.

[41]This is depicted in Naldi's poem to Ficino, *De Orpheo in ejus cythera picto*, in P.O. Kristeller, Ed., *Supplementum Ficinianum* (Florence, 1937), 2:37.

[42]Giovanni Corsi, "The Life of Marsilio Ficino," in *The Letters of Marsilio Ficino* (London: Shepheard-Walwyn, 1981), 3:138.

[43]*The Letters of Marsilio Ficino*, 1:32.

[44]Warden (Ed.), *Orpheus*, 85.

[45]Cf. Hillman's seventeen references to Ficino in his *Re-Visioning Psychology*.

[46]Ibid., 97.

[47]See Thomas Moore, *The Planets Within* (Lewisburg, PA: Bucknell University Press, 1982) for an imaginative attempt to adapt Ficino's "astrological psychology" to a contemporary context of therapy within a polytheistic, archetypal mode. Moore here suggests that "Hillman's concern for soul and his polytheistic position place him shoulder to shoulder with Ficino," (intro., 8).

[48]Rainer Maria Rilke, *Die Sonette an Orpheus*, 1.9. Translation by Eva Loewe and Noel Cobb ©1988.

[49]Jean Cocteau (from a talk given at the Theatre du Vieux-Columbier when the film *The Blood of a Poet* was shown there in 1932), in *Two Screen Plays*, trans. by Carol Martin-Sperry (London: Boyars, 1985), 67.

[50]Commenting on the ancient Delphic mural of the underworld by the artist Polygnotos, described by Pausanius (Bk. 10.25–31), Guthrie says that "it may be that in the eyes of some of his followers, [Orpheus] had an established position" in the underworld, "as it were, in his own right. No particular errand had to be supposed for his presence, for by the time of Polygnotos, he was certainly the patron of a religion in which all the emphasis was laid on eschatological dogma." Guthrie claims that "if Pausanius is to be trusted…this is our earliest piece of evidence for the presence of Orpheus among the dead." —W.K.C. Guthrie, *Orpheus and the Greek Religion* (London: Methuen, 1935/1952), 30.

[51]Pausanius, *Guide to Greece*, vol. 1, trans. by Peter Leuf (London: Penguin, 1971), 484–485.

[52]Hillman, *The Dream and the Underworld*, 102.

[53]Pablo Neruda, "Nothing But Death," in *Twenty Poems*, trans. by Robert Bly and James Wright (Madison, WI: The Sixties Press, 1967), 21.

[54]Hillman, *Re-Visioning*, 209.

[55]Alfred Ziegler, *Archetypal Medicine* (Dallas: Spring, 1983), 40ff.

[56]Hillman, *Dream*, 52–53.

[57]Hillman, *Archetypal Psychology*, 22.

285

[58] W.A. Anderson, "The Orpheus of Virgil and Ovid: Flebile nescio quid," in *Orpheus: The Metamorphoses of a Myth*. See note 38.

[59] James Hillman, "Pothos: The Nostalgia of the *Puer Eternus*," in *Loose Ends*.

[60] Sewell, *Orphic Voice*, 59.

[61] Linforth, *Arts of Orpheus*, 14.

[62] Ibid., 206ff.

[63] Guthrie, *Orpheus*, 41.

[64] See, further, the last sentence of Hillman's *The Myth of Analysis*, which reads: "It is so difficult to imagine, to conceive, to experience consciousness apart from its old identifications, its structural bedrock of misogyny, that we can hardly even intuit what this bisexual God might hold in store for the regeneration of psychic life."

[65] Guthrie, *Orpheus*, 127.

[66] Hillman, *Archetypal Psychology*, 16.

[67] See Hillman's survey of Dionysos in Jung's writings in *Facing the Gods* (Dallas: Spring, 1980).

[68] Richard B. Onians, *The Origins of European Thought: About the Body, the Mind, the Soul, the World, Time and Fate* (Cambridge: Cambridge University press, 1951), 100.

[69] In pointing out that "the contents of psychiatry and philosophy are of prime importance but the language they use to express those contents is soul-killing" (*Re-Visioning*, 214), Hillman is reacting, as he says, with Renaissance passion, like Petrarch, who also battled over language with the empirical practitioners and academic thinkers of his day: "Both their empty soulless nominalism and their 'infantile inability to speak' appalled his sense of eloquence where care for words meant care for soul" (Ibid.).

[70] Linforth, *Arts of Orpheus*, 127.

[71] Russell Hoban, *The Medusa Frequency* (London: Jonathan Cape, 1987), 31.

[72] Ibid., 33.

[73] Ibid., 100.

[74] Sewell, *Orphic Voice*, 171.

[75] Hoban, *Medusa Frequency*, 38.

[76] Ibid., 39. or, as archetypal psychology would say: "Myths never happened; they always are."

[77] Hillman, *Loose Ends*, 49ff.

[78] Hoban, *Medusa Frequency*, 33.

[79] Ibid., 119.

[80] Robert Graves, *Greek Myths* (London: Penguin, 1955), 1:115.

[81] Hillman, *Re-Visioning*, 57.

[82] James Hillman, "Anima *Mundi*: The Return of the Soul to the World," *Spring* 1982, 77.

[83] Ibid.

[84]Sewell, *Orphic Voice*, 413.

[85]Hillman, *Re-Visioning*, 169.

[86]Such a revision is attempted by Andrew Samuels, *Post Jungians*.

[87]Hillman, *Re-Visioning*, 144.

[88]Rainer Maria Rilke, *Die Sonette an Orpheus*, 1.5. Translation by Eva Loewe and Noel Cobb ©1988.

BORN IN 1938 in Grand Rapids, Michigan, Noel Cobb chose self-imposed exile from his country at the age of twenty-one. In 1959 in revulsion against the American way of life, Cobb embarked on a steamer sailing from New York to Oslo. He had a degree in philosophy, fifty dollars, a copy of Rilke's *The Notebook of Malte Laurids Brigge* and "a trunkful of existential dread." Twenty-four years later he returned for a short visit. He says that he has never regretted the exile.

As an expatriate in Europe, Cobb devoted the next twelve years to learning the customs and culture of the old world. While working as a stevedore on the waterfront in Oslo, he taught himself Norwegian, using a pocket dictionary and a copy of Knut Hamsun's *Pan*. Two years later he made his debut with a collection of poems in Norwegian and from this time on was an active member of an avant-garde group of young imagist poets in Oslo.

In 1966, having published four volumes of poetry and completed a six-year degree in psychology from the University of Oslo, he travelled to London where, on the invitation of Dr. R.D. Laing, he joined the now historic project of Kingsley Hall, the first experimental community in the world in which individuals diagnosed as schizophrenic lived together with professionals and were allowed their madness with no enforced form of pharmaceutical treatment. Cobb's novel from this time, *The Building*, was published in Norway in 1970.

Finding this extreme immersion in the pathologizing of the Western psyche somewhat one-sided, Cobb left England in 1971 for an exploration of non-Western cultures. After heading an expedition into the wilds of the Algerian Sahara and driving overland to India, he studied numerous forms of meditation with Tibetan yogis and meditation masters in the mountains of North India.

In 1976 Cobb returned to the West and to his practice of psychotherapy, adding a Jungian analysis and a training analysis to his previous experience. In 1985 he founded a charitable trust called The London Convivium for Archetypal Studies in order to create a forum in England for the new ideas of archetypal psychology. Since 1987 the Convivium has hosted yearly international conferences and published four issues of the annual *Sphinx*, a journal for archetypal psychology and the arts. Cobb has previously published *Prospero's Island—The Secret Alchemy at the Heart of The Tempest* (London: Coventure, 1984). He lives, and thrives, in London with his partner, the cofounder of the Convivium and *Sphinx*, Eva Loewe.